The Politics of Legality in a Neoliberal Age

This volume addresses the relationship between law and neoliberalism. Assembling work from established and emerging legal scholars, political theorists, philosophers, historians, and sociologists from around the world – including the Americas, Australia, Europe, and the United Kingdom – it addresses the conceptual, legal, and political relationships between liberal legality and neoliberal economics. More specifically, the book analyses the role that legality plays in the dominant economic force of our time, offering both a legal corrective to scholarship in economics and political economy that has paid insufficient attention to legal ideas, and, at the same time, a political economic corrective to legal scholarship that has only recently turned to theorizing neoliberalism. It will be of enormous interest to those working at the intersection of law and politics in our neoliberal age.

Ben Golder teaches courses on law and social theory, on public law, and on the politics of human rights in the Faculty of Law at the University of New South Wales. He is an associate editor of the journal *Contemporary Political Theory*, a member of the Editorial Committee of the UK-based journal *Law and Critique,* a member of the Editorial Board of the *Australian Journal of Human Rights*, and a member of the Editorial Board of the radical, open access publisher Counterpress. His most recent book is *Foucault and the Politics of Rights* (Stanford University Press, 2015).

Daniel McLoughlin is Senior Lecturer in the Law School at the University of New South Wales. He is the editor of *Agamben and Radical Politics* (Edinburgh University Press, 2016) and has published extensively on theories of sovereignty, biopolitics and government in journals including *Theory & Event, Law and Critique, Law, Culture and the Humanities*, and *Angelaki.*

The Politics of Legality in a Neoliberal Age

Edited by
Ben Golder and Daniel McLoughlin

Routledge
Taylor & Francis Group
LONDON AND NEW YORK

First published 2018
by Routledge

2 Park Square, Milton Park, Abingdon, Oxfordshire OX14 4RN
52 Vanderbilt Avenue, New York, NY 10017

Routledge is an imprint of the Taylor & Francis Group, an informa business

First issued in paperback 2018

British Library Cataloguing in Publication Data
A catalogue record for this book is available from the British Library

Library of Congress Cataloging in Publication Data
A catalog record for this book has been requested

ISBN: 978-1-138-12176-8 (hbk)
ISBN: 978-0-367-19182-5 (pbk)

Typeset in Galliard
by Taylor & Francis Books

Contents

Acknowledgements

This edited collection sprang from a symposium held at the University of New South Wales Law School, under the auspices of the Gilbert + Tobin Centre of Public Law's 'Public Law and Legal Theory' project (of which the editors of this volume are the joint Directors), on 1–2 August 2014. We are incredibly grateful to the Centre for their material support of the event, as well as the Faculty of Law itself, which financially supported both the event itself (through the provision of Workshop Support Scheme funding) and the publication process (through providing research assistance). We especially thank all the participants in that original symposium (many of whom are represented in the present volume), as well as those who attended it, for making it such a vibrant and productive event. Lastly, we are indebted to the editors (David Singh Grewal and Jedediah Purdy) and the publishers (Duke Law School) of the journal, *Law and Contemporary Problems*, for their permission to republish in this volume the following work: Samuel Moyn, 'A Powerless Companion: Human Rights in the Age of Neoliberalism' (2014) 77 *Law and Contemporary Problems* 147. Finally, Zeynep Kivilcim's chapter is dedicated to Turkey's 2212 Academics for Peace who are currently facing prosecution for terrorist propaganda for signing a petition for peace in Turkey.

Ben Golder and Daniel McLoughlin

Notes on contributors

Thomas Biebricher is a Professor of Political Theory and Philosophy at the Goethe-Universität in Frankfurt. He is currently completing a book manuscript on *The Political Theory of Neoliberalism.* His most recent publications include an edited volume, *Der Staat des Neoliberalismus* (Nomos, 2016) and 'Neoliberalism and Democracy' (2015) 22 (2) *Constellations* 255–266.

Javier Couso is a Professor of Law and Social Sciences at Universidad Diego Portales (Chile). His work focuses on comparative law and courts, with an emphasis on the interplay between constitutionalism, the rule of law, and legal cultures in new democracies. After graduating in law in Chile, he received a PhD in Jurisprudence and Social Policy from the University of California, Berkeley. He is the author of dozens of academic articles and books, including *Constitutional Law in Chile* (Wolters Kluwer, 2011), and (with Alexandra Huneeus and Rachel Sieder as co-editors), *Cultures of Legality: Judicialization and Political Activism in Latin America* (Cambridge University Press, 2010). Professor Couso has been a visiting professor at several academic institutions worldwide, including the University of Wisconsin-Madison; Melbourne University; Leiden University; Utrecht University; the University of California, Berkeley; the Instituto Tecnológico Autónomo de México (ITAM); and Bocconi University. Furthermore, he serves on the editorial board of a number of academic journals, such as *Law and Policy*, *International Journal of Law in Context*, *Journal of Law and Courts*, *Constitutional Court Review*, and *Griffith Law Review*. Lastly, he is currently an associate member of the International Academy of Comparative Law, after having served on the Board of Trustees of the Law and Society Association and on the Executive Committee of the International Association of Constitutional Law.

Michael Gardiner is Professor in the Department of English and Comparative Literary Studies at the University of Warwick. He writes for a number of online journals including *openDemocracy* and *Bella Caledonia*, and his books include *The Cultural Roots of British Devolution* (Edinburgh University Press, 2004), *From Trocchi to Trainspotting: Scottish Critical Theory Since 1960* (Edinburgh University Press, 2006), *The Return of England in English*

Literature (Palgrave Macmillan, 2012), *The Constitution of English Literature* (Bloomsbury Academic, 2013), and *Time and Action in the Scottish Independence Referendum* (Palgrave Pivot, 2015).

Ben Golder teaches courses on law and social theory, on public law, and on the politics of human rights, in the Faculty of Law at the University of New South Wales. He is an associate editor of the journal, *Contemporary Political Theory*, a member of the Editorial Committee of the UK-based journal, *Law and Critique*, a member of the Editorial Board of the *Australian Journal of Human Rights*, and a member of the Editorial Board of the radical, open access publisher, Counterpress. His most recent book is *Foucault and the Politics of Rights* (Stanford University Press, 2015).

Zeynep Kıvılcım is an Associate Professor of Public International Law. She is currently a Kosmos Project Fellow at Humboldt University and also a guest professor at Gottingen University. She received her MA and PhD degrees in Public International Law from University Paris II (Panthéon-Assas). She taught law and gender, international human rights law and critical approaches to public international law at Istanbul University between 2000 and 2016. She works on social movements, human rights and refugees' rights with a gendered and critical perspective. Her most recent work is the book *A Gendered Approach to the Syrian Refugee Crisis*, co-edited with Jane Freedman and Nurcan Özgür Baltacıoğlu (Routledge, 2017).

Martin Krygier is Gordon Samuels Professor of Law and Social Theory at the University of New South Wales, Honorary Professor at RegNet, Australian National University, and recurrent visiting professor at the Graduate School of Social Research, Warsaw, and the International Institute of Sociology of Law, Onati. He is a fellow of the Australian Academy of Social Sciences. His most recent book is *Philip Selznick. Ideals in the World* (Stanford University Press, 2012). In 2005, he published *Civil Passions: Selected Writings* (Black Inc, 2005), a selection of his essays on matters of public debate. *Between Fear and Hope. Hybrid Thoughts on Public Values* (ABC Books, 1997) is based on his Australian Broadcasting Commission 1997 Boyer lectures. He has edited and contributed to *Spreading Democracy and the Rule of Law?* (Springer Verlag, 2006), *Rethinking the Rule of Law after Communism* (CEU Press, 2005), *Community and Legality: The Intellectual Legacy of Philip Selznick* (Rowman & Littlefield, 2002), *The Rule of Law after Communism* (Ashgate, 1999), *Marxism and Communism. Posthumous Reflections on Politics, Society, and Law* (Rodopi, 1994), and *Bureaucracy: The Career of a Concept* (Edward Arnold, 1980). Apart from academic writings, he contributes to journals of ideas and public debate.

Zachary Manfredi is studying for a JD at Yale Law School and is a PhD candidate in the Department of Rhetoric at University College Berkeley. At Yale he serves as president of the American Constitution Society and participates in the Worker and Immigrant Rights Advocacy Clinic. His research interests include international human rights, humanitarian and criminal law, as well as domestic immigration law, worker and LGBTQ rights, equal protection jurisprudence and the First Amendment. Prior to coming to Yale he completed a Master's degree in political theory as a Rhodes Scholar at Oxford University. He has previously worked on international law issues at the Center for Constitutional Rights, the World Bank Inspections Panel, the Carter Center, Google Inc., and the Oxford Transitional Justice Research Project.

Daniel McLoughlin is Senior Lecturer in the Law School at the University of New South Wales. He is the editor of *Agamben and Radical Politics* (Edinburgh University Press, 2016) and has published extensively on theories of sovereignty, biopolitics and government in journals including *Theory & Event*, *Law and Critique*, *Law, Culture and the Humanities*, and *Angelaki*.

Samuel Moyn is a Professor of Law and Professor of History at Yale University. His most recent book is *Christian Human Rights* (University of Pennsylvania Press, 2015).

Ntina Tzouvala is a Laureate Post-Doctoral Fellow in International Law at Melbourne Law School. Her current research project focuses on the Greek Civil War (1946–1949) and the role of international law and international organizations in the framing and management of civil strife during the Cold War. Prior to this post, Ntina was a lecturer in law at Durham Law School where she taught various modules related to international law. She also completed her PhD on the history of international law as a method of capitalist state-building at the same institution. Her research interests include the political economy of international law, the nexus between international law, imperialism and capitalism, feminist legal studies, law and neoliberalism.

Miguel Vatter is Professor of Politics in the School of Social Sciences at the University of new South Wales. He works in the areas of history of political thought, biopolitics, and political theology. His most recent book is *The Republic of the Living. Biopolitics and the Critique of Civil Society* (Fordham University Press, 2014).

An introduction to the politics of legality in a neoliberal age

Ben Golder and Daniel McLoughlin

In popular parlance, the term 'neoliberalism' refers to 'free market' economic policies – such as maximised competition, privatisation, the lowering of tariffs, and deregulation – that have been pursued by states and international organisations since the 1970s.[1] These policies have led to the dismantling or transformation of much of the post-War Keynesian consensus – the welfare and planning state at the national level, and the Bretton Woods institutions at the international level. In the Anglophone North we associate the initial phase of neoliberal economic reform with parties of the political Right – Reagan and Thatcher – whereas in the Antipodean laboratories of neoliberal economic reform (New Zealand and Australia), these projects have been conducted by nominally social-democratic parties of the political Left: the economic policies of Roger Douglas (Finance Minister in the New Zealand Labour Government from 1984) and the Hawke and Keating Labor governments in Australia in the 1980s.[2] In the Global South, such policy prescriptions have been vigorously pursued by the International Monetary Fund through 'structural adjustment' programmes and by national governments seeking flows of international capital.

Since the Global Financial Crisis, neoliberalism has also become a particularly important term of art in the academy. A slew of books have appeared in recent years that use neoliberalism as a lens through which to understand the contemporary moment – titles such as Gérard Duménil and Dominique Lévy's *The Crisis of Neoliberalism*, Pierre Dardot and Christian Laval's *The New Way of the World: On Neoliberal Society*, Philip Mirowski's *Never Let a Serious Crisis Go to Waste: How Neoliberalism Survived the Financial Meltdown*, and Wendy Brown's *Undoing the Demos: Neoliberalism's Stealth Revolution*[3] In these works a more

1 For a helpful introduction, see David Harvey, *A Brief History of Neoliberalism* (Oxford: Oxford University Press, 2005).

2 On the Australian experience, see Elizabeth Humphrys and Damien Cahill, 'How Labour Made Neoliberalism', *Critical Sociology* (forthcoming). Pre-publication version available at: http://crs.sagepub.com/content/early/2016/08/03/0896920516655859.full.pdf+html (accessed 22 August 2016).

3 Gérard Duménil and Dominique Lévy, *The Crisis of Neoliberalism* (Cambridge, MA: Harvard University Press, 2013); Pierre Dardot and Christian Laval, *The New Way of*

detailed and complicated picture of neoliberalism emerges as, variously, a political theory, a (now bankrupt) account of political economy, a hegemonic ideology, a project for the restoration of class power, an authoritarian politics, and a mode of governing subjectivity and society.

The current collection of essays contributes to debates around neoliberalism and the contemporary moment by examining what we have called the 'politics of legality in a neoliberal age'. Yet this formula, which provides the title for our book, raises two major problems. The first is do we, whoever this we are, in fact live in a neoliberal age? Does the designation 'neoliberal' capture enough of what is important and meaningful about our present political and economic arrangements? Does it allow us to talk sensibly about changes that have occurred in the state, economy and society over the past thirty years, by grouping them at a level of analytic abstraction or polemic shorthand?[4] Or does the term, by contrast, function as a way not to think about these changes, as some kind of alibi or excuse, or as a displacement of our theoretical energies from other profitable objects of critical inquiry (such as capitalism or the state)? The second major problem is why it might be important, in an attempt to grasp the political dynamics of an ostensibly 'neoliberal age', to examine the problem of legality. This volume does not simply mean to draw attention to how neoliberalism might affect the doctrines and practices of discrete areas of law (neoliberalism and tort law, neoliberalism and family law, neoliberalism and criminal law, and so forth). It is, rather, interested in the more precise and yet encompassing idea of 'legality', by which we mean the particular type of political legitimacy that liberal states have traditionally drawn from the law. So why, then, do we think that the study of the institutions and discourse of legality is essential to understanding the thought and politics of neoliberalism?

The chapters in this volume, taken individually and in dialogue, constitute answers to these two fundamental questions. Before we introduce the chapters, however, we need to provide a sketch of our own thinking on these problems, and why we thought it important to invite our authors to reflect upon them.

Neoliberalism?

For all its popularity, one of the difficulties of talking about neoliberalism is that the term says both too much and too little. On the one hand, as with our book title, it is used as a shorthand for the economic and political trends of our time – much as the term 'globalisation' was brandished around the turn of the millennium. On the other hand, there are so many different policies and practices

the World: On Neoliberal Society, trans., Gregory Elliott (London: Verso, 2014); Philip Mirowski, *Never Let a Serious Crisis Go to Waste: How Neoliberalism Survived the Financial Meltdown* (London: Verso, 2014); Wendy Brown, *Undoing the Demos: Neoliberalism's Stealth Revolution* (New York: Zone, 2015).

4 Stephen Healey, 'Fuck Nuance', *Sociological Theory* (forthcoming). Draft available at: https://kieranhealy.org/files/papers/fuck-nuance.pdf (accessed 22 August 2016).

that are grouped under the term, and such a variety of ways of theorising the phenomenon, that to simply speak of 'neoliberalism' does not really give one a great deal of analytic or critical purchase. The present book is nonetheless premised upon the belief that neoliberalism is important to understanding the politics of our time, and that the indeterminacy of the term, and the rather loose way in which it is sometimes thrown about, simply demands a more thoughtful engagement with neoliberal ideas and their relationship to contemporary legal and political practices.

Each of the chapters provides, to an extent, an answer to the question: *what is neoliberalism?* And, in answering this question, the authors each pursue a different trajectory, with different theoretical tools and political commitments. For the reader's sake, then, we think it useful at the start of this book to lay out in bold strokes some of the ways that the term has been understood in political discourse and academic literature, as something of a user's manual to what follows, in greater detail and complexity.

We have already seen the way that the term neoliberalism is associated with a particular set of 'free market' economic policies that have, since the 1970s, played a crucial role in the development of global capitalism and the re-organisation of the relationship between state and economy. According to much of the popular political discourse on the left, however, neoliberalism is also characterised by a quasi-religious belief in the virtues of these economic policies. While they are in many ways strange bedfellows, bestselling political journalist Naomi Klein and former Australian Prime Minister Kevin Rudd share this account of neoliberalism as a fundamentalist ideology. In February 2009, Rudd published an essay arguing that the Global Financial Crisis could be traced to neoliberalism – 'that particular brand of free-market fundamentalism, extreme capitalism and excessive greed which became the economic orthodoxy of our time'.[5] 2009 also saw the release of the film version of Naomi Klein's *The Shock Doctrine*,[6] which paints an even more dramatic picture of the pernicious effects of neoliberalism. Beginning with the role that Chicago-trained economists played in drawing up the economic blueprints for Pinochet's dictatorship, Klein argues that the rise of free market economic policies has gone hand in hand with political authoritarianism and the manufacture and exploitation of crises for political gain. And, repurposing Cold War anti-Marxist tropes, she argues that it is the fundamentalist belief in free markets that leads to authoritarianism, because the attempt to fashion a free market utopia requires a strong state to impose the neoliberal vision upon an often resistant world.

The picture of neoliberalism that we get from academic discourse is rather more complicated than this left-wing demonology. There are, we would suggest, three dominant ways of understanding what neoliberalism is in contemporary academic debates: the political economy, normative political and legal theory, and

5 Kevin Rudd, 'The Global Financial Crisis', *The Monthly*, February 2009, 20–29.

6 For the book version of Klein's thesis, see *The Shock Doctrine: The Rise of Disaster Capitalism* (New York: Picador, 2007).

neoclassical economic analysis, of the neoliberal authors themselves; analyses of neoliberalism's governmental rationality and its effects on practice (analyses that are heavily influenced by the work of Michel Foucault); and the (usually Marxist) analysis of neoliberalism as a new phase of capitalism in which the hegemony of finance capital is legitimated by appeal to liberal ideals. Each of these theoretical approaches captures a different aspect of neoliberalism as a body of ideas and as a set of practices. Each of them tells us something different about the relationship between the theory and practice of neoliberalism. And each of them tells us something different about what exactly is new about neoliberalism – in what sense it institutes a break with the welfare state or continues its practices, in what sense it returns to classical liberalism or transforms its premises.

The intellectual origin of the 'neoliberal' economic thinking that has come to prominence since the 1970s is to be found in the work of political economists who, beginning in the late 1930s, began to return to and re-articulate classical liberal ideas such as the free market and the rule of law.[7] There are commonly thought to be three schools of thought that comprise the neoliberal intellectual movement. These include: the Austrian school (particularly Friedrich Hayek and Ludwig von Mises); German ordo-liberalism, which played a major role in the theoretical foundations of the German state after the Second World War (and includes such major thinkers as Wilhelm Ropke and Alexander Rüstow); and, lastly, the abovementioned Chicago School (including economists such as Milton Friedman and Gary Becker).

There are important differences between and within these schools. They comprise neoclassical economists, political economists, and political and legal theorists. They are, nonetheless, united by a common enemy – the state planning of the economy that began under Bismarckian socialism and the New Deal and which went on to became hegemonic after the Second World War. The grid of intelligibility for understanding state planning was provided by Nazism – in the famous polemics of Frederick Hayek, state planning of the economy paves the Road to Serfdom, because it expands the power of the state and diminishes the liberty of the individual.

In response to the alleged creeping totalitarianism of the welfare state, neoliberal theorists rallied to the classical liberal ideals and institutions that they believed were the font of freedom – in particular, the freedom of market exchange. Importantly, however, they re-articulated these ideas under the political and philosophical conditions of the twentieth century – the rise of mass society, the development of monopoly capitalism, and the increasingly positivist tenor of Western thought. What the neoliberals share then, is not only a common enemy, but a particular way of reformulating the relationship between market and state that responds to these conditions and thereby institutes a break with classical liberalism.

7 See Philip Mirowksi and Dieter Plehwe (eds), *The Road from Mont Pèlerin: The Making of the Neoliberal Thought Collective* (Cambridge, MA: Harvard University Press, 2009).

This, at least, is the thesis of one of the major influences on the critical debates around neoliberalism – Michel Foucault.[8] In 1978–79, Foucault delivered a series of lectures at the Collège de France that challenged the commonly held belief that neoliberalism involves a return to classical liberalism and the free market. 'We should not', he writes:

> be under any illusion that today's neo-liberalism is, as is too often said, the resurgence or recurrence of old forms of liberal economics which were formulated in the eighteenth and nineteenth centuries … in actual fact, something much more important is at stake in modern neo-liberalism … what is at issue is whether a market economy can in fact serve as the principle, form, and model for a state which, because of its defects, is mistrusted by everyone on both the right and the left, for one reason or another.[9]

According to Foucault, then, neoliberalism is not a matter of the state simply leaving things alone, not a matter of *laissez-faire* in the common understanding, and frequent ideological self-presentation, of neoliberalism, but rather a kind of regulation that supports the operation of the market, and an imposition of market models on the state.[10] It is not so much a free market as a competitive market, and one that the state needs constantly to reproduce and to guarantee through a range of different regulatory interventions.

Foucault's lectures are remarkably prescient, identifying the importance of neoliberal thought when the Thatcher government was only a year old. Yet the date of the lectures means that they can tell us precious little about what neoliberalism looks like in practice. However, since their translation into English, these lectures have been taken up to think through the effects of neoliberalism on state practices and policies.[11] Here, the emphasis has often been on how the 'governmental rationality' of neoliberalism – the market as the model and measure for the state – has effected both how states act, and how individuals understand and govern themselves.

8 Foucault's work on neoliberalism has *both* given rise to a series of studies indebted to his approach *and* become the object of critical attention itself. For an instance of the former, see the articles collected in the February 2009 special edition of the journal, *Foucault Studies*, dedicated to the theme of 'Neoliberal Governmentality'. For an instance of the latter, see the forum dedicated to 'Foucault and Neoliberalism' in Volume 54, Issue 3 of the journal, *History and Theory*, as well as the recently published Daniel Zamora and Michael C. Behrent (eds), *Foucault and Neoliberalism* (Cambridge: Polity, 2015).

9 Michel Foucault, *The Birth of Biopolitics: Lectures at the Collège de France 1978–79*, trans., Graham Burchell (Basingstoke: Palgrave Macmillan, 2008), 117.

10 For a recent, and very powerful, critique of the ways in which market models have colonised the democratic realm of contemporary capitalist societies, see Wendy Brown, *Undoing the Demos: Neoliberalism's Stealth Revolution* (New York: Zone Books, 2015).

11 See, for example, the special issue of the journal, *Foucault Studies*, mentioned above at note 8.

The other major influence in the critical literature around neoliberalism is political economy, often of a more or less explicitly Marxist stripe. From this perspective neoliberalism is, as Duménil and Lévy put it, 'a new phase in the evolution of capitalism that emerged from the structural crises of the 1970s'.[12] Here, the emphasis is not on the theoretical commitment to free markets, or the market-based rationality that this gives rise to, but the fundamental demand of our economic system – that the investment of capital return a profit. To put it very schematically, capital accumulation in the West in the post-war period was based on large monopolies and the strength of industrial capital, in conjunction with a degree of state planning, and a compromise between labour and capital. The economic crisis of the mid-1970s seemed to indicate that this model no longer functioned and that new strategies for capital accumulation were needed. This gave rise to many of the economic innovations that we associate with globalisation and the 'neoliberal age' – sending production offshore, the increasing precariousness of labour, privatisation, deregulation, the rise of finance capital and the debt economy, and the increasing importance of accumulation by dispossession – that is, the theft of land and resources.[13] These changes have consolidated economic and political power in the hands of capitalists – and, in particular, finance capital – and diminished the power of labour. The government policies that have facilitated these changes result from the role that the state plays in helping capital to reproduce and further accumulate – or in popular parlance, ensure economic growth – and from the influence on the state of monopoly, and particularly finance, capital. That is to say, from the perspective of Marxian political economy, all the fine neoliberal talk about individual liberty and free markets is simply an effective ideological aid to the project of restoring class power.[14]

The stakes of the theoretical and methodological choices that we make in studying neoliberalism are directly political. How we theorise neoliberalism matters a great deal, as different accounts of it can lead to very different conclusions about how to respond to the politics of our time. Writing in *Forbes Magazine* in 2013, Richard Salsman argues that the real cause of the financial crisis was not free market capitalism, but government intervention in markets – in particular, through the Federal Reserve artificially keeping interest rates low, and providing 'massive subsidies and regulations in housing, banking, and mortgages'.[15] From this perspective, neoliberalism is an unfinished project, and the only adequate response to the Financial Crisis is to finally liberate 'free market' capitalism from the last vestiges of the regulation restraining it. And there is certainly a sense in

12 Duménil and Lévy, *The Crisis of Neoliberalism*, 1.

13 See David Harvey, 'The "New" Imperialism: Accumulation by Dispossession', *Socialist Register* 40 (2004): 63–87.

14 See Harvey, *A Brief History*.

15 Richard M. Salsman, 'The Financial Crisis was a Failure of Government, Not Free Markets', *Forbes Magazine*, 19 September 2013, http://www.forbes.com/sites/richardsalsman/2013/09/19/the-financial-crisis-was-a-failure-of-government-not-free-markets/#58016a49449e (accessed 17 September 2016).

which arguments that extend these neoliberal conceptual premises about freedom and competition have purchase in contemporary politics – from the hard-core libertarianism of the Tea Party, to austerity budgets across the Anglophone world and the Eurozone, and the shift in political discussion of economic woes from the Financial Crisis to public debt – which locates the problem in the state, rather than in the market. However if, like Rudd, you believe that it was a fundamentalist approach to markets that led to the Financial Crisis, then the proper political response to our moment is to return pragmatism and rationality to government decision making – and this means a kind of Keynesianism that balances the virtues of open markets with the state's role in mitigating the inevitable inequities that they give rise to. Lastly, if, like David Harvey, you believe that neoliberalism is a new and particularly devastating phase of capitalism – and that the current crisis arose from deep within its economic forms and the structures of political power they gave rise to – then the appropriate response looks more like the revolutionary re-organisation of political power and economic production.[16]

Why 'the politics of legality'?

Disciplines such as political theory,[17] anthropology,[18] sociology[19] and geography[20] have been seriously thinking through the nature and effects of neoliberalism for more than a decade. By contrast, legal scholarship has tended to pay far less attention to the issue.[21] Given what this other literature is saying about the importance of neoliberalism to understanding the political and economic trends of our time, it is clearly important to create a space for a discussion about its impacts within the legal academy. If the analysis of neoliberalism is, as we have suggested, important to understanding contemporary politics and economics, why is it important to think about the relationship between neoliberalism and the 'politics of legality'?

We can begin to think through this problematic from the recent perspective of the history of human rights (which is the subject of the last part of our book). In what has become a classic reference point in debates about the historical origins of

16 See Harvey, *A Brief History*.

17 Ruth Blakely, *State Terrorism and Neoliberalism: The North in the South* (London: Routledge, 2009); Wendy Brown, 'Neo-Liberalism and the End of Liberal Democracy', *Theory and Event* 7, 1 (2003): 1–19, DOI: 10.1353/tae.2003.0020 (accessed 1 June 2010); 'American Nightmare: Neoliberalism, Neoconservatism, and De-democratization', *Political Theory* 34, 6 (2006): 690–714.

18 Aihwa Ong, *Neoliberalism as Exception: Mutations in Citizenship and Sovereignty* (Durham, NC and London: Duke University Press, 2006).

19 Melinda Cooper, *Life as Surplus: Biotechnology and Capitalism in the Neoliberal Era* (Seattle: University of Washington Press, 2008).

20 The most influential work in the field of geography is Harvey, *A Brief History*.

21 We have greatly profited from the excellent collection, 'Law and Neoliberalism', featured as a special issue in Volume 77, Issue 4 of the 2014 edition of the journal, *Law & Contemporary Problems*, edited by David Singh Grewal and Jebediah Purdy.

human rights, Samuel Moyn (one of our authors), argues in *The Last Utopia* that the breakthrough for human rights does not occur after the Second World War, but rather in the late 1970s.[22] Moyn's argument is predicated upon the idea that human rights are not simply a set of legal instruments and institutions, but a particular way of framing political critique and a particular mode of political activism. The success of this political vision in the 1970s was due to the fact that previously successful visions of a better world – particularly Marxism and national liberation – began to falter at this time. The political language of human rights, and the activism of transnational organisations such as Amnesty International, were successful because they provided a politics that suited the times. Rather than aiming at fundamentally transforming the world – a politics discredited by decades of Cold War ideological conflict and the failures of state socialism – human rights provided a 'minimalist utopia' that aimed to protect life and minimise suffering.[23]

This thesis raises two interesting questions that have begun to resonate in the critical human rights literature and beyond. The first question is primarily an historical one, namely that the political breakthrough for human rights (on the Moynian account) occurred at the same moment as that of neoliberal economic thinking – begging the question of the precise relationship between these two forms of liberalism (which, incidentally, is the topic of Moyn's contribution to this collection). The second question is whether human rights furnish adequate conceptual and political tools for political resistance, and in particular, resisting neoliberal capitalism – providing that one thinks, as we do, that it needs resisting. Now, we contend that both of these issues need to be understood in the context of a larger question around the relationship between neoliberalism and legality.

There were two things that led us to this rather broad problem. First, human rights are only one aspect of the architecture of liberal legality – the rule of law, for example, also plays a crucial role in our political discourse and institutional design; those concerned with the legal response to terrorism invoke the rule of law to criticise the expansion of executive powers; while the same executive pays meticulous attention to justifying actions such as torture in legal terms. Neoliberals argue that the planning state leads to totalitarianism because it violates the rule of law; meanwhile, critics argue that neoliberalism itself is leading to authoritarian forms of government that vitiate rule of law ideals. As such, we thought it

22 Samuel Moyn, *The Last Utopia: Human Rights in History* (Cambridge, MA: Harvard University Press/Belknap, 2010).

23 The kind of human rights minimalism that Moyn diagnoses historically is roughly the same kind that Michael Ignatieff normatively approves of, and that which contemporary leftist political theorists (such as Wendy Brown), inveigh against. For the references, see Michael Ignatieff, *Human Rights as Politics and Idolatry* (Princeton: Princeton University Press, 2001); Wendy Brown, '"The Most We Can Hope for …" Human Rights and the Politics of Fatalism', *South Atlantic Quarterly* 103, 2/3 (2004): 451–463; and, lastly, see the helpful Joshua Cohen, 'Minimalism About Human Rights: The Most We Can Hope For?', *The Journal of Political Philosophy* 12, 2 (2004): 190–213.

important to analyse the relationship between the hegemony of neoliberal economics and the ambivalent politics of liberal legality more broadly.

Second, there is a long theoretical tradition that interrogates the intimate relationship between liberal law and capitalist economy – one thinks, for example, of Marx's 'On the Jewish Question', Weber's account of the rationalisation of modern law and economy, or the work of the Soviet jurist Evgeny Pashukanis.[24] But neither state nor economy is what it was twenty or thirty years ago, let alone what it was in Marx's day – so it seemed to us to be important to return to the relationship between law and economy under present political conditions. This means, however, that we face a rather complicated field of analysis, as the question is no longer simply that of the relationship between different fields – the capitalist economy and liberal legal institutions – but also the temporal problem of how to think the relationship between these different moments in the history of liberalism. Framing law and neoliberalism in this way opened up a host of questions for us, to which we, in turn, asked contributors to respond. These included: What role does law play in neoliberal theory? How do neoliberal thinkers understand law and state authority? How do they re-interpret classical liberal legal ideas such as the rule of law and civil society? Have liberal legal ideas and institutions facilitated the rise of neoliberalism as a political project? Have neoliberal practices and policies transformed the way that law and state operate? Have neoliberal ideas changed the way that law and state are legitimated? If neoliberalism has transformed law, do traditional liberal legal ideas, such as the separation of the political and the economic or the restraint of arbitrary power, still have critical purchase in a neoliberal context? If the rise of neoliberalism has transformed the legal system and its mode of legitimacy, is this a betrayal of the liberal tradition and its commitment to political freedom? Or is it a result of that very tradition, arising from its commitment to contractual rights and private property and the capitalist economy that these legal forms presuppose and facilitate? Do traditional critiques of liberal law still have critical purchase? How might we reframe or update them to take account of changed political-economic circumstances? What purchase do new conceptual tools give us that these classical critiques did not?

The chapters

The first part of the collection is entitled 'The law and legality of neoliberalism' and, through the work of the first three contributors (Martin Krygier, Michael Gardiner and Miguel Vatter), it broadly engages the ways in which legal ideas have

24 Karl Marx, 'On the Jewish Question', in Karl Marx, *The Marx-Engels Reader*, ed., Robert C. Tucker (New York: W W Norton, 1972), 24–51. Evgeny Pashukanis, 'The General Theory of Law and Marxism', in Evgeny Pashukanis, *Pashukanis: Selected Writings on Marxism and Law*, eds, Piers Beirne et al. (London: Academic Press, 1980), 37–131; Max Weber, *Max Weber on Law in Economy and Society* (Cambridge MA: Harvard University Press, 1954).

been taken up and reworked within the writings of key neoliberal theorists. At stake in these discussions is the question of continuity; namely, to what extent neoliberalism marks a real break with the forms of liberalism that precede it (or whether, in fact, it represents a continuation, refinement or indeed intensification of the logics that are found within those forms of liberalism). Related to this question of temporal continuity is a separate conceptual question of continuity; namely, the continuity between the political and the economic dimensions of liberalism. Both of these questions, thought together, speak to the predicament that critics of the neoliberal age today find themselves in. Wendy Brown writes perceptively of this predicament and the ambivalence attending it:

> [H]owever much a Left analysis has identified a liberal political order with legitimating, cloaking, and mystifying the stratifications of society achieved by capitalism … it is also the case that liberal democratic principles of governance – liberalism as a political doctrine – have functioned as something of an antagonism to these stratifications. As Marx himself argued in 'On the Jewish Question,' formal political principles of equality and freedom (with their attendant promises of individual autonomy and dignity) figure an alternative vision of humanity and alternative social and moral referents to those of the capitalist order within which they are asserted. This is the Janus-face or at least Janus-potential of liberal democracy *vis a vis* a capitalist economy: while liberal democracy encodes, reflects, and legitimates capitalist social relations, it simultaneously resists, counters, and tempers them. Put simply, what liberal democracy has provided over the last two centuries is a modest ethical gap between economy and polity. Even as liberal democracy converges with many capitalist values (property rights, individualism, Hobbesian assumptions underneath all contract, etc.) the formal distinction it establishes between moral and political principles on the one hand and the economic order on the other has also served as insulation against the ghastliness of life exhaustively ordered by the market and measured by market values. It is this gap that a neoliberal political rationality closes as it submits every aspect of political and social life to economic calculation: asking not, for example, what does liberal constitutionalism stand for, what moral or political values does it protect and preserve, but rather what efficacy or profitability does constitutionalism promote … or interdict?

So, on Brown's account, part of what makes neoliberalism 'new' and different to earlier iterations of liberalism (which, even as they masked and enabled economic stratification nevertheless gestured beyond them to notions of equality and dignity) is this closing of the gap between the political and the economic. For Brown, the not insignificant challenge this raises for critics of neoliberalism in the present is not so much to prise them apart again, and to return to older and better variants of liberalism, but rather to rethink their relationship, to articulate an 'alternative vision of the good' beyond market value and to do this without longing to reinstate older, less compromised, forms of liberalism.[25]

By contrast, the author of our first chapter, Krygier, counsels a return to the oldest virtues of the rule of law tradition and a retrieval of the specifically *political* virtues of the rule of law. While Krygier shares with Brown a sense that neoliberalism is indeed something new, for him this means a corruption of the old, a telling 'subtraction' from it (whereas for Brown, earlier forms of liberalism were, at best, only Janus-faced, potentially useful). In 'Transformations of the rule of law: legal, liberal, and neo-', Krygier argues that the recent neoliberal popularisation of the rule of law (in his words, its uptake and transformation into a 'hurrah term' of the global rule of law promotion industry) comes at the cost of forgetting all that is valuable about the concept. On Krygier's account, the specifically political virtue of the rule of law ideal – as opposed to its incidental economic values – is the idea of *tempering* the exercise of public institutional power (rather than limiting or eviscerating it, as neoliberals publically claim to do). In stressing its instrumental values (of economic development, private property rights, securing investment, and so forth), neoliberal advocates of the rule of law hence lose sight of this key insight and, in the process, part company with the liberal tradition.

If Krygier wants both to emphasise a discontinuity between older and newer forms of liberalism, and to stress the differences between their political and economic dimensions and proponents, in his chapter, Gardiner aims to reconstruct a forgotten continuity. 'Thatcherism as an extension of consensus' is written against 'the usual story of neoliberalism' as it is understood to have taken place in Britain towards the end of the twentieth century. According to this story, Thatcher's neoliberal revolution and its undoing of post-war social bonds (indeed, its infamous proclaiming the very *impossibility* of these bonds) came, incomprehensibly, almost out of nowhere. 'Services and industries were nationalised, which meant they belonged to the population', writes Gardiner of this standard narrative, 'until in the 1980s the popular control over the economy was displaced by something different – a wave of privatisations undertaken by capitalist zealots who revived an obscure credo contrary to British values'. In fact, for Gardiner, the Thatcherite revolution was not the irruption of something new and alien but in fact the *restoration* of 'the most homely principles of a particular kind of constitution, a constitution whose power lies in its commitment to the universalism of "the economy" and its willingness to resist popular determination'. Gardiner traces this idea of British economic constitutionalism back, via post-war ideas of consensus and the nineteenth-century constitutional thinker, A.V. Dicey, to the English Enlightenment, not so as to deny that 'nothing new happened with Thatcherism', but rather to call attention more precisely to the way that the new was a restoration and an extension of the old.

25 Wendy Brown, 'Neo-liberalism and the End of Liberal Democracy', *Theory & Event* 7, 1 (2004). Online version (unpaginated) available at: https://muse.jhu.edu/article/48659 (accessed 22 August 2016).

Lastly, Vatter's chapter, 'Foucault and Becker: a biopolitical approach to human capital and the stability of preferences', like Gardiner's, seeks to reframe (or, as he puts it at the beginning of his chapter, less forcefully perhaps, 'complement') another familiar narrative surrounding neoliberalism. Whereas Gardiner assails the imagined historical discontinuity between older and newer forms of liberalism through a longer range genealogy of constitutionalism, Vatter addresses the relation between the politico-legal and the economic at stake in the question of neoliberalism. This relation, introduced for example by Brown in the extract cited above, and pursued more exhaustively in her most recent book, *Undoing the Demos*, is figured by her in terms of the onward march and expansion of economic rationalities to the public and political realms, indeed to all conceivable lifeworlds. However, as Vatter argues, such a view 'assumes that neoliberal rationality is essentially and exclusively "economic" and only in a secondary moment does it invest other spheres and their rationalities', when in fact, as he creatively suggests through a jurisprudential reading of the famous Chicago School economist Gary Becker and his theory of human capital, 'the very idea of *homo oeconomicus* would not have been possible had it not always already interiorised and recast the idea of *homo legalis*'. On Vatter's reading, then, Becker's *economics* presupposes a *jurisprudence* of human capital – suggesting a co-implication of the legal and the economic dimensions of neoliberalism.

The second part of the collection is entitled 'Constituting neoliberalism' and features contributions from Javier Couso, Thomas Biebricher and Ntina Tzouvala. Each of these contributions, in different ways, addressing different locations and times, contributes to our understanding of how neoliberal economic ideas and practices are constituted in law and sheltered from democratic contestation. Couso's chapter, entitled 'Constructing "privatopia": the role of constitutional law in Chile's radical neoliberal experiment', tells the story of the establishment of neoliberal economic doctrines in the Chilean Constitution after the coup that brought General Augusto Pinochet to power. One example of this, upon which a range of other constitutional rights and doctrines are dependent, is the '*Principio de Subsidariedad*' ('principle of subsidiarity'), which establishes that the 'State cannot intervene in the economy unless the private sector is unable to do so'. On Couso's account, the form of constitutionally embedded neoliberalism in Chile operated to 'end the political debate concerning economic matters, taking this discussion out of the realm of politics and into the realm of constitutional law'. Here neoliberal constitutionalism is not only counterposed to, but stifling of, popular democratic contestation of economic questions.

Biebricher's chapter moves the focus from the Southern Cone in the 1980s to contemporary fiscal debates within the European Union. In 'The rise of juridical neoliberalism', he addresses both the theory and the practice of what he calls 'juridical neoliberalism'. Like Couso, his focus is on the ways in which attempts to constitutionalise particular economic doctrines and requirements function to immunise them from popular mobilisation and dissent. Unlike Couso, however, Biebricher ends his chapter by pointing to an ambivalence that is embedded within this constitutional move – and that potentially opens the way for strategic contestation. Biebricher discusses the work of the Chicago-trained economist and public choice theorist, James Buchanan and, in particular, his well-known ideas around the balanced-budget amendment (BBA) (a constitutional rule constraining state fiscal policy by requiring a state not to spend more than its income). Biebricher discusses various examples of European-level BBA agreements that 'aim to ensure that Eurozone member states achieve balanced budgets, avoid excessive deficits and prevent/correct macroeconomic imbalances' but, tellingly, points to a tension embedded within these documents. On the one hand, they try to achieve a 'depoliticization of fiscal policy', but, on the other hand, these constitutional attempts to vouchsafe fiscal policy from exercises of popular sovereignty do not just remain exercises of technocracy but are overlaid with a certain morality (of debt, austerity, fiscal discipline and responsibility – for the future of Europe). Biebricher hence observes:

> one can argue that the moralization of law serves to immunize it even more from challenges, but at the same time this moralization negates the strictly technocratic character of the BBA ... [and hence charges] these rules with moral implications [that] might inadvertently rekindle and fan the flames of political passions that the strategy of juridification was trying to put out.

Lastly, moving the geographical focus again, this time to the global arena, Tzouvala's chapter engages international trade law. In 'Neoliberalism as legalism: international economic law and the rise of the judiciary', she discusses the General Agreement on Tariffs and Trade and, later, the World Trade Organization. The logic she traces is one of the increasing legalisation (and internationalisation) of economic governance and the particular role that the judiciary plays in this process. Extending and applying the Marxist theorist, Nicos Poulantzas's concept of *authoritarian statism* to the domain of international trade law, Tzouvala argues that (like the examples discussed by Couso and Biebricher in the preceding chapters) the rise in importance of the judiciary in trade dispute resolution can be seen as part of a neoliberal trend towards 'reduc[ing] the influence of mass politics, organised labour and democratic imperatives on [economic] policy-making'. Indeed, as democratic and popular critics of strong form judicial review have argued for a long time in domestic constitutional contexts, and as she pithily puts it, 'the judiciary is the ideal agent for consolidating market discipline' due to its structural independence, political insulation and technocratic-formalist training.

The final part of the collection is entitled 'Human rights and neoliberalism' and returns us to the set of questions that we raised earlier. If human rights have become the predominant emancipatory discourse of our time then how can we understand their historical relation to neoliberalism in the late 1970s and, in our own day, what are the political possibilities opened up (and potentially closed off) by human rights when it comes to contesting neoliberalism? This concluding part features contributions by Samuel Moyn, Zachary Manfredi and Zeynep Kıvılcım which, respectively, address these questions in a historiographical, a theoretical and, finally, an empirical, register. Moyn's chapter, entitled 'A powerless companion: human rights in the age of neoliberalism', challenges those who (like Naomi Klein, Wendy Brown and the international lawyer, Susan Marks) point to the historical coincidence of the joint breakthrough of human rights and neoliberalism in the 1970s as evidence of their political compatibility such that human rights are cast as the accomplice of neoliberal economic restructuring. Contrary to this, Moyn suggests, the historical evidence for such a reading is scant and we should in fact think of human rights not as enabling the privations of neoliberalism, but as simply being powerless to prevent them. On Moyn's account, the more valid critique of human rights consists in pointing out just how moderate its demands for economic justice really are, and the more pressing challenge for the left hence consists not in castigating human rights for what it never really aimed to achieve, nor for alleging its complicity with neoliberalism, but for (as Wendy Brown herself calls for) demanding 'another politics' that would seriously address the economic problems of the neoliberal age.

Zachary Manfredi begins to think through this question, namely the political prospects of human rights, in his chapter, entitled 'An unlikely resonance? Subjects of human rights and subjects of human capital reconsidered'. Instead of moving beyond human rights, or supplementing them somehow with an alternative understanding of politics, Manfredi is interested in re-engaging the political possibilities of human rights themselves. Manfredi wants to complicate the framing of the relationship between human rights and neoliberalism. 'On my account', he writes, 'neoliberalism and human rights need not be treated as independent notions whose compatibility can be judged by comparing their normative principles and historical aspirations'. Rather, Manfredi argues, in a chapter that draws upon the substantive and methodological insights of Foucault's Collège de France lecture courses on *The Birth of Biopolitics*, 'in different historical configurations, both terms may prove co-constitutive. Neoliberal political rationality may, in certain contexts, amalgamate with human rights in ways that transform both concepts'. To work out when and in what contexts human rights will be transformed, or transform neoliberalism, demands attention to what Manfredi calls the particular 'configuration' of each. And so his chapter chooses to focus upon the intersection of human rights, human capital theory and late twentieth-century international development discourse in an attempt to show how the latter 'yoke[s] both theories of human "capital" (or human "capabilities") to notions of human rights in complex, ambivalent and potentially promising ways'.

Lastly, Kıvılcım's chapter, 'Articulating human rights discourse in local struggles in a neoliberal age', concludes this part and the collection itself by focusing empirically upon a particular instance of popular mobilisation against neoliberal economic policies. The instance that Kıvılcım focuses upon is the campaign against the Turkish state's plan to construct two thousand hydroelectric power plants (HPPs) by the end of 2023. These HPPs are to be 'constructed and operated by private companies licensed for the exclusive use of the water derived from those rivers'. Kıvılcım's chapter is an attempt to reckon with the ambivalence of one particular dimension of the resistance to the Turkish state's plans, namely the emerging and as-yet-undetermined human right to water. Through a wide-ranging study informed by the ideas of Antonio Gramsci, Ernesto Laclau and Chantal Mouffe, and drawing upon interviews with several key actors in different sections of the nationwide anti-HPP movement, Kıvılcım provides a fascinating map of the uptake of (but also strategic resistance to) the language of rights in the fight against water commodification.

Part I

The law and legality of neoliberalism

Chapter 1

Transformations of the rule of law

Legal, liberal, and neo-

Martin Krygier

'Neo' is a curious prefix. Supposed to mean 'new', it often has come to mean 'not'. Imagine, for example, what Edmund Burke or Michael Oakeshott might say of neo-conservative foreign policy adventurism: not much cautious 'pursuit of intimations'[1] there! Neo-liberalism presents a similar paradox. An ideal, the rule of law, prominent in discourses about power over millennia, and that remained so – indeed was a central element – in liberal and related political thought, has become a 'hurrah term' in many quarters in recent years, including 'neo-liberal' quarters. This boost in popularity, however, has not always gone with a more illuminating grasp of the *point* of concern with such matters. In particular, neo did not so much *add* to classical liberalism, as subtract from it. For liberalism was a powerful tradition of *political* thought, with a strenuous political morality, which also had an economic component. By contrast, like old-fashioned orthodox Marxism, with which it shares more features than either would enjoy to contemplate, neo-liberalism has powerful political implications and perhaps motivations, but its central inspiration and focus is economic. And its main thoughts on the rule of law have been economically focussed and derived as well. My fear is that much has been lost in the move: not merely a shift of domains, but the shrinking and repositioning of a worthy ideal, to its and our cost. I seek to show this by considering the character and fate of a particular disposition – a wish to temper power – that I take to have been central to the rule of law ideal for a very long time.

Tempering power

The rule of law is one of a number of overlapping ideas, among them constitutionalism, due process, legality, justice, that make claims for the proper character and role of law in well-ordered states and societies. Among these, rule of law has in recent times come into its own. It is lauded by international agencies, pressed upon conflictual, post-conflict, and 'transitional' societies, touted as the key to economic development and relief of poverty, security of human rights, and

1 Michael Oakeshott, 'Political Education', in Michael Oakeshott, *Rationalism in Politics and Other Essays*, new and expanded edition (Indianapolis: LibertyPress, 1991), 66–69.

many other good things. It is examined in political theory and jurisprudence, and also, though less often, has been subjected to sociological investigation. This all aside from its traditional role of being talked up by politicians and lawyers, particularly judges, on ceremonial occasions.

Whatever else might be said of it, the rule of law has to do with the exercise of power. And while the concept of law itself may or may not be normatively neutral about that relationship, depending on your jurisprudence, the rule of law is not. Rule *by* law might occur whenever and however law serves as a vehicle for the exercise of power; the rule *of* law, its partisans have insisted, is not compatible with every way in which power and law are yoked together, but only with some ways.

Appeal to the rule of law signals the hope that law might contribute to articulating, channelling, disciplining, constraining and informing – rather than merely serving – the exercise of power. I refer collectively to such contributions as *tempering* power, rather than, as is common among both liberals and neo-liberals, *limiting* it. The difference has implications, which I will explain shortly. But either way, tempering or limiting, we are already some distance from those who see law simply as one of the means by which power is exercised, neither better nor worse than any other. For there are lots of ways to exercise power, and lots of ways to enlist law in that exercise; partisans of the rule of law believe it is incompatible with many of those ways, including many of the worst of them.[2]

Why bother about that? Because, as over centuries countless thinkers have observed, a pervasive problem is that power untempered bids fair at least to be capricious and at worst wild. And as too many people over too many centuries have not only observed, but also experienced, capricious power is terribly unsettling and wild power is simply terrible. More generally, the potential is alive even when power is not wild, but merely, to use the more common epithet, arbitrary. Arbitrary power is not necessarily wild, but it is usually and already objectionable. Among the reasons identified by its opponents are at least five that have been emphasised by different thinkers at different times. Where arbitrariness is linked with significant power, it is liable to threaten the *liberty* of anyone subject to it; generate reasonable and enduring *fear* among them; deprive citizens of reliable sources of expectations of, and *coordination* with, each other and with the state; and reject both the *dignity* and the moral equality of all who find themselves mere objects of power exercisable at the whim or caprice of another. More can be said about all of this,[3] but not in the present chapter. One hope for the rule of law is that it might contribute to limiting the potential of power to generate such effects.

2 See Kristen Rundle, 'The Impossibility of an Exterminatory Legality: Law and the Holocaust' (2009) 59 (1) *University of Toronto Law Journal* 65–125.

3 I discuss these reasons more extensively in Martin Krygier, 'Four Puzzles about the Rule of Law: Why, What, Where? And Who Cares?', in *Getting to the Rule of Law*, ed., James E. Fleming (New York: New York University Press, 2011), 78–81.

Implications

Even at this throat-clearing stage, there are some implications to be uncovered. First, to oppose arbitrary or wild power is not to say that power of itself is obnoxious. Contrary to the view of Hayek, which he attributes to 'the great individualist social philosophers of the nineteenth century', that 'power itself has always appeared the archevil',[4] we could not do without power in many forms and for many purposes. We should not want to deny the need or emasculate the capacity for power to keep peace, defend populations, enforce legal judgments, collect taxes, balance other powers, and so on. Anyway, we are stuck with power; it will not disappear.

The problem with wild or arbitrary power is not the noun itself, but what the adjective does to it. Arbitrariness is a specific and obnoxious vice when added to power. A few masochists aside, few of us want to endure circumstances where significant power can be exercised over us in an arbitrary manner. There are many other vices which depend on the specific purpose or consequences of the exercise, but arbitrary power is vicious enough even without them and, moreover, can be vicious even when intentions are honourable. It is a free-standing vice, as it were, that has to do with the *ways* power is exercised.

The concept of arbitrariness is complex and insufficiently theorised. We can point to examples though. Exercises of power which depend on nothing but the caprice, unreasoned prejudice, untrammelled whim, of a power-holder are arbitrary. So too are those which, whatever their source, affect people in ways they have no way to predict. A third example is where the power-wielder is free to ignore the perspectives, circumstances and interests of those whom it would affect. What makes each of these exercises of power arbitrary is the fact that the act of power 'is subject just to the *arbitrium*, the decision or judgement of the [power-wielding] agent; the agent was in a position to choose it or not choose it, at their pleasure.'[5] Conversely, those subject to such power cannot manifest their voice and perspective, or take account of it ahead of time in choosing how to act; it is like lightning.

Law

Law has often been seen as an apt vehicle for institutionalising constraints on arbitrariness, though that is never all that law does; often it does not do it, not just any legal arrangement will do, and there are many other social practices and institutions necessary to accomplish it. And that is not even to mention uses and kinds of law that deny the values of the rule of law altogether. There are many such uses and kinds. The ideal of the rule of law rejects them. From the specific

4 F.A. Hayek, *The Road to Serfdom*, with a new introduction by Milton Friedman (Chicago: University of Chicago Press, 1994), 159.

5 Philip Pettit, *Republicanism: A Theory of Freedom and Government* (Oxford: Clarendon Press, 1997), 55.

perspective of the rule of law, law does well to the extent that and only insofar as public power is effectively constrained and channelled, so that it is routinely and reliably exercised in non-arbitrary ways. The role of law in the rule of law is to contribute to this state of affairs.

Of course, it is possible to be hostile to wild or arbitrary power without invoking law to remedy it. One might be suspicious that the law will always be in the sway of the powerful, which many have thought and is often the case. Or one might think law too weak a thing to temper power, and often this is true also. Or, and I am coming to hold such a view, one might emphasise the extent to which any good law does will depend on many things going right outside the law, and think it in principle an open question, with answers that vary with circumstance, how much official state law, as distinct from other social forces, practices and traditions might contribute to the tempering of power.

On the other hand, it does not seem to me surprising that the congeries of law-connected (and often well-connected) actors, that Halliday and partners call 'the legal complex', have been found again and again to be active defenders of a certain limited form of what they call 'political liberalism', which demands: (1) 'a moderate state, where power within the state is divided'; (2) civil society; and (3) 'a foundation of basic legal freedoms: negative rights to protect citizens against state tyranny or arbitrary state action; core political rights that permit freedoms of speech, association, and movement; and property rights, which give citizens inalienable claims to property'.[6] That lawyers might also be otherwise conservative, interested in money and status, not concerned with larger social and moral questions, justice in a large form, human rights broadly conceived, might not say much for their professional character, but it can be at least conjecturally explained in my terms: the ways power is exercised, and the ways it might legitimately be exercised are their special concern. That is unlikely to be everyone's concern, and there are many other equally and maybe ultimately more important concerns, but theirs is an important concern too. One does not expect to find a surfeit of heroes or revolutionaries among lawyers, but they are intimately acquainted with the exercise of public power, and it might well be an occupationally generated calling to prefer it to be exercised in non-arbitrary ways. *Mutatis mutandis*, the same might be said of dentists' interest in clean teeth.

Certainly, some traditions of legal thought have long maintained that law is crucial to tempering of power, and some have sought to build that ambition into the structure of law itself. The English common law tradition is distinctive for the length and strength of such beliefs and effort. And compared to pretty well any place one could name, the English have not done badly in their efforts, at least at home.

The rule of law is an English phrase, and even without the phrase there is a distinctive tradition of thought about law that can sensibly be referred to as an

6 See Lucien Karpik and Terry Halliday, 'The Legal Complex' (2011) 7 *Annual Review of Law and Social Science* 217–236.

English rule of law tradition. From at least the thirteenth century until well into the eighteenth century, the common law tradition maintained that even the king was subject to a law that he had not made, indeed that made him king. For the king, for anyone, to ignore or override that law was to act arbitrarily.[7] Liberties, and procedures to protect them, such as *habeas corpus* and due process, came to be enshrined in that law, and encroachment on such liberties was barred, even to the monarch, by the law. For the king, like his subjects, was subject to 'the law of the land', which had come down by various means over many generations.

This was not mere moral exhortation. Old in English traditions of thought about law are attempts to institutionalise the ambition to frame and channel the exercise of power within a legal order that is simultaneously an instrument of power. It was classically described by Charles McIlwain,[8] and its rationale has recently been recovered and re-articulated by Gianluigi Palombella as central to the rule of law. According to this tradition, the point of the rule of law is 'to prevent the law from turning itself into a sheer tool of domination, a manageable servant to political monopoly and instrumentalism.'[9] It requires that, besides the laws that bend to the will of governments, '"another" positive law should be available, which is located somehow outside the purview of the (legitimate) government, be it granted by the long standing tradition of common law or by the creation of a "constitutional" higher law protection, and so forth.'[10] The common law writers spoke of a *balance* between the sovereign's untrammelled right to pursue the ends of government (*gubernaculum*), on the one hand, and legal protection of the right (*jurisdictio*), on the other. The former must not overwhelm the latter, even if it is unlimited in its own sphere.

The solution was found in the common law, viewed not just as a moral limit, but a binding legal one. Written and binding constitutions are more recent examples of such an ambition. In all these the ruler is supposed to be bound, or 'bridled' in Bracton's usage, by something that is truly law, but not his to rule, not able to be bent to his will. Note that the rule of law in this interpretation requires a *balance* between protection of right and pursuit of the common good. It does not deny the responsibility of governments to look to the latter, so long as they do not infringe the former. If the notion of balance denies that *gubernaculum* can overwhelm *jurisdictio*, it also implies the converse: the sphere of *gubernaculum* is a legitimate sphere of government activity, whatever contemporary neo-liberals might be tempted to say against it. This implication is captured in Palombella's recovery of the medieval notion, and is well brought out by Neil Walker:

7 See John Philip Reid, *The Rule of Law* (De Kalb: Northern Illinois University Press, 2004); Leonardo Morlino and Gianluigi Palombella, eds, *Rule of Law and Democracy: Inquiries into Internal and External Issues* (Leiden: Brill, 2010).

8 Charles Howard McIlwain, *Constitutionalism: Ancient and Modern*, rev. edn (Ithaca, NY: Cornell University Press, 1947).

9 Gianluigi Palombella, 'The Rule of Law as an Institutional Ideal', in Morlino and Palombella, *Rule of Law and Democracy*, 4.

10 Palombella, 'The Rule of Law', 31.

> Tellingly, the idea of the Rule of Law … is often reduced in the canonical literature to one side of law's duality – to the rights-based protection against arbitrary public power. For Palombella, however, it is better conceived of as an integrative achievement. His Rule of Law is concerned with acknowledging and maintaining an equilibrium that allows each *desideratum* to prosper, and permits all the virtues of law – both the deep autonomy-respecting virtues of individual Right and the collectively self-realising virtue of the common Good, to be placed in balance.[11]

Liberalism

Political thinkers have asked many things of political arrangements, among them, fulfilment, liberation, justice, mercy, prosperity, social equality. The list is long and it can be inspiring. There is, however, a strain of thought which appears to ask for little, and that is quite austere, but does so insistently. It asks for security from the evils that flow from arbitrary power. People of this disposition might ask for more than such security, but they insist that it is central. Many traditions, legal and political, have exhibited this disposition. It has, for example, been central to the republican tradition. It has also been central to many thinkers and thoughts we call liberal.

Liberalism, a term only coined in the nineteenth century, has many ancestors and many variants, few canonical texts of the sort that Marxism boasts, and no single orthodoxy that covers the field. But what Judith Shklar, one of the most recent, uncompromising and eloquent exponents of this way of thinking about politics, has aptly named the 'liberalism of fear' is a prominent participant in the tradition. The various strands of thought that Shklar characterises as the liberalism of fear can be understood as moments in an extended meditation on ways to institutionalise the tempering of power, consistent with the rule of law ideal.

The products of such meditations are various. Different rule of law regimes have often embodied different judgments about how to achieve this goal, and have different legal and other histories and traditions which have influenced the particular shape of the institutions they have. These differences are not automatically fatal, once one recognises that the rule of law is not a recipe for detailed institutional design, but rather a cluster of values which might inform such design, and which might be – and have been – pursued in a variety of ways.[12]

This concern to tame major sources of fear has had deep resonance among thinkers about public affairs over several hundred years; it was not confined to the English. Roman Republicans expressed the concern, and their influence has lasted from Polybius in Rome (though he was Greek) to Pettit in Princeton and Canberra (though he is Irish). It is expressed among other places in the writings of

11 Neil Walker, 'Law's Global (Re)connection' (2014) 3 (1) *Rivista di filosofia del diritto* 102.

12 See Philip Selznick, 'Legal Cultures and the Rule of Law', in *The Rule of Law after Communism*, eds, Martin Krygier and Adam Czarnota (Aldershot: Ashgate, 1999).

Montesquieu (though he is French), and these greatly influenced the American Constitutional Founding Fathers, among other things, to misunderstand the English constitution (as containing a strict separation of powers) in an inspired and at least until recently relatively useful way. They, in turn, influenced us all, even if today tempering of sources of fear commonly finds more eloquent partisans among those who have suffered its absence than those who live off the fruits of its presence.

Shklar, similarly, considers escape from arbitrary power the fundamental virtue to be sought from legal and political arrangements, and insists that it cannot be achieved without the rule of law. Indeed, her position is quite simple and stark. As she explicates and approves Montesquieu's institutional recommendations, designed to ensure what he described and valued as 'moderation' in government:

> [t]his whole scheme is ultimately based on a very basic dichotomy. The ultimate spiritual and political struggle is always between war and law ... The institutions of judicial citizen protection may create rights, but they exist in order to avoid what Montesquieu took to be the greatest of human evils, constant fear created by the threats of violence and the actual cruelties of the holders of military power in society. The Rule of Law is the one way ruling classes have of imposing controls upon each other.[13]

Implications

Shklar is not alone in her combination of a high regard for the rule of law with a negative view of it. This is only an apparent, verbal, paradox. For it is common to understand it as good, less for what it enables and creates than for what it might prevent. On this interpretation, its point is to *block* and *limit* the possibility of unruly power, to curb and restrain power's exercise. This is not a new view, and it is still popular among liberals, and even more neo-liberals. Thus Hayek: 'The effective limitation of power is the most important problem of social order',[14] and it is the job of constitutionalism and the rule of law to impose the limits. The characteristics most associated with law changed over the centuries, particularly moving from custom to legislation, and with those changes went different conceptions of what the law needed to be like to do its proper work. However, the identification of the rule of law's purpose with what it strives to rule out rather than what it rules in; what it seeks to prevent, rather than what it hopes to generate and encourages to flourish, remains prevalent.

I find this negative emphasis powerful, above all because it takes 'the circumstances of politics'[15] much more seriously than a lot of so-called political theory

13 Judith N. Shklar, 'Political Theory and the Rule of Law', in Judith N. Shklar, *Political Thought and Political Thinkers*, ed., Stanley Hoffmann (Chicago: University of Chicago Press, 1998), 25.

14 Friedrich A. Hayek, *The Political Order of a Free People*, vol. 3 of *Law, Legislation and Liberty* (Chicago: University of Chicago Press, 1979), 128.

15 See Jeremy Waldron, *Law and Disagreement* (Oxford: Oxford University Press, 1999).

does. Politics is, after all, not just a matter of the ends we should seek, but of conflict, violence, oppression, domination, their consequences, and its study needs to be concerned with what might be needed to avoid them;[16] it is not all, as both Bernard Williams and Jeremy Waldron have emphasised, 'just applied moral philosophy'.[17]

And yet, the liberalism of fear can also limit and distort one's understanding of politics, and of law. Avoiding the worst is not the sum of politics, or of the contribution of the rule of law. That is one reason I prefer to speak (as Cicero and Bracton, *inter alia*, did) of *tempering* power, not limiting it, or any of the other words – taming, restraining, etc. – usually associated with the rule of law.[18] Tempering suggests both moderating (for example, justice with mercy) and strengthening (for example, of steel), and that combination is what the rule of law promises. Power is not to be lessened but refined, balanced, mixed; and it might be strengthened. For the negative conception is not the only way of viewing the rule of law, and arguably not the best.

Jeremy Waldron has criticised views of constitutionalism according to which '[e]verything is seen through the lens of restraint and limitation',[19] and has insisted on the empowering role and potential of constitutional provisions. Similar points might be made about the rule of law. Again, Stephen Holmes has long stressed the empowering consequences of law; what, in contrast to the more common negative conception, he calls 'positive constitutionalism'.[20] Appropriately configured laws, on this view, provide 'enabling constraints'.[21] For the 'paradoxical insight' here, as Holmes describes it, is that:

> Limited government is, or can be, more powerful than unlimited government … that constraints can be enabling, which is far from being a contradiction, lies at the heart of liberal constitutionalism … By restricting the arbitrary powers of

16 See Bernard Williams, 'The Liberalism of Fear', in Bernard Williams, *In the Beginning Was the Deed: Realism and Moralism in Political Argument*, ed., Geoffrey Hawthorn (Princeton, NJ: Princeton University Press, 2005).

17 Jeremy Waldron, '*Political* Political Theory: An Inaugural Lecture' (2013) 21 (1) *Journal of Political Philosophy* 1–23.

18 See Martin Krygier, 'Tempering Power', in *Bridging Idealism and Realism in Constitutionalism and Rule of Law*, eds, Maurice Adams, Ernst Hirsch Ballin and Anne Meuwese (Cambridge: Cambridge University Press, 2016), from which this section of this chapter is largely drawn.

19 Jeremy Waldron, 'Constitutionalism: A Skeptical View' (Public Law & Legal Theory Research Paper Series no. 10–87, School of Law, New York University, 2010), 25.

20 Stephen Holmes, *Passions and Constraint: On the Theory of Liberal Democracy* (Chicago: University of Chicago Press, 1995).

21 I believe this is a coinage of David Stark and László Bruszt, *Postsocialist Pathways: Transforming Politics and Property in East Central Europe* (Cambridge: Cambridge University Press, 1998), chap. 6. See also Martin Loughlin, *The Idea of Public Law* (Oxford: Oxford University Press, 2003); Jon Elster, *Ulysses Unbound: Studies in Rationality, Precommitment, and Constraints* (Cambridge: Cambridge University Press, 2000).

> government officials, a liberal constitution can, under the right conditions, *increase* the state's capacity to focus on specific problems and mobilize collective resources for common purposes.[22]

On this view, like a swimmer (or a scholar) who must master, and in a sense come to be mastered by, techniques and disciplines to marshal and channel raw energy (or intelligence) for effective performance, so the ability of a state to concentrate its powers where and how it should is enhanced by legal requirements, procedures and institutions which, among other things, block its ability to splash around where and how it should not.

And there is another point, well made by Philip Selznick. Selznick also saw reduction of arbitrariness as the central point of the rule of law, and he also viewed protection against the brute vices of unrestrained power as primary. But that was not always and everywhere a problem of the same intensity and urgency. Arbitrariness, just to stay with that, comes in many kinds and degrees, and one needs to attend to many things short of war, cruelty and fanaticism. One might also hope for better from rule of law constraints on the exercise of power than avoidance of such terrible forces. In well-established legal orders with strong traditions, institutions and professions, one can ask more of legal institutions than mere restraint on power, notwithstanding the preciousness of that. Rather:

> In contemporary discussions of the rule of law we find much that goes beyond the negative virtue of restraining official misconduct ... This thicker, more positive vision speaks to more than abuse of power. It responds to values that can be *realized*, not merely protected within a legal process. These include respect for the dignity, integrity, and moral equality of persons and groups. Thus understood, the rule of law enlarges horizons even as it conveys a message of restraint.[23]

In this understanding, arbitrariness, and its antidote the rule of law, both take on a larger meaning, attached to values to be vindicated, rather than simply to a set of institutions and practices imagined to serve them. Arbitrariness is not found merely when a strict rule is overstepped but equally when law is 'inflexible, insensitive, or justified *only* by history or precedent'.[24] 'Going by the book'[25] generates its own forms of arbitrariness, as anyone who has sought to deal with officious bureaucrats might testify. To counteract such forms of arbitrariness, space needs to be made for an expanded understanding of the rule of law, more open-ended and open to the world.

22 Holmes, *Passions and Constraint*, xi.
23 Selznick, 'Legal Cultures and the Rule of Law', 26.
24 Selznick, 'Legal Cultures and the Rule of Law', 27.
25 See Eugene Bardach and Robert A. Kagan, *Going by the Book: The Problem of Regulatory Unreasonableness* (Philadelphia, PA: Temple University Press, 1982).

Lastly, as with most political values, the rule of law is not the only game in town. If there are tensions between tempering power and other important values, those tensions need to be examined and dealt with, sometimes simply put up with, lived with. We do that with tensions all the time, after all. We have few absolute and universal trumps in these games.

Neo-liberalism

These days 'neo-liberalism' is a term used far more by enemies than friends. It was actually coined by its friends, the German 'Ordo-liberals' of the 1930s, but it was not they who made the term pervasive and they are not the subject of this chapter. I focus on those today called neo-liberals, whose influence is thought by many to be pervasive in the contemporary world.

I should confess that I am suspicious of social explanation which reduces all that is distasteful (since it is some time since 'neo-liberal' was a boast) to the machinations of some omnipresent and omnivorous neo-liberal imperative, ambition, ideology or system. Such homogenising efforts have a flavour which matches in reverse some neo-liberal tendencies to attribute everything bad to 'collectivism' (Hayek) or the state (Reagan). They flatten out differences among alleged neo-liberals; whereas these can be significant, particularly between those whose writings began before the Second World War, such as Hayek, and a later generation, galvanised by Milton Friedman, who were more populist, more activist and more radical.[26] They also flatten out the explanation of often complex social phenomena, in search of one, often pre-determined, causal agent. Reality is typically more complex, however, than enthusiastic neos and con-neos (not to be confused with neo-cons) concede.

However, there are certain modern dispositions of thought, to use that phrase again, which seem to me incontestably to be found wherever 'neo-liberals' seem to cluster, and which have seeped into many domains of life (not least the modern university where it is not immediately obvious that they have a place). Here I will limit my observations to a few of them that involve law.

Neo-liberalism began within, and in relation to, developed Western countries, where it was revived by economists, perhaps best known among them Friedrich von Hayek and Milton Friedman, in reaction to perceived inadequacies in, and normative objections to, the welfare states and Keynesian economics that had been prominent through much of the second half of the twentieth century. It achieved political influence in the late 1970s, propelled and symbolised by the political leadership and rhetoric of Margaret Thatcher and Ronald Reagan. Particularly after the collapse of European communism, it became a key influence on, and vehicle for (though perhaps less confidently today), the evangelical export industry of rule of law promotion in countries allegedly in need of it. I will start with the West and move to the rest.

26 See Angus Burgin, *The Great Persuasion. Reinventing Free Markets since the Depression* (Cambridge, MA: Harvard University Press, 2012).

Home

There are at least two levels at which the welfare and regulatory activities of modern states offend neo-liberals. One appears wholesale, as it were, and covers the gamut of modern welfare and regulatory state activities. It has to do with the purpose and scope of much such activity, and its alleged social, economic and political consequences. The other focuses on the effects of this activity on the character of the *laws* that this active modern state comes to rely upon, and in particular on the *form* of law. I will sketch them in turn.

One of the major developments of the twentieth century was the growth of the welfare and regulatory state, and with it unprecedented expansion of state activity, both in quantity and in kind. Numbers soared – people employed, money spent, activities pursued – and so too did the range and substance of state activities, central among them the provision of welfare, services and regulatory activity. A tag line for neo-liberal responses, buttressed by somewhat more sophisticated if arguable economic theory, is Reagan's inaugural pronouncement that 'Government is not the solution to our problem; government is the problem.' So what is the solution? Again not as simple as this, but in this direction: the activities of individuals and corporations in open and free markets. And what is the proper role of law? To secure the conditions of free and efficient market exchange: particularly property rights, contract, law of bankruptcy, but also criminal law, without which all else would be vulnerable. Otherwise, '[t]he fundamental principle [is] that in the ordering of our affairs we should make as much use as possible of the spontaneous forces of society, and resort as little as possible to coercion.'[27] Governments are necessary to provide some public goods, services and facilities (for example, monetary system, land registration, roads, sewers) not provided by the market,[28] that secure 'a favourable framework for individual decisions'.[29] However, coercive meddling with private freedom, say by way of intrusive regulation derived not from 'general and timeless purposes' but from 'particular preferences which guide the government of the moment or from any opinion as to how particular people ought to be situated'[30] both is inconsistent with the freedom necessary for efficient market transactions, and takes the form of laws that in their very *character* – imprecise, variable, discretionary, purpose-oriented – undermine the rule of law itself.

Libertarians and so-called neo-liberals in theory (Friedrich von Hayek, Milton Friedman, Robert Nozick) and in power (Margaret Thatcher, Ronald Reagan) objected on political and/or economic and/or philosophical (epistemological and moral) grounds to what they took to be the hyperactivity of the modern state. Hayek had great influence here. He had both moral and epistemological

27 Hayek, *The Road to Serfdom*, 21.
28 Hayek, *Political Order of a Free People*, 41; and see F.A. Hayek, *The Constitution of Liberty* (London: Routledge, 1976), 215, 221.
29 Hayek, *The Constitution of Liberty*, 223.
30 Hayek, *The Constitution of Liberty*, 226.

objections to the welfare state's 'instrumentalisation' of law. Morally, intervention that purports to further the 'will-of-the wisp of "social justice"'[31] is the pursuit of a 'mirage'.[32] Only the conduct of individuals or organisations could be either just or unjust. Collective states of affairs, results of aggregated social action, could not. In particular, the concept had no place in regard to the 'spontaneous order' that is a society, since 'nothing that is not subject to human control can be just (or moral)'.[33] To try to characterise the justice of a society is nonsense, a category mistake,[34] and not an innocent one; '[I]t is bound to lead back to socialism and its coercive and essentially arbitrary methods'.[35] For Hayek, the notion that law must flexibly 'respond' to social needs – other than basic ones for a clear framework of general rules to assist individuals in guiding their actions and interactions – emanates from a flawed social theory and presages a damaged polity. It also pretends to a knowledge that no individuals but only markets, which aggregate more knowledge than anyone separately has, can possess.

Friedman's hostility to state interventions and regulations was even more thorough-going than Hayek's (which was already not slight). Post-Friedmanite neo-liberals have typically taken the rule of law to be associated with a restricted state, the appropriate functions of which were to be strictly limited and few, though those few were important: primarily to keep the peace and frame, facilitate and secure the conditions of free individual coordination and choice. The real action was properly elsewhere and by others: in the market, populated and driven by private individuals and corporations, and free from restrictions that hamper its natural self-correcting propensities. In the context of what neo-liberals saw as bloated welfare states of the seventies, not to mention post-communist states of the nineties, this therefore would require, *inter alia*, large scale privatisation of the assets and activities, and outsourcing of many services, hitherto provided by states. The state was certainly not to row, and only on occasion to steer. Or, to change the metaphor, the state was necessary to establish and enforce the constitutive rules of the game;[36] not to be a player. These rules were needed to provide a reliable normative frame for market activities, which generates clear signals of the rules of the game, lends stability to, and allows coordination among, the expectations of market actors. And that, roughly, was to be it. Attempts to use law

31 Friedrich A. Hayek, *Rules and Order*, vol. 1 of *Law, Legislation and Liberty* (Chicago: University of Chicago Press, 1973), 143.

32 Friedrich A. Hayek, *The Mirage of Social Justice*, vol. 2 of *Law, Legislation and Liberty* (Chicago: University of Chicago Press, 1977). See at 133: '"social justice" is an empty phrase without determinable content. … Like chasing any mirage it is likely to produce results which one would have done much to avoid if one had foreseen them. Many desirable aims will be sacrificed in the vain hope of making possible what must forever elude our grasp.'

33 Hayek, *The Mirage of Social Justice*, 32.

34 Hayek, *The Mirage of Social Justice*, 31.

35 Hayek, *The Constitution of Liberty*, 260.

36 See Milton Friedman, *Capitalism and Freedom*, reissued with new Preface (Chicago, IL: University of Chicago Press, 1982, 25).

to 'respond' to social problems, and attend to matters of 'fairness' or 'social justice', were seen as counter-productive non-solutions to non- or insoluble problems, which in turn create their own problems, among them for the rule of law.

On this model, the job of state and law, when highly constrained, is crucial but not central. Its rules should be clear, stable, precise and general, but not too numerous. Such rules can give security to private interests, particularly those of investors, property-owners and market contractors, without which the market cannot work efficiently. The job of the state is to enforce these basic normative rules of the game, an important job, but not a particularly extensive or active one. If it goes further than that, to mess with matters of distribution and regulation, it will threaten the market order.

Apart from the inappropriateness of modern goals, a second neo-liberal objection was to the effects of modern state activity on the legal *means* used by the welfare and regulatory state. Again Hayek, who thought more than many economists about law, was influential here. Free markets depend *on clear, general, abstract, impersonal and negative* legal rules of the game, 'rules of just conduct',[37] interpreted and enforced by independent arbiters, and essentially made up of private and criminal law. They could not withstand blizzards of open-ended policy directives of public law, increasingly vague and unspecific in their terms, full of appeals to substantive criteria and specific social purposes to be achieved, open to discretionary implementation by goal-directed bureaucrats increasingly free (actually required) to adjust their interpretations to the specificity of particular cases in pursuit of governmentally prescribed specific ends.[38] Bad goals in turn generate bad means, laws that do not guide, frameworks that keep being adjusted, prescriptions too vague and malleable to be followed, but altogether labile in the hands of their wielders.

Much of this governmental regulatory and distributive activity of the modern state devolved upon administrators (though the derisive epithet of choice was usually bureaucrats), well supplied with open-ended legislative provisions, regulatory discretions, and particularised decisions to make. Many writers, prominently but not only neo-liberals, have been concerned that however well-meaning the motives of such activity, their pursuit exacts a high price in terms of the ability of law to constrain power and contribute to coordination, even if their goals are likely to be achieved, which many such critics also doubt. Again, a significant part of the cost of the pursuit, it has often been alleged, is borne by the rule of law.[39]

37 Hayek, *Rules and Order*, 143.

38 See Hayek, *Rules and Order*; Hayek, *The Mirage of Social Justice*; Hayek, *Political Order of a Free People.*

39 See, e.g. Geoffrey de Q. Walker, *The Rule of Law: Foundation of Constitutional Democracy* (Carleton: Melbourne University Press, 1988); Hayek, *Law, Legislation and Liberty*; E. Kamenka and A.E-S. Tay, 'Beyond Bourgeois Individualism – The Contemporary Crisis in Law and Legal Ideology' in *Feudalism, Capitalism and Beyond*, eds, E. Kamenka and R.S. Neale (Canberra: ANU Press, 1975). And from a different political perspective, see Brian Tamanaha, *Law as a Means to an End: Threat to the Rule of*

Implications

How should someone who shares the disposition of thought I began with respond to this twofold critique: the wholesale rejection of non-market responses to questions of 'social justice' and the retail critique of the sort of law that generates?

First, there is a serious conceptual difficulty with identifying the state as 'the problem, not the solution' and the market as that solution, because the market depends heavily, and in many ways unacknowledged by modern neo-liberals, on the state, and in particular on a state that can tax and spend. As several authors have reminded us, while a common sense distinction between state and society or state and market can be understood, to erect a dichotomy out of it makes no sense. Karl Polanyi already showed that a market society is no natural phenomenon, but depends on particular forms of state law and regulation.[40]

Of course, supporters of 'minimal' states agree that some sorts of legal (and therefore state) activity are necessary for the state to support civil societies, but only those they say are primarily protective, negative activities; not positive, active. They distinguish the former laudable and modest state activities from the latter intrusive and immodest ones of modern welfare states. But on what ground can this distinction be made?

It is common to distinguish between classical liberal rights – so-called negative rights, rights against interference – and more socialistic, 'positive', welfare rights which depend on state provision. However, even the most classical of the liberal rights depend on very substantial state provision. Markets and private property, not to mention contract, copyright, intellectual property and corporations, are products of systematic state interference in society. They exist owing to laws which enforce certain rules and not others, embody certain images of social interaction and not others, penalise certain behaviours and reward others.[41] None of this is small game, and none of it involves simply tracking and backing autonomous social activity. What form this activity takes, what consequences it will have, what is to be tracked and what is to be backed, and how, and with what implications, are all state decisions. How effectively any of this happens depends on state solvency, integrity, institutional design, trained personnel, and an ethos of office which can withstand the variety of corruptions that high stakes will, without counteraction, attract.

Law (Cambridge: Cambridge University Press, 2007). More complex appraisals of such developments include Otto Kirchheimer, 'The *Rechtsstaat* as Magic Wall', in Otto Kirchheimer, *Politics, Law, and Social Change* (New York: Columbia University Press, 1969), 428; Philippe Nonet and Philip Selznick, *Law and Society in Transition. Toward Responsive Law* (New Brunswick: Transaction Publishers, 2001); and, for a bracing critique of such 'crisis talk', David Nelken, 'Is there a Crisis in Law and Legal Ideology?' (1982) 9 (2) *Journal of Law and Society* 177–89.

40 Fred Block and Margaret R. Somers, *The Power of Market Fundamentalism. Karl Polanyi's Critique* (Cambridge, MA: Harvard University Press, 2014), 27.

41 See Cass R. Sunstein, *Free Markets and Social Justice* (New York: Oxford University Press, 1997).

As Holmes and Sunstein make clear, popular but false dichotomies, like that between negative rights that allegedly require no or merely negative state intervention and positive rights that depend upon lots of it, are spurious. Rights, as they emphasise, all rights, including property and contractual rights, depend on government recognition, enforcement, financial and institutional provision, adjudication, remedy. All these things cost, and so all rights cost, often a great deal. There is no categorical distinction to be made.

Think what the state must provide just to allow citizens the potential to sue each other, let alone the state itself. And then to expect, and then to get, a fair trial. And then to have a decision enforced. None of these rights is just a negative protection, freedom *from* interference by others. They are constituted by state decisions, underwritten by state provision, and made good by state intervention, on legal cause proven by state sanctioned methods in state institutions. They are, as Holmes insists, entitlements to state action; just as welfare rights are. And, like welfare rights, they are hollow without such action. As Holmes has observed, 'Rights protection and enforcement depend on state capacities. Statelessness, therefore, means rightlessness'.[42]

A historical reflection might not go amiss here. Many neo-liberals, most notably Hayek, in that remarkable feat of elision, *The Road to Serfdom*, predicted a slippery slope from the welfare state to totalitarianism. Indeed, characteristically, Hayek denied that there could be any third way between a market order and dictatorship:

> There is no other possibility than either the order governed by the impersonal discipline of the market or that directed by the will of a few individuals; and those who are out to destroy the first are wittingly or unwittingly helping to create the second.[43]

Hayek had the Nazis primarily in mind, though he considered that they shared common socialist, collectivist origins, objectives and illusions with Italian fascists and Soviet communists. When only communism survived the Second World War, later neo-liberals focused on it as the great 'other' in the conceptual geography of the world.

It is therefore worth remembering that no society has ever slid down that slope. Germany was at least modern, though more a 'predatory warfare society' than a welfare state.[44] Moreover, no communist state ever began as a welfare state in decline, and no welfare state has ever delivered the comprehensive political, moral, economic and ecological degradation that communist states did. On the contrary. All success is relative and most is transient, but given those caveats, western liberal

42 Stephen Holmes, 'Cultural Legacies or State Collapse? Probing the Postcommunist Dilemma', Public Lecture no. 13, Collegium Budapest, Institute for Advanced Study, Budapest, Hungary, November 1995, 35.

43 Hayek, *The Road to Serfdom*, 219.

44 See Heinz Lubasz, 'The Nazi Welfare State' (1968) 11 (11) *The New York Review of Books*, 19 December.

democracies were the success story of the past century. Yet these polities, at the moments of their greatest success, were liberal social democracies, with government activity and welfare services greater than have ever existed in the history of the world. One can say that they would have done immeasurably better if they had never been welfare states at all; but then one can *say* anything.

Try excising the 'problem' state from the market 'solution' and it is not clear what will be left. That being the case, the *actual* controversy is not between more and less state provision but rather about the proper *kind* of state provision. Notwithstanding the best efforts of neo-liberals, state provision and expense have not diminished in recent years, but have changed in goals, beneficiaries and those whom they burden. Seen in that light the debate takes a very different form from that which many neo-liberals suggest, and it cannot be settled within the terms they offer.

So, there is a lot for states to do. One needs a state strong enough to do what it must, and restrained enough not to do what it must not. Therein lie the point and virtue of long liberal and republican political traditions of institutional design, whose central aim is not to emasculate, but to temper and channel the exercise of governmental power. In these circumstances, and from this perspective, the various liberal nostrums that we know so well – limited government, the rule of law, an independent judiciary, a free press, and so on – have the twofold importance of allowing governments the strength they need, while requiring that as much as can be contrived they act through channels, and in ways, and under the watch of other forces which might temper the exercise of power. Such institutionalisation makes power at the same time safer and more effective.

Moreover, even apart from the inextricable dependencies of markets on states, what sense does it make from the point of view of the rule of law to identify the state as the exclusive source of rule of law problems? Let us recall that, on the interpretation I am endorsing here, the key anti-hero of the rule of law story is arbitrary power. I have emphasised that the rule of law is not hostile to power itself. It is the addition of arbitrariness that hurts.

Neo-liberals, in this case not eccentrically but with a vengeance, have focused their hostility on state power, virtually exclusively. So too did the rule of law tradition more generally. But why would anyone with the disposition I have advocated accept such a limit? If other forms and sources of power – social, economic, religious, ethnic – have significant public impact, why imagine that their arbitrary exercise will be benign, simply because it is not the state that exercises it? Indeed, one should put it more strongly than that. If the reason we are talking about the rule of law is because wild or arbitrary power is so potentially horrible, then whenever an institution or group, more occasionally individual, is in a position to wield arbitrary power with significant public consequences, that should be the subject of concern for anyone who is persuaded of the dangers of such power. Of course there are limits. Not every exercise of power should be a matter of public concern. Distinctions have to be made, and matters of scale, character and consequence really matter. But state/non-state cannot be the pivot, I think, for people who fear arbitrary power.

Once, but far from always in human history, one might have been confident that states are uniquely more powerful than all other forces, and that is why they are at the centre of attention. But always it is an empirical and variable matter whether threats to the rule of law are going to come from the state or somewhere else or both. And today things are more complicated. If non-state power is arbitrarily exercised by oligarchs, Mafiosi, warlords, tribal elders, Al Qaeda, business executives, finance speculators, international ratings agencies, financial institutions or, indeed, university administrators, it too has the potential to bring with it the vices of arbitrariness mentioned above. Banks can do a lot of damage too and, in recent relatively unregulated years and countries, they have. We have an interest in tempering significant public power, whoever is doing the exercise.

Taking the rule of law seriously requires acknowledgement that many of the most significant sources of, goods generated by, and dangers to the rule of law are to be found in the wider society, including the market, not merely in or even near the obvious institutional centres of official law.[45] Sources of power are many, and they vary. There are numerous societies in which arbitrariness flows as much or more from extra-state exercises of power, sometimes aided by suborned official agencies, sometimes opposed to them. Moreover, possible constraints on it may come, or fail to come, from many domains of social life, and from many agencies other than legal ones. Not only might this happen, but it already does, and in spades. There might be other reasons to be chary of interfering with non-state actors wielding arbitrary power, but a concern to temper arbitrary public power does not of itself suggest them.

I now move to the retail dimension, the allegedly transformative and degrading effect of an active state on the form and character of modern law, and its ability to serve the rule of law. It must be admitted that Hayek is a clear thinker, but that is not always a virtue. He is often too clear. His thought is full of what John Dewey used to castigate as 'pernicious dualisms', where one pristine logically coherent ideal type, say of a free market or the private law of just conduct, contradicts another, say the regulatory state, or public law. But these are not real-world contradictions. Neo-liberal anxiety can only distinguish itself from paranoia, and can only make plausible claims about the effects of different forms of law in the world if neo-liberals are prepared to take circumstances, and variations in institutional strength, support and resilience, into account. Many who understand the power of evil and corruption in the world are genuinely and rightly reluctant to compromise the capacity of law to frame and give cues to social conduct, and the autonomy from other pressures which a law of stable general rules seems to promise. Comparing relatively autonomous legal orders with repressive and arbitrary ones, they prefer the former. And rightly so. But these are not the only alternatives; there are many possibilities in between, and that is where many of us live.

But why would one want to compromise the ruliness of law? Basically because, while we need institutions and the rule of law to protect us we might need to

45 For more on this, see Krygier, 'Four Puzzles'.

enlist them for other purposes as well, and characteristics apt for one purpose might not be equally apt for others, however legitimate they both are.[46]

Conservatives and neo-liberals in rule-of-law-rich countries, suspicious of any falling-off from some idealised version of its supposed legal vehicles, often over-react to, say, injection of any substantive concerns into adjudication or discretionary authority in administration, indeed to any number of welfare state incursions. These are interpreted as dangers to the existence of the rule of law as we know it, whereas they might be dangers only in circumstances where legality is already weak, and has no other resources with which to defend itself. Such reactions show little reflection on what the rule of law might depend upon, what it would be like to really threaten what they have of it, and what it would really mean to lack it. Radicals in the same societies, on the other hand, who treat some indeterminacy in appellate decision-making as testimony to fraudulence or at least to absence of the rule of law, exhibit a similar frivolousness about what it might really be to have to live without a good measure of it.[47]

This suggests that not every potential source of threat to the rule of law will be equally salient in different legal orders: some will be much threatened, others less so, by the same things. It also suggests that different threats in different circumstances might require different defences. Not to mention that we might want to do more than ward off threats. Of course, the rule of law can be seriously threatened even where it appears to be in good shape. If we needed to recall it, the war on terror reminds us of that, as it does of the dangers of complacency in such circumstances. Yet there is still a lot to draw on, even there, which is unavailable in a tyranny, a failed state, illiberal democracy, and so on.

Away

The international career of the rule of law took off in the 1990s, spurred dramatically and quickly by the collapse of European communism in 1989. Given the dichotomies that dominated the conceptual space of most of the preceding century – liberal democracy in politics and market capitalist in economics versus Party-state dictatorship and command economy – the collapse of one of its protagonists was taken by many observers to mean not merely the signal victory of the other, but that the sources of its superiority would be found in institutions and practices that were the *reverse image* of those that had failed. This particularly was taken to refer to the state and public administration.

Dissidents under communism were rarely economists, and the opposite was also true. However, they often converged in their identification of the Other. Political opposition within communist states had been increasingly articulated in zero-sum

46 For more on this point, see Martin Krygier, *Philip Selznick. Ideals in the World* (Palo Alto, CA: Stanford University Press, 2012), 188–96.

47 I have particularly in mind critical legal studies, a now dated movement but which has occasional echoes.

terms: civil society versus the state, us against them, society against power, anti-politics versus the polity. Economists advocated minimal state intervention in place of the pervasive maximalism of the communist state; in place of no property rights, untouchably secure ones, and so on. This was a great boost to the neo-liberal 'take' on Western achievements which already had other sources, for some time squeezing out other interpretations of a more mixed, complex and variable sort, of possible relations between states, laws and civil societies. For some time, and to some people, the notion that there were indispensable 'virtuous circles',[48] rather than stark oppositions between states and civil societies, for example, or property-securing rule of law on one hand, and regulatory interventions, on the other, could only seem to be squeamish temporising.

These two projects, the political one connected with democracy and the economic one that Trubek calls 'the project of markets and the discovery of institutions', quickly dominated the scene. The latter:

> stressed export-led growth, free markets, privatization, and foreign investment as the keys to growth. To pursue these goals, it was necessary to create all the institutions of a market economy in former command economies and remove restrictions on markets in *dirigiste* economies such as those in many Latin American countries.[49]

With roots in the institutional economics of the 1960s and the Hayekian/Friedmanite transformations of the 1980s, the new economic approach laid great stress on law, property rights and security of contract guaranteed by law, and more general economic predictability, also said to flow from law.

While there were overlaps between the democracy/human rights project and the economic project, they had different goals, priorities and targets. Securing property rights is not the same as a commitment to temper arbitrary power in its many manifestations. Though it might be a part of it, it is certainly not sufficient, nor for many purposes even the main game. You might want both, but typically those interested in one had less to say about the other. Nevertheless, as often happens in matters of rhetorical fashion, they fastened onto the same slogan, and together pushed it along.

Economic development is a major ambition of donor countries and agencies, and it became conventional wisdom that an institutional package which came to be called the rule of law – focusing particularly on formal institutions of private (and some aspects of criminal) law – is necessary for it. So the rule of law was popular because its proponents believed there is this causal connection and they support the rule of law because they value the economic results said to flow from it. More

48 Martin Krygier, 'Virtuous Circles: Antipodean Reflections on Power, Institutions, and Civil Society' (1997) 11 (1) *Eastern European Politics and Societies* 36–87.

49 See David M. Trubek, 'The "Rule of Law" in Development Assistance: Past, Present, and Future', in *The New Law and Economic Development: A Critical Appraisal*, eds, David M. Trubek and Alvaro Santos (New York: Cambridge University Press, 2006), 84.

recently, the situation has been complicated since the rise of China and the Great Financial Crisis, and the rhetoric has changed considerably, prompting Trubek and others to suggest there might be a new model, the 'new developmental state' coming to replace neo-liberal prescriptions of 'the Washington Consensus', but the situation is in flux, and many of the older nostrums and procedures remain strong.

There is now a huge literature in economics and political science devoted to testing the connections between the rule of law and economic growth. From the point of view of a liberal devotee of the former, there are some problems here. I cannot assess neo-liberal rule of law prescriptions from an economic point of view, but since the centrepiece of many of them is the rule of law, it matters how well they think about that. The results are not altogether encouraging.

Implications

First, particularly for ideological purists influenced by Hayek, there is a considerable preliminary embarrassment. For he insisted that the growth of markets and of the laws that undergird and adapt to them should be primarily a spontaneous process only likely to be derailed by purposive, 'constructivist' government intervention. Indeed, he compares the writings of English socialists, 'the Totalitarians in our Midst', with those of the Nazis '[w]hich destroyed the belief in Western civilization in Germany and created the state of mind in which nazism could become successful.' Both shared a similar 'temper with which the problems are approached than of the specific arguments used – a similar readiness to break all cultural ties with the past and to stake everything on the success of a particular experiment.'[50]

Rejecting that temper did not mean there was nothing to do, but rather that '[t]he attitude of the liberal towards society is like that of the gardener who tends a plant and in order to create the conditions most favourable to its growth must know as much as possible about its structure and the way it functions'.[51] In the foreign ventures of the economic rule of law, however, not gardeners but social engineers have been in charge. They have commonly ignored, or sought to overcome rather than cultivate, their beneficiaries' 'cultural ties to the past', about which they equally commonly knew little, in a confident bet on 'the success of a particular experiment'. Indeed, often – and in post-communist societies in spades – ties to the past were treated like noxious weeds more than plants deserving the ministrations, at least the careful attention, of devoted gardeners. Too often there has been little but purposive foreign intervention, and that in often the most challenging of circumstances, plagued by civil strife, poverty, ethnic and religious division, and a host of rarely or barely understood 'spontaneous' legacies which are precisely what neo-liberal reformers want to eliminate. Rule of law promotion in its current incarnation seeks to do what Hayek seems to have

50 Hayek, *The Road to Serfdom*, 203. On the pathologies of 'constructive rationalism', see especially Hayek, *Rules and Order*.

51 Hayek, *The Road to Serfdom*, 22.

rejected in principle: *build* rather than 'cultivate' the rule of law in circumstances in which it is weak, or non-existent, on the basis of institutions transplanted from radically different contexts. After all, at least the German and English ideas he attacked were largely home grown; the 'Washington Consensus' on development assistance abroad was only at home in Washington.

And Hayek apart, the problems of institutional transplantation are still massive. The modern West is usually taken as the model for neo-liberal export, but those exports have depended on social, political, economic understandings and practices that do not always make the journey. And when they arrive it is not to an empty field (unless because it has recently been laid waste). Societies are patterned in differing ways. Many of these patterns endure over time, and they matter for most things, among them legal institutional function, form, social salience and performance. Societies exhibit internal continuities and differences from each other; regions and sub-societies differ too, in the character and texture of relationships they generate, enforce and suppress. The extent to which social configurations are apt to support and resist specific institutional arrangements also varies.

If one's interest is the extent to which the exercise of power is successfully tempered in a society, these contextual differences are key. The salience of features of legal institutions, formal and procedural characteristics usually nominated to constitute the rule of law, depends on how successfully they support the attainment of this value, in the wider society. To the extent they do, they have aided us in identifying what the law needs to be like to serve the end of the rule of law – at least *there*. To the extent that they do not, however, it is not at all clear why we fix on them so, still less try to extend them to places where they might merely have parodic roles. The challenge for anyone seeking the rule of law anywhere is not primarily to emulate or parody practices that seem to have worked elsewhere, but to find ways of reducing the possibility of arbitrary exercise of power, whatever that takes, here.

Transplanting institutions with the hope to transform behaviours is an ambitious enterprise of social engineering which depends as much or more on context than on the institutions transplanted, but economic analysis has rarely had much to say about context. All this might sound like banal truisms were it not for the fact that it has so often been ignored in the law-transplantation business by, among others, neo-liberal reformers.

The World Bank signalled a significant rhetorical change in its 2011 World Development Report,[52] when it advocated 'best fit' rather than 'best practice', but if that is to be more than rhetoric, it will need to display more understanding than any of us has on what 'best fit' might mean and generate in societies in the midst of fighting, legacies hostile to programmatic innovations, etc. There is a sociological innocence in neo-liberal enthusiasms and prescriptions, as indeed in much

52 *World Development Report 2011: Conflict, Security, and Development* (Washington, DC: World Bank, 2011), https://www.wdronline.worldbank.org/handle/10986/4389

rule of law promotion more generally, which is striking given the difficulty of the problems of social transformation that they ambitiously confront.

Given these uncertainties and complexities, neo-liberals and other enthusiasts would do well to heed the invocation of the Hippocratic Oath by Haggard and his colleagues:

> This review has taken a highly instrumental view of the rule of law, stressing its utility for growth in particular. But our final and most important point is that the rule of law is of great importance as a value in its own right and as a contributor to other values, such as human freedom. Yet precisely for that reason – because we believe in the rule of law – it is all the more important that those who would offer development assistance make sure, first, to do no harm.[53]

This warning has not always been heeded.

Even were we more confident than we have reason to be that neo-liberal reforms were guaranteed to produce the economic outcomes intended, the selectiveness of neo-liberal interests should worry anyone committed to the rule of law. Neo-liberals are particularly interested in encouraging investment and trade. That explains what institutional reforms they advocate. It also explains *where* and for whom they advocate them. That is rarely everywhere or for everyone. So, note the reflections of one of the most sophisticated and dedicated advocates of the importance of the rule of law, as reforms were made in its name in Latin America in the 1990s:

> nowadays legal and judicial reforms (and the international and domestic funding allocated to support them) are strongly oriented toward the perceived interests of the dominant sectors (basically domestic and international commercial law, some aspects of civil law, and the more purely repressive aspects of criminal law). This may be useful for fomenting investment, but it tends to produce a 'dualistic development of the justice system, centred on those aspects 'that concern the modernizing sectors of the economic elite in matters of an economic business or financial nature ... [while] other areas of litigation and access to justice remain untouched, corrupted and persistently lacking in infrastructure and resources.'[54] For societies that are profoundly unequal, these trends may very well reinforce the exclusion of many from the rule of law, while further exaggerating the advantages that the privileged enjoy by means of laws and courts enhanced in their direct interest.[55]

53 Stephan Haggard, Andrew MacIntyre and Lydia Tiede, 'The Rule of Law and Economic Development' (2008) 11 *Annual Review of Political Science* 205–234, 221.

54 Pilar Domingo, 'Judicial Independence and Judicial Reform in Latin America', in *The Self-Restraining State: Power and Accountability in New Democracies*, eds, Andreas Schedler, Larry Diamond and Marc F. Plattner (Boulder, CO: Lynne Rienner Publishers, 1999), 165.

55 Guillermo O'Donnell, 'Polyarchies and the (Un)Rule of Law in Latin America: A Partial Conclusion', in *The (Un)Rule of Law and the Underprivileged in Latin*

Haggard et al. make a complementary point when they observe that 'Much of the property rights literature focuses on the security of property rights, but the corruption literature suggests it is possible to have secure property rights that favour an inefficient allocation of resources because of private capture'. Moreover, as with the post-communist successes of 'oligarchs' whose billions came from plundering the state, just getting the property out of state hands and into (securely held) private ones is often no solution to a (real) problem.

There is a broader point here. The neo-liberal interest in what they call the rule of law flows from the belief that it is good for the economy. Until economists believed that, they did not concern themselves with law or advocate the rule of law. Now that they do, billions are spent on it, but what if they are wrong? In the various 'post-' countries where the money goes – post-conflict, post-dictatorship, post-communist – the results are not especially encouraging, nor are the theoretical underpinnings. Enthusiasts for rule of law promotion might, as enthusiasts so often do, blame inadequate zeal in pursuing the reforms they promote. So the answer is more of the same. However, as the authors of one survey of the field have observed:

> we really have no robust evidence that shortcomings with respect to property rights are a result of 'bad' institutions or the much more fundamental problem of state failure and anarchy. This is hardly a trivial issue![56]

We are not overrun with economic successes to report from neo-liberal legal reforms. Even where there does seem to be some correlation between the reforms and economic development, we still have not established causation, in two senses. One unsettled question is whether institutional reform is likelier to cause economic success; is the causal sequence perhaps the other way around (the 'reverse causality' problem)? The usual templates for such reforms are legal institutions in economically successful countries, but several writers have questioned what came first: the economic development or the institutions. It makes a difference. If, as Chang and Mungiu-Pippidi[57] argue, contemporary legal institutions in economically developed countries followed rather than preceded economic development, then perhaps those interested in the latter should focus on policies rather than institutions to spur it. If they are right, does that mean we should cease to be

America, eds, Juan E. Mendéz, Guillermo A. O'Donnell and Paulo Sérgio de Moraes (Notre Dame, IN: University of Notre Dame Press, 1999), 319–20.

56 O'Donnell, 'Polyarchies', 210.

57 Both cited in Bojan Bugaric, 'Law and Development in Central and Eastern Europe: The Neo-liberal Development State and Its Problems', in *Law and Development in Middle-Income Countries: Avoiding the Middle-Income Trap*, eds, Randall Peerenboom and Tom Ginsburg (Cambridge: Cambridge University Press, 2014), 136. And see Erik G. Jensen, 'Postscript: An Immodest Reflection', in *The International Rule of Law Movement: A Crisis of Legitimacy and the Way Forward*, ed., David Marshall (Cambridge, MA: Harvard University Press, 2014), 298–99.

interested in the rule of law? Might it suggest that we should worry less about implanting new formal institutions which might merely have a 'parchment' existence, and more about adopting policies that might generate economic growth? I am not competent to judge the economists' debate, and have no confident answers to these questions, but confidence is not always the most reliable mood with which to approach these matters. Another question is whether both economic and institutional success and failure, where they occur, might depend on other factors; in particular, settings that we have yet to account for (the 'endogeneity' problem).[58]

What should we think about the rule of law, were we to conclude that it did not produce economic growth? Should we lose interest in it? The older tradition is unequivocal in saying no. As Stephen Holmes has stressed: 'The ideal-typical liberal … saw economic liberty as only one kind of right, of no greater importance than, say, freedom of speech, the right to a fair trial, freedom from bodily fear, freedom of conscience, the right to education, or the right to vote'.[59] We still have every reason to fear despotism and anarchy, to welcome regulated political and personal liberty, to value human dignity, and also to live in a world made safe from wild power, even if we were to discover it is not worth a dollar in gross national product. And even were it to be worth that dollar, we would still have the same reasons to support it in areas that do not attract international trade or investment. That is to say, we have every interest to value what the rule of law was supposed to ensure.

To put the point more broadly, the rule of law can be likened to what Rawls called 'primary social goods', both in the sense in which he originally described such goods in *Theory of Justice* – 'things which it is supposed a rational man wants whatever else he wants. Regardless of what an individual's rational plans are in detail, it is assumed that there are various things which he would prefer more of rather than less'[60] – and in his later more moralised revision – 'what persons need in their status as free and equal citizens, and as normal and fully cooperating members of society over a complete life'.[61]

But today we typically think of the rule of law instrumentally, as good to the extent that it leads to some other specific good, in other particular domains of life. Claims that all sorts of such goods flow from the rule of law – economic development, human rights, democracy, etc. – are the lifeblood of the international rule of law promotion industry, as we have seen. But apart from those

58 See, e.g. Stephan Haggard and Lydia Tiede, 'The Rule of Law and Economic Growth: Where Are We?' (2011) 39 (5) *World Development* 673–685, and Haggard, MacIntyre and Tiede, 'Rule of Law and Economic Development', 221.

59 Stephen Holmes, 'The Liberal Idea', in *Passions and Constraint: On the Theory of Liberal Democracy*, ed., Stephen Holmes (Chicago: University of Chicago Press, 1995), 27.

60 John Rawls, *A Theory of Justice*, rev. edn (1971; repr., Cambridge, MA: Belknap Press, 1999), 79.

61 Rawls, *A Theory of Justice*, xiii.

external, purported blessings allegedly bestowed by the rule of law, we should value diminution of the possibility of arbitrary power for its own sake and at large.

There are intuitively plausible reasons, and some evidence, to support the belief that lessening of the possibility of arbitrary power might support other good things, such as economic development, human rights or democracy. But if it were shown that, in an order where the rule of law in the sense sketched here was strongly in evidence, the economy had tanked, this would not be in itself a reason to conclude that there was no rule of law. Nor that the diminution in the possibility of arbitrary exercise of power was therefore not a good. Unfortunately, we still have a bit to learn about how to secure and extend that value in all those domains that make up the lives of people when they are not trading or investing. It is not clear that neo-liberals have much to teach us in this regard.

Chapter 2

Thatcherism as an extension of consensus

Michael Gardiner

In Britain the usual story of neoliberalism goes like this. The mass effort of World War II created a pressure from below that forced a broad policy agreement within which the economy was forced to work, at least in part, for the benefit of the people. Services and industries were nationalised, which meant they belonged to the population, until in the 1980s the popular control over the economy was displaced by something different – a wave of privatisations undertaken by capitalist zealots who revived an obscure credo contrary to British values. And finally, although neoliberalism has been effective in taking over the levers of power, it has never quite fully captured these values, which remain a defence against markets getting out of hand. This chapter suggests that there are serious problems with this story of neoliberalism as an alien imposition that follows a popular control of industry and services – even though this story's iconography (the 'spirit of '45', nostalgia for Attlee and Bevan, welfare consensus) remains important to much of the British Left. It suggests that the particularly 'pure' form of British neoliberalism did not so much *displace* as *depend on* the mass psychology of wartime and post-war consensus, and form a continuum with it. It suggests moreover that far from being an alien credo, Thatcherism represents a return to the most homely principles of a particular kind of constitution, a constitution whose power lies in its commitment to the universalism of 'the economy' and its willingness to resist popular determination.

The state as arithmetic core

Even the most telling of the histories of neoliberalism that have appeared over the last decade or so (Boltanski, Harvey, Crouch, Mirowski, Peck, Davies) have had relatively little to say about specific state constitutions, and how and to what extent they might accommodate market sovereignty. Most accounts have (rightly) described neoliberalism as multi-centred and as having to graft itself onto existing government forms – but this stress has risked making existing government forms seem oddly neutral, as benevolent bodies to which neoliberalism happens. This has a particular significance in the case of the British state, which is also the economic underwiring of empire and which is based, *as by nature*, in a financial guarantee.

Under neoliberalism the idea of the economy as the eternal and natural basis of civil society comes to seem indisputable. But an economic understanding of nature is also specific to the conditions of British state creation at the end of the English Enlightenment, an era sometimes described as the Financial Revolution (1680s–1710s). The Hanoverian coup of 1688 that crystallises the Financial Revolution and creates the modern British state is both a *restoration* – it returns government to the condition of nature – and a *revolution* – it shifts authority from the 'random, despotic' power of monarchs towards the enfranchisement of individual property owners. For the apparently natural and allegedly minimal state, government is only the guarantee of property, a universalisation of the terms of exchange, and therefore a stabilisation of value, across the time and space of an expanding empire. As the ascendant Whigs understand it, franchise should be open to all individual property-owners – but property has to be continually created, through the labour that makes nature useful. Government is only an economic mechanism that allows a natural exchange to go on: parliament is convened to manage budgets, the party system is conceived as a competition of financial narratives, the great national credit-raising banks are set up in the 1690s, and in the 1700s the Acts of Union formalise the new pan-British state in these terms. The new state that arises from the 1680s–1700s consolidation is at once a promise to keep power away from despotic authority that might threaten value, and an accounting convention – or as it was put in 1709 by the British-unionist pamphleteer and chronicler of the imperial adventures of money, Daniel Defoe, the new government was created 'draw the balance of interest, or state … the affairs of both nations [England and Scotland] into one account current'.[1]

Elsewhere I have described how, in the context of the English Enlightenment, this new state's turn to the laws of nature to describe the spread of franchise was a Newtonian one.[2] Since the laws of the economy are universal and natural, they are not written out, but are discovered, and at their base is the self-evident good of individual property As described by that key translator of Newtonian cosmology to government, John Locke, not only is property 'the great and chief end … of men's … putting themselves under government', but this principle is not specific to any place, it is simply 'natural reason'.[3] Modern progressive government only exists to ensure that the universal and natural laws of the economy are left to do their work without political interference, and its force is just protection from despotic interruptions to these natural laws, that is, from threats which are to be understood as *political*. Political threats to the universal laws of exchange are then seen as threats to the foundations of society as such, to progress and

1 Daniel Defoe, *History of the Union* (Dublin: J. Exshaw, 1799 (1709)); cf. Michael Gardiner, *Time and Action in the Scottish Independence Referendum* (Basingstoke: Palgrave, 2015), 20–21.

2 Gardiner, *Time and Action*, 8–15.

3 John Locke, *Second Treatise on Government*, II-9, 'Of the Ends of Political Society and Government', para 124: http://www.gutenberg.org/files/7370/7370-h/7370-h.htm#CHAPTER_XI

enfranchisement for all, and so must be seen as treasonous – as in Newton's support, as Keeper of the Mint, for death sentences for counterfeiters, and more generally in the explosion of definitions of 'financial crimes' after 1688. It thus turns out that 'restricting' the state to the laws of the economy creates a natural and therefore in principle limitless mandate for the state to expand itself to protect these laws. The constitution behind this state, implied, not codified natural not historical, is also, as it would later be put by that most influential Victorian commentator, A.V. Dicey, absolutely *flexible* – it is beyond 'political considerations', by which he means determination by the people.[4] The culturing of Britishness grows around the refusal to write out the natural laws of exchange as if they had been determined, rather than discovered, which would undermine their universality and limit their authority. The 'flexibility' of the constitution is key to the British way of life, and becomes the non-negotiable principle for which the British empire will go to war, from the eighteenth-century battles against republicanism and Jacobinism to the mass psychological mobilisation of World War II. Since the constitution is, as Dicey says, beyond politics, it is based in a belief in an undeterminable essence – yet since it is ultimately anchored to the arithmetic of terms of exchange that are natural and universal, its core is discovered empirically. All the cultural paraphernalia of the British imperial constitution, gentlemanliness, good English, parliamentary ceremony, and so on, circle this core, or the centre which that other canonical Victorian commentator, Walter Bagehot, described as its 'efficient secret'.[5]

Commentators on neoliberalism have often suggested that this kind of arithmetic core rises in the late twentieth century – civil society is given over to evaluation, audit, target-setting, the reduction of relationships to numerical values. William Davies for example has expanded on Philip Mirowski's description of the economy's capture of the legislature and its reduction of political *metaphysics* to political *physics*, of *ethical* aims to *empirical* and *evaluative* aims.[6] The point to add to this is that the Newtonian-Lockean state is already such an empiricising machine – and there is a kind of patriotism in the British return to dynamic liberalism, the desire to see relationships as ultimately evaluation, audit, and accounts.[7] This, in large part, is the genius of Thatcherism – a patriotic hardening of the state to protect an arithmetic core, and, in this case, to make this protection a personal matter and a matter of individual adaptation. But in this personal sense especially, it was reliant on the cohesion created by that other great adaptation of

4 A.V. Dicey, *England's Case Against Home Rule* (Richmond: Richmond Publishing (1886)); Dicey, *An Introduction to the Law of the Constitution* (London: Macmillan, 1979 (1885)), 127, 133; Will Davies, *The Limits of Neoliberalism: Authority, Sovereignty and the Logic of Capitalism* (London: Sage, 2014), 47.

5 Davies, *The Limits of Neoliberalism*, 111.

6 Davies, *The Limits of Neoliberalism*, 13–16; Luc Boltanski and Laurent Thévenot, *On Justification: Economies of Worth* (Princeton: Princeton University Press, 2006).

7 Davies, *The Limits of Neoliberalism*, 56.

the personal that rises from the patriotic Churchillian vision of war defence, and its echoes in the welfare state.

The financial blitz

In the neoliberal era we know all about the endless demands of labour, the way work seems to extend into every aspect of our lives, to be relentless and precarious and exceed any fixed hours, to become ever more closely bound up with our wants and our self-expression.[8] However, the demand for continuous property-creation is a condition of British democracy: in the Lockean understanding, labour must be continuously added to new nature to make new property, and new property is the basis of franchise. Labour must keep adapting and expanding – for British democracy (for the 'Protestant Work Ethic', as it is cultured), labour is endless. To adapt Dicey's term, the *flexible constitution* always points towards *flexible labour*. Thatcherism then can be seen as a neo-Lockean demand to maintain property-creation by helping it towards new realms of nature, not only physical nature (industry, colonies, areas of 'decline'), but also increasingly 'human nature' (the subjective economy). But this move to the personal demands a strong shared language of belonging, and this builds on the great upheaval of World War II in a way rarely accounted for in the post-1970s' concentration of most histories of neoliberalism. Evacuation, war service, rationing, home defence – the existing forms of 'collectivity' and shared effort arising from the people form an imagery to be drawn on heavily by post-war British governments to further the regime of property and labour, and is an essential part of neoliberalism that comes from consensus.

Part of the power of Thatcherism is in recognising that the post-war consensus has to be modified into a militarisation of the resistance to political threats, that is, threats to property, whether by communists, trade unionists, or Irish republicans. What Thatcherism describes as a 'small state' is thus ever more militarised: counter-subversion policing is imported from Northern Ireland, 'enemies within' are identified, a small Atlantic war is made to resonate in Churchillian terms to help pave the way for a second election and the greatest financial reforms, and nuclear weapons are common sense – extending their role in welfare consensus (as Nye Bevan said of the nuclear arsenal even in the austerity of the 1940s, we've got to have it and 'we've got to have a bloody union jack on it').[9] In one sense British consensus's post-war extension of military spending into

8 John Locke, *Two Treatises on Government*, especially II-9, 'Of the Ends of Political Society and Government', http://www.gutenberg.org/files/7370/7370-h/7370-h.htm#CHAPTER_XI

9 Anthony Barnett, *Iron Britannia: Why Parliament Waged Its Falklands War* (London: Allison and Busby, 1982); cf. Tom Nairn, *Pariah: Misfortunes of the British Kingdom* (London: Verso, 2002), 51; Bevan quoted in Nottingham Fabian Society, 'The Disaster of Scottish Independence?', 26 August 2014, http://nottsfabians.org.uk/scottish-indepedence/; see also Gardiner, *Time and Action*, 61–65.

a generalised patriotic emergency is something like a version of what J.K. Galbraith described as 'Military Keynesianism' – a permanent emergency which becomes understood in financial terms as the need for competitiveness. There is, in turn, an important continuity between this consensus politics of emergency and the neoliberal condition that Davies has described, drawing on Giorgio Agamben, as a 'state of market exception', a generalised anxiety that can 'compel leaders to do whatever is necessary to defend their political communities against the "threat" of rival nations'.[10] The patriotic effort within the state of emergency that characterised consensus then becomes the basis of a neoliberal reality that, as Davies puts it, only '"holds together" if individuals already possess a shared narrative commitment to certain ways of doing things … [a]chieving concerted action in pursuit of competitiveness requires building on forms of collectivity that already exist'.[11]

In the 1940s the Nazi enemy moreover provides a particularly potent and ongoing symbol of threat, at base the threat of political 'systems' to a constitution organised by the economy. It is not just that the Nazis trigger a 'racial' taboo – indeed perception of a racial crime against the universal only really rises with the demands for the absolute equivalence of market actors in neoliberalism (and for that matter, much of the liberal establishment, including Beveridge, Keynes and Chamberlain, had advocated eugenics until a rethink in the 1940s, when they turned towards the needs of individual aspiration). More fundamentally it was the Nazis' celebration of 'random, despotic' political force that galvanised the mass psychological defence of the informal constitution, a defence that was between 1939 and 1942, cultured as organic, eternal and natural, through a widespread conglomeration of cultural agencies (the BBC, MOI, GPO and others). The consensus idea of the Nazis echoed previous threats to natural reason, most potently, that of the French Jacobins.[12] In Dicey's terms, meant for the French, the Nazis were not flexible: they were a reminder of the consequences of limiting government by seeing it not in terms of universal principles, but a specific history or people. The threat of Nazism was turned into a call to defend universal and natural laws – Newtonian laws of the economy, ultimately, which can and should never be determined or defined, and which can only be described impressionistically.

The mass allegiance to an impressionistic, undeterminable constitution is a staple of the 'socialism' of consensus, and seen for example in one of the most familiar repositories of consensus-era values, one seized on by needy parliamentarians ever since – George Orwell's 'England, Your England'. Placing itself immediately within Blitz defence ('As I write this, highly civilized beings are flying

10 J.K. Galbraith, *The Age of Uncertainty, Part 7: The Mandarin Revolution* (BBC TV, 1977); Davies, *The Limits of Neoliberalism*, 172–177, 134.

11 Davies, *The Limits of Neoliberalism*, 134, 156.

12 Cf. Michael Gardiner, *The Return of England in English Literature* (Basingstoke: Palgrave, 2012), 36–48.

overhead, trying to kill me'), Orwell's sketch describes 'England' (Britain) not as a constitutional power like European nations, but as a series of impressions – bad teeth, gardening, old maids cycling – and demands not constitutional change, but an extension of the makeup of the managerial classes within the existing unwritten constitution.[13] This socialist vision of consensus is then constitutionally substantially the same as the Thatcherite vision – it relies on a citizenship that is ultimately economic (the reverence for 'privacy' lauded by Orwell), in a civil society whose sovereignty is always mediated in these terms. Whatever rebuilding there will be after the war will depend on a patriotic personalisation of the universal and natural properties of the existing constitution.

One of the most telling depictions of the Thatcherite use of the mass psychology of the wartime defence of the eternal-natural constitution appears in Adam Curtis's documentary *The Attic*, which describes how the Churchillian idealisation of empire exerted a 'mesmeric hold' on post-war administrations, leaving them 'possessed by the memory of a golden age'.[14] Not least amongst these was the young Margaret Thatcher, whose defences of neoliberal policy would take a Churchillian tone – 'repeating, almost like a mantra, "Churchill in 1940, Churchill in 1940"'.[15] It is because the wartime defence, as associated as it may be with Orwellian socialism, is a defence of the economic constitution, that its trace becomes so important again during neoliberalism's various crises after 2008. In British parliamentary and media output the banking crisis was often figured as a kind of new Blitz, a foreign threat to our way of life demanding a rallying defence of the economy – the Blitz was a frequent touchstone, for example, for the speeches of Prime Minister Gordon Brown. The post-2008 defence of neoliberal realism is full of images of the Blitz – a return to a 'Home Front' aesthetics drawing from rationing (austerity recipes, 'Bake-Offs', food banks as the Big Society), to bombing and evacuation (evictions, DIY), to altruistic debt for the greater good ('the housing ladder', tuition fees). The term 'austerity' itself has strong retro associations, and connotes the shared struggles of the rebuilding that followed the Blitz. The appearance of the 'Keep Calm' motif has by now been well documented, with its moral imperative to muck in to help the 'collective' good founded on individual competition, taken as a protection of Britain's market sovereignty ('Buy More Shit or We're All Fucked', as one Keep Calm parody has it).

Indeed, we need look no further for a repository of 1940s' images repurposed for neoliberal realism than the opening ceremony of the 'Second Austerity Olympics' in 2012 (the First Austerity Olympics of 1948 were often echoed). By this point, consensus images could be openly mined for market value: 1940s' NHS

13 George Orwell, 'The Lion and the Unicorn: Socialism and the English Genius', in George Orwell, *Essays* (London: Penguin, 2007 (1941)), 138–187, 171.

14 Wr. and dir. Adam Curtis, *The Living Dead, Episode 3: The Attic*, 1995, archived at https://www.youtube.com/watch?v=iu4RymE14xs&list=PL399F0ABDF4DA0320&index=3; cf. Gardiner, *Time and Action*, 27–28.

15 Curtis, *The Attic.*

uniforms, the BBC, commonwealth, London as world city, austerity as socialism, even the phrase *This Is For Everyone* projected into one of the world's most privatised and securitised environments. The background to this was a city whose fame had become tied up with its ability to adapt the terms of the communal to the natural reason of property creation. In a short 2013 piece for *openDemocracy*, Davies described how Olympic developments had been able to make aspirational an architecture oddly bereft of human determination, recalling Brezhnev's Soviet Union (or, ironically, the socialist 'plan' so feared by Hayekian neoliberals).[16] Political determination is always naturally giving way to an economic interpellation of the people without any meaningful determining action taking place, and:

> *repetition* becomes the key trope … Words are recited, truths are repeatedly affirmed, routines are performed repeatedly … certain things have to be spoken – delivery, efficiency, security, competitiveness – but in order to hold the edifice together, rather than to reveal anything as objectively 'delivered', 'efficient', 'secure' or 'competitive' for fear that otherwise questions might be asked.[17]

Tom Nairn has long described the British drive to perform a phantom 'past', a drive that becomes particularly central in Blairism, which in many ways completes the Thatcherite project by extending the audit economy over any possible ground of determinability so successfully that, as Nairn says of the 2001 election, people have to be reminded to vote.[18] Blair's New Labour, indeed, has a greater reach into the consensus cohesion needed by neoliberalism, since it can better lay claim to mass enfranchisement and to the 'people's victory' of 1945, so that the demand to adapt the economy to the subjective or personal seems to come from the mass itself (an irony repeated in the party's name, of course, since in the Lockean understanding, all labour is always new labour, seeking out new realms of nature). New Labour finally confirmed neoliberalism's settlement within the British tradition of socialism, and was highly adept at using the figure of the 'people' as attributed to the 'people's victory' of 1945 – People's Lottery, People's Vote, Diana as 'People's Princess' (after Diana's death in 1997 Blair was able to re-stage the Whig rise of parliament over the 'despotic, random' monarchy by showing that his own tribute was more progressively attuned). In 'neoliberal socialism', a terminology of values, principles, and convictions becomes useful as currency (as an arithmetic), without having to hang on to any 'political' idea of determining the environment. This sense of perpetual adjustment to the mass cohesion of market actors, under which personal determination seems naturally to

16 Will Davies, 'Britain's Brezhnev-style capitalism', *openDemocracy*, 6 April 2013, www.opendemocracy.net/ourkingdom/will-davies/britains-brezhnev-style-capitalism; cf. Davies, *The Limits of Neoliberalism*, 196.
17 Davies, 'Britain's Brezhnev-style capitalism'.
18 Nairn, *Pariah*, 3, 147.

disappear, leads to the strange doubling of the self-described of 2000s–2010s Britain by Davies as Brezhnevesque, by Nairn as Kim Jong-Ilesque, and by Mark Fisher as Stalinist, and of course drawing from Orwell's own powerful description of constant patriotic self-monitoring as 'doublethink'.[19]

The serious point here, often hinted at by Nairn, is that constitutionally Britain is *only* ever a repetition without an ultimate referent. Since civil society is never really determined, it is constituted by an endless series of adjustments to prior universal laws that themselves seem to stand beyond any political power. Welfare consensus had to make these adjustments familiar, in its role as a mass-psychological defence against any popular sovereignty not mediated by the economy – and Blairism now makes such economic adjustments culturally desirable. Or as Ross McKibben puts it, New Labour aims 'to depoliticize political action'.[20] Crucially, the relation of British neoliberalism to the founding principle of labour-franchise allows it to recognise that this work of adapting the imagescape of consensus to the defence of the flexible constitution itself has an 'industrial' role. After the decline of manufacturing industry, and behind it the decline of physical empire, property-creation, and so the spread of franchise in the Lockean sense, must increasingly embrace the 'nature' of the national image itself. Thatcherism had helped with this push, with its strong understanding of the need to build on the togetherness creating during war. Under Thatcherism, the economy is confirmed as a kind of eternal return. One 1979 Thatcher campaign ad by Saatchi and Saatchi, 'Going Backwards and Forwards', reversed and fast-forwarded film to rally the population – besieged by trade unionists and communists – to the work of reinventing the national image for a competitiveness that was to be understood a shared good just as the war effort had been a shared good.[21] Thatcherism recognises that the national memory must now itself become the 'nature' on which labour works to create property, and moreover that this 'enclosure' of experience is a patriotic duty. Thus the growth of the heritage business under Thatcher, as in the launch of English Heritage in 1984 – a 'privatising' demand to repackage the debris of industry for profit, but also a recognition that consensus had made the economy 'personal'. George Caffentzis has described Locke's labour theory of value as a 'memory theory of property' demanding that the terms of exchange are stable across time. Under neoliberalism this Lockean understanding of value adapts to the demand to rework the personal itself – for which work it relies on the cohesion of consensus.

This migration of labour from physical production to subjective production of course is not unique to the UK, and it has been placed in the mid-twentieth century in various ways – in the description of immaterial labour by autonomist marxists, in Michel Foucault's biopolitics, in C. Wright Mills's 'competitive

19 Mark Fisher, *Captialist Realism: Is There No Alternative?* (Winchester: Zero, 2009).
20 Ross McKibben, 'Treading Water', *New Left Review* 4, July–Aug 2000, quoted in Nairn, *Pariah*, 61.
21 Curtis, *The Attic.*

personality', and in the 'one-dimensional' consumer subject described by the New Left. But perhaps nowhere outside of the realm of the British flexible constitution does the mass protection of the economy as nature lead so seamlessly to a mass competitive subjectivity. Thus the examples of Nikolas Rose's classic (Foucauldian) account of consensus *Governing the Soul*, in which British institutions during the great post-war rebuilding mobilised the inroads made into the realm of the personal during the war emergency (the lessons of evacuation, rationing, and the imperative of 'morale') to expose everyday relationships and desires to wider organising forces.[22] Developments in social and mental health were marshalled for national efficiency via the emerging realm of management.[23] Attitudes surveys and other corporate feedback mechanisms, psychotherapy and human resources all fed into unified exercises of personality assessment to maximise 'the expertise of productive subjectivity'.[24] In these contexts consensus, often understood as a reward for war effort involving the agreement of multiple institutions, is perhaps better understood as a longer mass move to the subjective economy. So Rose describes how the mass adjustment of war allowed 'the personal and subjective capacities of citizens [to be] incorporated into the scope and aspiration of public powers', and the most celebrated document of welfare consensus, the Beveridge Report, in this sense aimed to 'conceptualis[e] and regulat[e] the bonds that tied individuals into social groups'.[25] These regimes of audit swept across the institutional realms of the expanding public *within* consensus, commanding a patriotic competitive remaking on the part of each individual, taking place in corporations, public health, prisons, and most notably in education, in which sphere it is best known as *meritocracy*.

Equal opportunities versus equality

Anchored to that cornerstone of welfare consensus, the Education Act 1944, meritocracy extends franchise by ensuring that individual betterment is possible for more people. To do this is must posit a universal, or as near universal as possible, desire for mass individual adjustment to a regime of measurement or audit, an educational 'arithmetic'. Meritocracy helps the arbiter state reach into each household and each subject, and it also makes it possible for an overall loss by the people to be celebrated as an increase in the possibilities for individual aspiration presented in quasi-collective terms. The power of unified mass testing to turn collective action into bureaucratic individualism was recognised deep within consensus, in Michael Young's 1958 satirical speculative fiction *The Rise of the Meritocracy*, which projects the current competition for places in grammar schools to a time in which personal audit by examination has come to define all relationships,

22 Nikolas Rose, *Governing the Soul: The Shaping of the Private Self* (London: Free Association, 1999 (1989)).
23 Rose, *Governing the Soul*, 82.
24 Rose, *Governing the Soul*, 22, 32, 47, 59, 73–74, 117.
25 Rose, *Governing the Soul*, 228, 103.

and this audit itself has become the mainstay of everyday work.[26] Mass testing now effectively creates new persons, and indeed is a kind of alter-eugenics that stands in contrast to 'despotic', physical eugenics by having individuals self-select according to a national imperative to competitiveness. The real fear of Young's meritocrats is the possible political rupture of a 'Populist' revolution – a revolution of popular sovereignty – that they imagine might look like 1789 or 1848.[27] In meritocracy, the desire for individual self-improvement is open to all, and culturally it is demanded of all – but this also instrumentally stands as an important part of the defence of the aspirational individual against political collectives, and so such a spread of 'opportunities' remains almost intact, or even enhanced, in the neoliberal subject. This naturalisation of the competitive individual creates an environment in which arch-conservatives can also be militant meritocrats – a position championed by Margaret Thatcher, whose own consensus-era journey becomes iconic of the grammar school route to success.

Indeed, post-war British public institutions are defined by a moral crusade for equal opportunities in a way that would be crucial to neoliberalism's demands for individual self-making, and its fierce policing of participation. As Young's meritocrats realise, the work of inclusion-policing can then become a central means for the development of 'private' power – a language of equal opportunities can become instrumental to the perpetual defeat of equality. Today we are quite familiar with the way a proficiency in the language of inclusion can be used to defend class privilege, the overwhelmingly middle-class makeup of diversity panels on the BBC for example, or the uses of inclusion training in universities to secure individual careers and protect waning privileges. Conversely, of course, failures of inclusion (usually described in terms of grounds of race, sex or other limiting factors often associated with the physical or biological), have to be perpetually sought out and exposed – in which sense, such failures echo the proliferation of 'financial crimes' of the post-1688 period: there is a constant, naturalised, background demand that people remain attuned to property-creating by reinventing themselves as competitive individuals, and any attempt to limit these equal opportunities becomes an outrage to be turned on by the whole of society.

Neoliberalism then is able to build on a meritocratic desire for individual personal audit and adjustment that has existed since early consensus. Thatcherites insisted that all actors be seen as equal before the market, and its more influential thinkers described 'equivalence' as both a basis of justice and a source of national belonging.[28] The competitive subject is understood as internalising a quasi-egalitarian framework of universal 'equivalence' as something like the common good. Davies usefully cites Adam Smith's conception of 'sympathy' in this regard (and indeed Smith has a specific role in the firming up of the British

26 Michael Young, *The Rise of the Meritocracy, 1870–2033: An Essay in Education and Equality* (London: Thames and Hudson, 1958).
27 Young, *The Rise of the Meritocracy*, 11.
28 Davies, *The Limits of Neoliberalism*, 37.

constitution during the eighteenth-century growth phase when he was a key figure in 'culturing' the universality of terms of exchange in a language guide for ambitious provincial boys even before *The Wealth of Nations*).[29] The key post-industrial business of enforcing equal opportunities might then be described as the neoliberal version of the demand for universal laws of exchange, helped into an era of subjective economy by the great meritocratic institutions of welfare consensus.

We can see the importance of the meritocratic demand for equal opportunities, for example, in one of the key mid-1970s' market-fundamentalist London think tanks, the Institute of Economic Affairs (IEA), an organisation much exercised by the moral basis of the 'equivalence' of individuals as market actors. In his 1977 IEA pamphlet Lionel Robbins, founding member of the elite neoliberal Mont Pelerin Society, and the LSE Chair who brought Friedrich Hayek to London, emphasises that the equivalence of market actors – institutionally backed by a broad meritocracy – is a natural foundation of the law.[30] Dismissing 'positive liberty', a phrase by then often pejoratively used by neoliberals to imply political determination (a 'confusion … caused by the use of the word liberty, which essentially involves freedom of choice and action'), Robbins stresses that the equal opportunities of economic actors is the *origin* of law – 'a *condition* of any behaviour capable of being placed in a moral category'.[31] Many other IEA papers similarly stress equal opportunities as a condition of lawful civil society – and they do so at a moment (1974–77) in which communists and trade unionists seem to be catastrophically undermining the equivalence of market actors. A general crisis of law then comes to have an *arithmetic* explanation, in the damage done to property by the failure to maintain a widespread equivalence of market actors, rather giving rein to *political* actors – as seen in inflation and, increasingly, in money quantity.

Part of the ingenuity of the Thatcherite restoration is in this understanding of crises of *social* values as crises of *arithmetic* values – inflation measures moral problems, or what the IEA contributor William Rees-Mogg calls a 'disease of inordinacy'.[32] Rees-Mogg's 1974 defence against the 'inordinacy' of inflation has a markedly patriotic and Churchillian tone and its models often come from the shared acceptance of privation in the 1940s. As we would expect from the Lockean settlement's tendency to strengthen the state, the fight against the enemies of value was also often militant and paramilitary, involving coalescing private armies, intelligence-finance-police-based market fundamentalist organisations including Great Britain 75, The Freedom Association, and flying strike-breakers (and Stephen Dorrill and Robin Ramsay, amongst others, have described Thatcherism as a kind of military coup in these terms).[33] This

29 Davies, *The Limits of Neoliberalism*, 59; Adam Smith, *Lectures on Rhetoric and Belles Lettres* (Oxford: OUP, 2001 (1748–)).

30 Lionel Robbins, *Liberty and Equality* (London: Institute of Economic Affairs, 1977).

31 Robbins, *Liberty and Equality*, 7, 8.

32 William Rees-Mogg, *The Reigning Error: The Crisis of World Inflation* (London: Hamish Hamilton, 1974), 10.

33 Robin Ramsay and Stephen Dorrill, *Lobster* 21, 1991: http://www.lobster-magazine.co.uk/issue21.php

new Battle of Britain waged against inordinacy and political attempts to create equality was in turn watched carefully by the global mainstream of neoliberals – James Callaghan's famous 1976 Labour Party speech for example, usually seen as signalling the end of palliative inflation ('We used to think that you could spend your way out of a recession … I tell you in all candour that that option no longer exists') was quoted in the Nobel Prize speech of IEA contributor Milton Friedman in the same year, and duly published as an IEA pamphlet.[34] At the same time a wave of dystopian warnings portrayed the consequences of the arithmetic failure (inflation, currency), and the disastrous unintended consequences for desires for equality rather than the acceptance of equal opportunities before the market – Robert Moss's *The Collapse of Democracy*, Patrick Hutber's *Decline and Fall of the Middle Class*, and a rash of '*Nineteen Eighty-Four* Revisited' polemics such as Anthony Burgess's *1985*, in which trade unions' destruction of money paralyses society to leave a few rogue patriots defending value as if from Nazi bombers.[35] Equal opportunities are homely, fair, natural, consensual, oriented towards property, and ultimately economic. Equality is alien, unfair, unnatural, despotic, destructive of property, and ultimately political.

The IEA are clear that threats to the universal terms of exchange, and so to British civil society, are the fault of politics, with its vague and misguided (and European-esque) promises of equality. Ministers create problems by trying to buy favour from specific groups through wage concessions and inflating money-supply (the Conservative Edward Heath, as it happens, had been particularly guilty during the previous parliamentary term, which is why monetarist liberals had to break away behind intellectual leaders such as Enoch Powell and Keith Joseph). Politicians in general refuse to admit that while financial concessions may garner short-term popularity, they also erode the integrity of property, and so the rule of law. Restoring a Newtonian regularity to money is then necessary to avoid what Rees-Mogg calls, looking at the fate of what he describes as an otherwise sound French *ancien régime*, 'ruin and revolution'.[36] As we might expect from Locke, political sovereignty is seen as less reasonable than shareholder sovereignty, and direct redistribution is a liability that prevents the natural justice and good circulation of economic equivalence.

Moreover crucially, for many Thatcherites this is how the ideas of Keynes should be understood, despite having been hijacked by inflationary politicians. Within the IEA there grows a tradition of 'Keynes versus the Keynesians' – the title of T.W. Hutchison's 1977 paper – and a search for a Keynesian 'quantity

34 Milton Friedman, 'Inflation and Unemployment', Nobel Prize speech, 1976: http://www.nobelprize.org/nobel_prizes/economic-sciences/laureates/1976/friedman-lecture.pdf; Jim Callaghan, speech to Labour conference in Blackpool, 1976: http://www.britishpoliticalspeech.org/speech-archive.htm?speech=174

35 Robert Moss, *The Collapse of Democracy* (London: Maurice Temple Smith, 1975); Patrick Hutber, *The decline and fall of the Middle Class – and how it can fight back* (London: Associated Business Programmes, 1976); Anthony Burgess, *1985* (London: Arrow, 1980 (1978)).

36 Rees-Mogg, *The Reigning Error*, 29, 49.

theory', for the Keynes who in the *General Theory* wanted to complete Locke's work on money quantity, and whose only real mistake was in overlooking the time-lag (the 'Hume-Jevons' time lag') between inflationary policy and the inevitable social destruction that follows.[37] So for Rees-Mogg '[t]he leading British monetary economist of the 20th century is unquestionably Maynard Keynes, though unfortunately the development and the ambivalence of his thought make him self-contradictory'.[38] This neoliberal push for an 'authentic' Keynes bound to the arithmetic of money supply was not lost on Thatcher herself – as Peter Clarke reports, '"No, no, no", she told one interviewer in 1979, "I am afraid Keynesianism has gone mad and it wasn't in the least little bit what Keynes thought". Nor was this a stray remark – she returned happily to this theme on numerous occasions'.[39] And, Keynes's understanding of probability could be reappropriated as support for the arbiter state – government is not a political dictator but, in this liberal tradition, as the arithmetic high ground from which personal chances – underwritten by market equivalence – are refereed. Such a general equivalence, grounded in an economic vision of disciplined money supply, should provide the country with what the IEA see, following Hayek, as the *right kind* of uncertainty – the uncertainty of market outcomes between equivalent actors – whose apparently limitless dynamism is necessary, paradoxically, to minimise the uncertainty they describe as coming from politics.

From politics to brand

The means for this virtuous acceleration of economic uncertainty is found not merely in some alien market-lust, as some accounts of neoliberalism imply – it is found also within the big public brands established (or massified) during consensus, the NHS, the BBC, the universities, and so on. Such often-consensus-themed institutions are important because they can become absolutely 'private' while still commanding public loyalty. Colin Crouch has described Britain's 'privatized Keynesianism', a property understanding of the 'collective' good that the great institutions of consensus allowed to become 'a kind of bizarre collective good, however nested in private actions it was'.[40] Jamie Peck has described a neoliberal 'roll-out' phase that, following the 'roll-back' more usually associated with Thatcherism, sees the bureaucratic embedding of institutions monitoring efficiency – an era of '[p]roactive statecraft and institution-building in service of neoliberal goals'.[41] But of course, such a network of institutions already concretely existed in Britain, complete with the ability to command a near-universal participation as the public good. Again, the need for neoliberalism to act as a dynamic amplification of

37 William Rees-Mogg, *Democracy and the Value of Money: The Theory of Money from Locke to Keynes* (London: Institute of Economic Affairs, 1977), 12, 16–18.

38 Rees-Mogg, *Democracy and the Value of Money*, 26.

39 Peter Clarke, *Keynes: The Twentieth Century's Most Influential Economist* (London: Bloomsbury 2009), 17.

40 Crouch, *The Strange Non-Death*, 117.

41 Peck, *Constructions of Neoliberalism*, 26.

consensus is intellectually set during early Thatcherism, but becomes particularly visible under New Labour. Adapting a Gramscian term already used in Stuart Hall's seminal description of Thatcherism as a 'Great Moving Right Show', Nairn describes New Labour's performance of emancipation as a kind of *transformismo*, or the performance of change, an exhortation to socialist progress that can now reveal itself in the form of market realism.[42] The good of the 'nation' is now performed by a collection of competitive individuals whose national experience is always and naturally mediated by the economy, an understanding of the nation not as a people, but as a *brand*.

While the Thatcherite promotion of heritage, or the post-industrial work of redefining the national image, had already moved towards seeing the nation as brand, this becomes easier to see with New Labour's terminologies of 'creative industries' and, especially in music and film, the party's claims on its own mass-industrial past. The early phase of creative industries known as Cool Britannia, sometimes dated from Blair's hosting of stars of Britpop at Downing Street in 1997, was a particularly clear depiction of this – decaying post-industrial landscapes acted as backdrops to the dogged performance of equal opportunities, communities were devastated but proud, and pressed the toughest and most enterprising individuals to prevail, and usually to escape the shell of the industrial collective (*Billy Elliot*, *The Full Monty*, *Trainspotting*, *Brassed Off*, *Purely Belter*). Industrial workplaces could be repurposed for the cultural work of national branding, and collectives defined as groups of individual entrepreneurs inheriting the pride of the collective. And perhaps most importantly, the form and themes of these productions were favoured for cultural dominance since they fitted the ideological needs of competitive funding, for example via National Lottery money. Increasingly, in competitive bids to auditing quangos or licensed boards, culture has to prove that it has a proactive attitude towards national branding (as, for that matter, does academic research – the AHRC for example have gradually increased their demand that academic work show its use to 'the British economy', a demand that it figures not as a political claim, but as a rational and neutral one). As the key term in national competitiveness, cultural production must be able to send a branding message overseas, but it must do so by being performed at home: Melissa Aronczyk describes how nation-branding demands that people '"live the brand" … to perform attitudes and behaviours that are compatible with the brand strategy … "immersing" themselves in the brand identity'.[43] And while this vision of the national is patriotic, it is for Aronczyk now also visibly 'rooted in the unifying spirit of benign commercial "interests" rather than in the potential divisions of political "passions"'.[44]

42 Nairn, *Pariah*, 66–67; Stuart Hall, 'The Great Moving-Right Show', repr. in Stuart Hall and Martin Jacques, eds, *The Politics of Thatcherism* (London: Lawrence and Wishart, 1983), 19–39.

43 Melissa Aronczyk, *Branding the Nation: The Global Business of National Diversity* (New York: OUP, 2013), 76.

44 Aronczyk, *Branding the Nation*, 17, 25.

Behind this image of a dynamic youthful 'lived' Britain, of course, are the huge interconnected systems of trading and cultural prestige that were created around the empire's universalist extension of its arithmetic core. Or as Nairn puts it, '[m]ost of late-Britain's unceasing regime-slogans about its ineffable Constitution, "flexibility", "adaptability", "realism" (and so on), apply much better to the radioactive element at its heart, the City of London'.[45] The neoliberalism unfolding under the early Blair described by Nairn here had already been extremely effective in reconciling the mythologies of eternal British freedom with their origins in value measurements and the 'culturing' of these measurements in the financial city. The nation-branding of the UK thus involves a continuum of prestige from imperial beliefs and imagery through to their arithmetic core – gentlemanliness, the canon of timeless literary greats, Britain as nation, London as cultural capital, and ultimately the arithmetic grounding of the financial City – between these levels there may be few formal 'political' alliances, but there will be deeply naturalised informal connections, only sometimes glimpsed, for example in universities' role in the literary heritage business. The ultimately economic structure of this continuum, the way each level of belief can be both financially rational and seeming politically neutral, helps explain why the ability to shift to a subjective economy or cultural production is not even, but has particularly British and indeed London resonances – in fact, as Aronczyk shows, virtually all the active nation-branding consultants to be found anywhere in the world are based in London.[46]

Economic patriotism, political nationalism

The extraordinary ability of British consensus to naturalise this 'lived' branding reveals a level of patriotism that critiques of neoliberalism rarely discuss. It is not that these critiques have ignored neoliberalism's relationship with the state. Jamie Peck describes neoliberal doctrine as necessarily two-faced since it gestures towards anti-state purity in full knowledge of its own need for the impure 'capture and reuse of the state'.[47] Colin Crouch points to neoliberalism's strengthening of the state against interference in its own market project revealing the way that '[n]eoliberals have been centralisers'.[48] And David Harvey's *Brief History* describes how after the economic crises of the 1970s, states had to become proactive in modifying their economies to restore profitability and reinvigorate their class system.[49] (Indeed, despite some Marxists' tendency to 'flatten out' constitutional contexts, critique of the British state specifically as the basis of cohesive beliefs in credit can be traced back to *Capital.*[50]) And yet Harvey still sees nationalism as an

45 Nairn, *Pariah*, 40.
46 Aronczyk, *Branding the Nation*, 66.
47 Jamie Peck, *Constructions of Neoliberalism* (Oxford: OUP, 2010), 7–9.
48 Colin Crouch, *The Strange Non-Death of Neoliberalism* (Cambridge: Polity, 2011), 22.
49 David Harvey, *A Brief History of Neoliberalism* (Oxford: OUP, 2005), 69.
50 Karl Marx, trans. Ben Fowkes, *Capital: Critique of Political Economy* (London: Penguin, 1990 (1867)), chap. 31, 914–926.

anomaly, an unintended weakness of neoliberalism, and as puzzling in the Thatcherite environment since it is 'antagonistic to the neoliberal agenda'.[51] I have suggested that if we understand the unwritten constitution's basis in the economy, this is not an antagonism at all – 'privatisation', or the rationalisation of public bodies in property terms, is patriotic, and the great outpouring of national pride that underpins the great public institutions of the 1940s–50s can shift pretty seamlessly to the public good of competition. It is not just that neoliberalism is forced to compromise with the state, but that the state relies on a basis of property adapted from physical to personal labour and the demand to perpetually self-invent, and the groundwork for this is done by the post-war consensus. Thatcherism was impatient with manufacturing industry not in the narrow sense of being 'unviable', but relatedly in the wider sense in which class-based blocs of power with political demands would hold up the progress of marking out new forms of individual property and precipitate a democratic crisis. The need for a conclusive end to the Miners' Strikes of 1972–85 was then fundamentally a constitutional need. Thatcherism strengthens consensus by subjecting it to a Lockean restoration: where the Hanoverians abrogated unlimited power to protect the natural laws of property, Thatcherism similarly extends the powers of the arbiter state and attempts to redefine all the terms of public exchange in terms of a mass behavioural adjustment to the sanctity of property, most obviously with the use of city centre CCTV, trialled in High Streets in the second Thatcher administration and growing into the greatest surveillance penetration per person on earth.

And yet although this militarised state must thus expand the existing settlement to a tremendous and oppressive scale, it will go to any lengths to avoid being described as *nationalist*: nationalism, in the sense of a defined political people, is the one thing it is defined against. Nationalism in this sense is what is not reducible to the economy. So the fervent flagwaving and branding around the summer of 2012 (the summer of the Olympics and the Queen's Diamond Jubilee) could seriously be presented as something other than nationalism, and indeed, paradoxically, as a kind of fairness standing against nationalism. This is the context of the 2014 Scottish independence referendum: the Diceyan demand for universality is so naturalised that even while some of Tory Britain reverted to old bluster about the need to be free of Celtic parasites (*Telegraph* comments pages, for example), the demand for economic sovereignty to be universal and undefined always drew them back into the unionist case – as it had in Dicey's own support of the Ulster *coup d'état* exactly a century before.[52] The term *nationalist* is so outrageous to neoliberal thinking because it implies that the universal laws of the economy can be limited, or interrupted, by some determining people – something like what the IEA described as the attack on property that would always have disastrous, communist results.

51 Harvey, *A Brief History of Neoliberalism*, 78–79.

52 Iain McLean, *What's Wrong with the British Constitution?* (Oxford: OUP, 2010), 6–8, 100–125.

Indeed, so beyond the pale is this term, nationalism, that even when enormous nationalist efforts are made on behalf of the economy, they have to be called *patriotism*. And this formula, 'patriotism, not nationalism', comes straight from wartime consensus, specifically Orwell's 1945 'Notes on Nationalism', an essay notorious for contrasting the benevolent necessity of British patriotism to the fascistic menace of Scottish and Irish nationalism.[53] There is a particularly vivid demonstration of the revival of this consensus formula in the 2014 referendum: when David Cameron's February 2014 'lovebombing' speech to the Scots, from (bizarrely enough) the London Olympic stadium, warned explicitly about the dangers of the political challenge to the *British brand*, it was reported as his stressing the need to 'fight Scottish nationalism with British patriotism'.[54] Throughout the campaigns, anti-independence campaigners stressed their own credentials as patriots (Scottish and British) to a peculiar and sometimes embarrassing degree, while describing themselves as anti-nationalist.[55] The Labour Party itself had long been casting around for a renewed language of patriotism, from 'Blue Labour' to the Attlee iconography that flourished in social media after 2008 and the rise of retro-themed celebrity commentators such as Owen Jones ('the Orwell of our generation').[56] A tremendous amount of nationalist work can then be concealed in universalist claims, in a blindspot that now looks quite peculiar, and is wonderfully summarised in the formulation in Tony Blair's memoirs, 'I supported the UK [and] distrusted nationalism as a concept'.[57] However, the sovereignty issues surrounding the referendum put the Labour Party in a tricky position (one culminating in their near-wipeout in Scotland in 2014–15), as gestures towards the people made in a language of neoliberal realism largely sank against a revived tradition of actual popular sovereignty perceived even by many who had never voted in a general election.[58] This show of popular sovereignty was awkward for those '45ist consensualists who had always claimed to hold that ground even while sunk into an everyday language of neoliberal realism: before

53 George Orwell, 'Notes on Nationalism', in George Orwell, *Essays* (London: Penguin, 2007 (1945)), 300–317.

54 Kate Devlin, 'Cameron evokes spirit of Team GB with pro-Union speech', *Herald*, 7 February 2014: http//:www.heraldscotland.com/politics/referendum-news/Cameron-evokes-spirit-of-team-gb-with-pro-union-speech.23375921

55 Cf. Scottish Independence 2014 Blog (2013) 'From Poisonous Little Acorns ...', 25 May, http://scottishindy2014.wordpress.com/2013/05/25/from-poisonous-little-acorns/

56 Russell Brand, cover puff for Owen Jones, *The Establishment, and how they get away with it* (London: Penguin, 2014).

57 Tony Blair's memoirs quoted in Gerry Hassan, 'The Future of the "Global Kingdom"', in Claire Westall and Michael Gardiner, eds, *Literature of an Independent England: Revisions of England, Englishness, and English Literature* (Basingstoke: Palgrave, 2013), 31–45, 33.

58 *MacCormick v Lord Advocate* SC 396 (1953), extracted at http://en.wikisource.org/wiki/MacCormick_v_Lord_Advocate; discussed in Gardiner, *Time and Action*, 40–47; on the Labour wipeout, cf. 48–60.

the referendum *The Guardian* admitted that although 'the independence referendum campaign in Scotland has been a reassertion of some of the things that matter most to this newspaper and its readers', still economic sovereignty had to be defended, since political determination was nationalism, and '[n]ationalism is not the answer'.[59]

Constitutionally, 2014 helped reveal Scotland, like Ireland before it, as a sovereignty trigger area, and a kind of coda for the limitations of neoliberal realism. The country had long been a fly in the ointment of economic sovereignty, but this has stood more visibly in relief since the Thatcherite restoration of 1979. Sovereignty claims made by Scottish Constitutional Convention's 1988–89 *Claim of Right*, for example, represent a different order of demand from the devolution plans by the Labour Party in the previous decade. However, this scepticism over the British parliament as absolute financial manager in fact goes right back into consensus: the celebrated 1953 test case *MacCormick v Lord Advocate* nominally challenged the title of Queen Elizabeth II in Scotland (she was Elizabeth I of Scotland and of Britain), but more fundamentally showed that the British state's claims to be 'natural, universal' (monarchs not changing regnal number even when the state form changed) were in fact specific and historical.[60] The case's judgment that 'the unlimited authority of Parliament has no equivalent in Scotland' marked a serious problem for economic sovereignty: the whole territory of the British Empire had *not* always come under the natural reason of economic sovereignty – there were pockets of popular sovereignty right at home. Within the context of the Thatcherite restoration this situation was known as *democratic deficit* – a term sometimes written off as a minor voting oddity ('they don't get the party they vote for'), but really denoting an unevenness in sovereignty. Although the eighteenth-century Union had built on the universal reach of the parliamentary management of the economy, popular sovereignty had never been formally relinquished in Scotland, where it remained a sleeper issue – to be revealed eventually as a threat to the 'flexible' state built on in neoliberalism. Such a political 'nationalism' must be denounced and closed down by economic patriotism, and this economic patriotism draws heavily on the consensus images of togetherness that precede it.

When popular sovereignty arises like this it *must* be described as nationalist, to show its scandalous limitation of universal economic laws. Nationalism is partisan, closed-minded, and so on – it is a failure of inclusion. The term nationalism, then, means something like *political action* – the interruption of the economy by an actually determining people. The Labour Party in Scotland (tellingly rebranded after 2014–15 as 'the Scottish Labour Party'), had long used this term,

59 The Guardian, 'The *Guardian* view on the Scottish referendum: Britain deserves another chance', 12 Sept 2014: http://www.theguardian.com/commentisfree/2014/sep/12/guardian-view-scottish-independence

60 *MacCormick v Lord Advocate* SC 396 (1953), extracted at http://en.wikisource.org/wiki/MacCormick_v_Lord_Advocate

nationalism, as a jibe towards the social democrats slightly to their left (the SNP), with their vaguely European and republican politics – now in 2014, in the context of the real prospect of the unpicking of economic naturalism, this term could revert to its more familiar role of describing all political threats to a way of life. Indeed, 2013–14 saw all major British political parties joined against the nationalist threat (Conservative – Labour – Lib Dem alliances were common, and at times Labour applauded UKIP and BNP votes, weirdly, as part of a 'pro-UK' alliance against nationalism).[61] In fact, the dismissal of politics crystallised in this term has long been recognised as a staple of neoliberal reason, which, as Michel Foucault showed, casts any ground of sovereignty outside the economy as ludicrous.[62] Scottish campaigns for self-determination were indeed frequently seen as a kind of comic Jacobinism or comic Nazism – one excruciating contribution by 'Save the Union', for example, adapts the opening titles of *Dad's Army*: 'Who do you think you're kidding, Mister Salmond, if you think Great Britain's done'.[63] The joke here is not only the implication that one campaigner (not in fact the leader) is Hitler-like, but, more fundamentally, the idea that sovereignty can be determined by the population rather than by an eternalism it can never reach.

In large part the patriotic answer to the constitutional threat that became clear in 2013–14 has been to move the debate back onto something like Defoe's 'accounts' vision, to reduce questions of determination to questions of 'audit'. During the 2014 campaigns it became something of a standing joke that the Strathclyde University analyst John Curtice was the go-to man for BBC commentary, not because Curtice's analysis was incompetent, but because it reduced sovereignty questions to an arithmetic of 'voting behaviour'. To a large extent the arguments over Scottish self-determination in 2014 *were* enunciations of a threat to the arithmetic core, or to the Hayekian good of market uncertainty protecting us from political uncertainty. Political uncertainty, for neoliberals, is always a dystopian interference with the natural functioning of the market, and is always to be avoided, whether the reasons are clear or not. So the anti-independence organisation Better Together, which an internal memo showed embracing the nickname 'Project Fear', produced a stream of terror stories about political uncertainty (including the notorious '500 Questions' – 'What will be the international dialling code of an independent Scotland?).[64] The great consensus-era public institutions were enlisted to enforce this sense of danger as they had to be defended as a public good *no matter how given over to market goals they are.* A perpetual 'crisis' of the NHS then becomes something that binds us in a Blitz spirit, demanding that we defend it even if this means, as in 2014, defending it

61 Stuart Campbell, 'Friends and Enemies', *Wings Over Scotland*, 26 May, http://wingsoverscotland.com/friends-and-enemies/; cf. Gardiner, *Time and Action*, 49–50.

62 Michael Foucault, trans. Graham Burchell, *The Birth of Biopolitics: Lectures at the Collège de France* (Basingstoke: Palgrave Macmillan, 2008 (1979)), 131.

63 Save the Union, 'Salmond Song', https://youtube.com/watch?v=-ckoqeTHQe8

64 Better Together, '500 Questions' pamphlet, http://b.3cdn.net/better/38a382b210f856a0e2_5zm6b1yew.pdf

against the political threat of *free healthcare*. Thus the bizarre situation in which Labour Shadow Chancellor Ed Balls could claim that Scottish self-determination would mean 'perils' for public services, while his own party guaranteed the economic safety of greater 'privatisation' (prescription fees, OAP provision, service outsourcing).[65] From this point of view it is telling that around the time of the referendum, although shouldering the common image of themselves as benefit junkies, Scots showed *less* faith in the 1940s' welfare consensus model than did the rest of the UK.[66]

Conclusion

The argument here is not that nothing new happened with Thatcherism. Thatcherism's extension of the economy into new subjective realism was certainly far-reaching and revolutionary, in the Whig sense of the term, which always implies *restoration*. But it could only be so by relying on the mass psychological binding to the eternal constitution enabled by wartime and post-war consensus, which it reduced to its barest, most 'arithmetic' terms. Neoliberalism's adaptation of consensus has been so powerfully naturalised that not only was it not seriously troubled by the banking crisis of 2008, but this crisis provoked a defensive wave of patriotic welfare state that celebration demanded a protection and extension of the subjective economy. Nevertheless, neoliberal realism is thrown into relief by the combination of post-2008 critiques and 2014's scepticism over the claim that the economic constitution as natural and universal. Just as the fissures made obvious by the referendum of 2014 tested the strength of the Olympic moment, so they also continue to test the imagery of consensus that lay behind it. Rather than taking the Thatcherite rhetoric of 'rolling back the state' at its word, as critiques of neoliberalism sometimes seem to do, we might instead see a personalisation and expansion of the state through a long roll-out phase from the early 1940s to the early 1970s, only stuttering through a half-decade or so of crisis before a Thatcherite restoration set it back on its right path.

65 Andrew Whitaker, 'Balls: Independence would bring inequality rise', *Scotsman*, 28 May, http://scotsman.com/news/politics/top-stories/balls-independence-would-bring-inequality-rise-1-3424520

66 Bob Duncan, 'Poll shows Scots have least faith in UK Welfare System', *Newsnet*, 11 February 2013: http://newsnet.scot/2013/02/poll-shows-scots-have-least-faith-in-uk-welfare-system/

Chapter 3

Foucault and Becker

A biopolitical approach to human capital and the stability of preferences

Miguel Vatter

Neoliberalism and the priority of the *homo oeconomicus*

On the received account, neoliberalism names that regime in which the different spheres and rationalities of the life-world are progressively colonised by economics. As Wendy Brown has recently put it, neoliberalism is 'a peculiar form of reason that configures all aspects of existence in economic terms.'[1] This chapter puts forward a complementary hypothesis with respect to neoliberalism: it claims that the condition of possibility for the fact that neoliberal governance treats us as if 'we are everywhere *homo oeconomicus* [economic man] and only *homo oeconomicus*' requires economics to interiorise certain jurisprudential categories and normative assumptions, such that the neoliberal *homo oeconomicus* is always at the same time a neoliberal *homo legalis*.[2] This seems to be what Foucault meant when he claimed that the neoliberal project introduces 'the principle of the Rule of law in the economic order.'[3] This hypothesis is quite different from saying that 'law becomes a

1 Wendy Brown, *Undoing the Demos. Neoliberalism's Stealth Revolution* (New York: Zone Books, 2015), 17.

2 On *homo oeconomicus*, see Gebhard Kirchgaessner, *Homo Oeconomicus. The Economic Model of Behaviour and Its Applications in Economics and Other Social Sciences, The European Heritage in Economics and the Social Sciences* (New York: Springer, 2008).

3 Michel Foucault, *Birth of Biopolitics: Lectures at the Collège de France, 1978–1979* (New York: Picador, 2010), 171. Thus, Foucault was always clear that neoliberalism contained two dynamics, one that introjects legal discourse into economics, and the other that projects economics into other spheres. As he says, on the one hand, neoliberalism tests the hypothesis that 'the overall exercise of political power can be modelled on the principles of market economy' (131). On the other hand, neoliberalism works from the beginning by denying the 'naturalness' of economic relations, and instead posits the principle that the juridical 'informs' the economic: 'the economy must be a game: a set of regulated activities … but in which the rules are not decisions which someone takes for others. It is a set of rules which determine the way in which each must play a game whose outcomes is not known by anyone. The economy is a game and the legal institution which frames the economy should be thought of as the rules of the game' (173). It is this latter part of the argument that I intend to pursue in this analysis of Becker. This is the real point of Foucault's claim that 'an enterprise society and a judicial society, a society oriented towards the enterprise and a society framed by a multiplicity of judicial institutions, are two faces of a single phenomenon' (150). Or, as Brown says in *Undoing the Demos*, 'modern

medium for disseminating neoliberal rationality beyond the economy'[4] because the latter view assumes that neoliberal rationality is essentially and exclusively 'economic' and only in a secondary moment does it invest other spheres and their rationalities. The hypothesis pursued in this chapter, conversely, is that the very idea of *homo oeconomicus* would not have been possible had it not always already interiorised and recast the idea of *homo legalis.*

On nearly all accounts of neoliberalism, Gary Becker's concept of human capital plays a central role in illustrating the first hypothesis of a colonisation of the life-world by economic rationality. His well-known claim that the 'economic approach is a comprehensive one that is applicable to all human behaviour'[5] would seem to epitomise this standard understanding of neoliberalism. At first sight, Becker's theory seems to offer a counterexample to Foucault's claim that postulates a juridification of economics as the ground of neoliberalism. Indeed, Foucault first made this claim in relation to his brief discussion of Hayek's 'Austrian School' of neoliberalism in *The Birth of Biopolitics*, and the differences between the Austrian and Chicago Schools are well-known.[6] Additionally, some recent Foucault commentators have argued that the French thinker 'did indeed have a liberal moment' at the time of these lectures: Foucault, it is argued, was particularly sympathetic to the neoliberalism of the Chicago School, exemplified by Becker's work.[7] Michael Behrent has argued that Foucault was attracted to the Chicago School due to their 'anti-statism', and even more by the promise of a form of government that would not presuppose law.[8] The problem with this reading, as far as this chapter is concerned, is that it collapses Foucault's understanding of the state with his conception of the law. However, Foucault never identified the sphere of law with the destiny of sovereign power: the coupling of sovereignty with law is only one possible modality of law, one which was being surpassed by a conception of the law as limit to the state precisely during the aegis of liberal 'governmentality',

citizenship features a double persona, juridical-legal, on the one hand, economic on the other' (85). It is not merely that Foucault reduces the political to the legal and forgets 'the subject of politics, a demotic subject' (87).

4 Brown, *Undoing the Demos*, 151.

5 Gary Becker, 'The Economic Approach to Human Behavior', in *The Essence of Becker*, eds, Ramón Febrero and Pedro S. Schwartz (Stanford: Hoover Institution Press, 1995), 7.

6 Davies, for example, distinguishes between 'an ordoliberal [Freiburg School] project of extending legal analysis into economics, and then in a Chicago School Project of extending economic analysis into law', William Davies, *The Limits of Neoliberalism. Authority, Sovereignty and the Logic of Competition* (London: Sage, 2014), 75. For an argument to bring all neoliberal Schools under one umbrella, see now *The Mont Pelerin Society: The Making of the Neoliberal Thought Collective*, eds, Philip Mirowski and Dieter Plehwe (Boston: Harvard University Press, 2009). For an extensive reading of Foucault and Hayek, see Miguel Vatter, *The Republic of the Living. Biopolitics and the Critique of Civil Society* (New York: Fordham, 2014), chap. 6.

7 Michael C. Behrent, 'Liberalism Without Humanism: Michel Foucault and the Free-Market Creed, 1976–1979', *Modern Intellectual History* 6 (2009): 545.

8 Behrent, 'Liberalism Without Humanism', 561–563.

starting in the late eighteenth century.[9] What remains unquestioned here is the neoliberal, anti-statist conception of law.

Other commentators have argued that in these lectures Foucault sought to criticise neoliberalism as a form of 'biopower'.[10] As Lemke argues, Foucault identified 'biopower' as a form of power and subjectivation that is particularly self-reflexive because it relies on the subject's own freedom in order to operate: security goes hand in hand with freedom.[11] The problem with this reading is that it leaves undetermined the structure of the neoliberal, economic conception of freedom and thus leaves unexplained the connection between neoliberal economic theory and biopower.[12]

This chapter suggests possible ways to address these problems. It employs Foucault's reading of Becker to argue that Becker's 'economic approach' is not simply the elimination of the *homo legalis* (as well as of the *homo politicus*) and its replacement by the *homo oeconomicus* because Becker's innovations in microeconomics presuppose an implicit theory of juridical conduct that, in turn, made it possible for economic rationality to expand beyond its traditional limits. Beckerian microeconomic analysis has recently found a popular expression in bestsellers dedicated to 'freakonomics'. One could say that this chapter seeks to identify Becker's 'freak-jurisprudence' that shadows his 'freakonomics'. This chapter also makes a contribution to discussions of the neoliberal economic conception of freedom and the reason that it is so conducive to biopower, although in so doing it leaves Foucault's reading aside and analyses Becker's writings. The chapter

9 Behrent cites Jeremy Bentham's utilitarianism as one of the main sources of an 'economic liberalism' that 'effectively dispenses with the need for juridical foundations', Behrent, 'Liberalism Without Humanism', 562, seemingly forgetting that Bentham is the source of a crucial revolution in jurisprudence. Discussing Ewald's understanding of Foucault's treatment to neoliberalism, Behrent picks up on Foucault's claim that neoliberalism is a 'juridical regression', although later it becomes clear that Foucault and Ewald are talking about a shift from 'disciplinary norms' towards the 'regulatory norms' that are constitutive of biopower. Michael C. Behrent, 'Accidents Happen: Francois Ewald, the "Antirevolutionary" Foucault, and the Intellectual Politics of the French Welfare State', *The Journal of Modern History* 82 (2010): 616–617. But the connection between such norms and Beckerian economics remains unthematised in Behrent.

10 See in general Michael Hardt and Antonio Negri, *Multitude: War and Democracy in the Age of Empire* (Cambridge: Harvard University Press, 2005); Thomas Lemke, *Foucault, Governmentality, and Critique* (London: Routledge, 2012); and Mitchel Dean, 'Michel Foucault's "apology" for neoliberalism', *Journal of Political Power* 7 (2014): 433–442.

11 See Thomas Lemke, 'The Risks of Security: Liberalism Biopolitics and Fear', in *The Government of Life. Foucault, Biopolitics, and Neoliberalism*, eds, Miguel Vatter and Vanessa Lemm (New York: Fordham University Press, 2014), 59–77.

12 Attempts by Harcourt and Ewald to make this connection by imputing to Becker an argument for eugenics and/or a strong behaviourism are rejected by Becker himself. See Gary Becker, Francois Ewald and Bernard Harcourt, '"Becker on Ewald on Foucault on Becker": American Neoliberalism and Michel Foucault's 1979 *Birth of Politics* Lectures' (lecture, University of Chicago Law School, Chicago, 2012).

argues that this conception of freedom is crystallised around Becker's approach to the economic idea of 'revealed preference' (the idea that choices reveal preferences), and in particular his axiom concerning the 'stability of preferences'. It turns out that preferences, understood as expression of subjective freedom, can be seen as the medium for a process of subjectivation that is internally related to the exercise of biopower, understood as the power to conduct or govern 'populations' or aggregates of individuals.

Normativity beyond discipline and punishment

Although Becker is famous for arguing that his 'economic approach is a comprehensive one that is applicable to all human behaviour',[13] he does not, for the most part, establish the conditions of possibility of such an 'economic approach', and when he does, he tends to think about it as the application of rational choice methodology. Yet, I would argue that it is better to think about it not as an application of so-called 'methodological individualism', but rather as a synonym of what Weber and Foucault would actually recognise as *ethos*, as a methodical 'conduct of conduct'. Seen from this perspective, Becker's microeconomics is not simply an 'economic' theory as much as a contribution to the constitution of neoliberal governmentality.

There are three determinants of this *ethos* or 'approach': 'assumptions of maximizing behaviour, market equilibrium, and stable preferences'.[14] Economists of the Austrian School have often questioned these assumptions as purely 'theoretical' or 'abstract', as if they have no purchase on how human beings 'really' act. From a purely economic perspective, this may or may not be true, but from a biopolitical perspective which focuses on the problem of how human conduct is 'governed', as I show below, this objection misses the point entirely. If one considers these assumptions purely from an economics standpoint, then as Becker says, there follow well-known theorems of neo-classical economics: 'rise in price reduces quantity demanded'; 'rise in price increases quantity supplied' (i.e. curves of demand and supply); 'competitive markets satisfy consumer preferences more effectively than monopoly markets' (*eidos* of market as competition); 'tax on the output of a market reduces the output' (for example, stricter penalties reduces crime, punishment as 'tax' on crime). Additionally, prices (real or shadow ones) 'measure the opportunity cost of using scarce resources'. So, all commodities (even non-material ones) have a 'price' that one has to pay in order to consume them. 'In equilibrium the ratio of these prices must equal the ratio of the marginal utilities.'[15] The 'right' price will then be that which allows most 'utility' for all people dealing with that commodity.

13 Becker, 'The Economic Approach to Human Behavior', 7.
14 Becker, 'The Economic Approach to Human Behavior', 5.
15 Becker, 'The Economic Approach to Human Behavior', 6.

One of the rare sustained Foucaultian readings of Becker in the literature is Bernard Harcourt's *The Illusion of Free Markets*. Harcourt's analysis of the Chicago School is centred on an internal change within the paradigm of normativity characterised by 'discipline and punishment'. Thus, he writes:

> Becker's model could have led to a definition of crime based on welfare maximization: in this view, crime could have been defined as any human behaviour that can be most efficiently regulated by means of the criminal sanction. Or, more robustly, any human behaviour that, when criminalized properly, maximizes social welfare ... It would have been possible, according to the Beckerian model, to determine for each behaviour whether it contributes to social welfare or whether instead it would maximize welfare to criminalize and enforce prohibitions on such behaviour.[16]

Although Harcourt acknowledges that this is not at all the direction in which Becker's work develops, it does betray Harcourt's own view that neoliberalism drives a thorough criminalisation of social behaviour.

Yet Harcourt never discusses Becker's 'economic approach' from the biopolitical perspective opened up by Foucault's own analysis of neoliberalism and of Becker's work in particular. In the *Birth of Biopolitics* Foucault's treatment of Becker is mainly focused on the revolutionary consequences for the traditional idea of the *homo oeconomicus* when he or she becomes conceived as an enterprising human being characterised by maximising the utilities derived from his or her 'human capital'. However, the manuscript of Foucault's two lectures dedicated to Chicago School neoliberalism, of 14 March 1979 and 21 March 1979, actually ends with some notes in which he considers whether Becker's theory does not make it necessary to 'change the conception of law', in order to move beyond the dualism between 'legality', based on sovereign power, and 'normalization', based on disciplinary power, that had characterised Foucault's previous discourse on law.[17] These concluding and undeveloped notes on Becker suggest a way of reading neoliberal economics from an alternative, if not opposite, direction to Harcourt's emphasis on discipline, by adopting a biopolitical understanding of normativity.

16 Bernard E. Harcourt, *The Illusion of Free Markets. Punishments and the Myth of Natural Order* (Cambridge: Harvard University Press, 2011), 135. Hence Harcourt adds: 'in this sense, it would have replicated in a more modern vocabulary the cameralist reading of Beccaria'. I am instead advocating the hypothesis that Beckerian jurisprudence is not Beccarian, pun included. This perspective which ties economic behaviour to techniques of discipline and surveillance rather than to biopolitics is still in evidence in later works by Harcourt, for instance his comments in Becker, Ewald and Harcourt, '"Becker on Ewald on Foucault on Becker"', as well as in Bernard E. Harcourt, 'Fantasies and Illusions: On Liberty, Order, and Free Markets', *Cardozo Law Review* 33 (2011–2012): 2413–2428.

17 Neoliberalism signals 'a massive withdrawal with regard to the normative-disciplinary system ... It is necessary 1. To change the conception of law', Foucault, *Birth of Biopolitics*, 260. On Foucault's previous discourse on law, see Ben Golder and Peter Fitzpatrick, *Foucault's Law* (London: Routledge, 2009).

Foucault suggests that neoliberalism moves away from an idea of law as 'human technology' based on 'discipline-normalization', and towards a conception of law as 'action on the environment. Modifying the terms of the game, not the players' mentality ... You must consider everyone as a player and only intervene on an environment in which he is able to play'.[18] This new 'environmentalism' of jurisprudence corresponds to a third kind of technology of power, associated with biopolitics and biopower. This chapter attempts a first approximation to what 'modifying the terms of the game, not the players' mentality' means, by analysing Foucault's treatment of Becker's concept of human capital, and then by moving to an analysis of Becker's theory of the stability of preferences.

Foucault's most extended development of a biopolitical conception of norms and normativity is found in the 1977–78 lectures *Security, Territory, Population.*[19] One of the Greek terms for law, *nomos*, originally appears to refer to the interrelation of the three terms (security, territory, population).[20] Indeed, a great deal of twentieth-century jurisprudence, from Schmitt to Fuller and Hayek, seems to turn around the idea of law as *nomos*. It is thus no coincidence that Foucault would choose this title for a volume that gives the most explicit biopolitical articulation of this idea of law. As he explains it, the key presupposition for a biopolitical conception of *nomos* as security is a renewed idea of how populations are to be distributed in a given territory so as to maximise their life-forces. Territory becomes conceived in terms of 'common space' rather than of 'enclosures'. In turn, populations are analysed into different sub-populations that can be mixed together in a regulated way so as to form an 'ecology' or an evolutionary niche within the 'open' free market or complex networks of communication. On this neoliberal idea of security, the norms that bring about securitisation[21] – the norms that Foucault later associates with the 'regulatory power' of the police[22] – make possible the circulation, the flow, of things and people in, and through, and out of a given territory, rather than cordoning off this territory from other ones.

A simple illustration of such securitisation is the process of (neoliberal) gentrification. Here, a 'bad' part of town, historically riddled by high crime and high unemployment rates, becomes slowly gentrified not by imposing round-the-clock police patrols, but, rather, by providing a minimum level of security sufficient to make the neighbourhood attractive to a 'bohemian' part of the population and allowing it to settle this territory. Bohemians do not want to live in crime-free suburbia: they require just enough crime to make it 'dangerous' for a majoritarian

18 Foucault, *Birth of Biopolitics*, 260–261.

19 See Michel Foucault, *Security, Territory, Population: Lectures at the Collège de France, 1978–1979* (New York: Picador, 2009). For analyses of these terms in Foucault, see now the essays in *The Government of Life. Foucault, Biopolitics and Neoliberalism*, eds, Vanessa Lemm and Miguel Vatter (New York: Fordham, 2014).

20 See the discussion in Miguel Vatter, *The Republic of the Living. Biopolitics and the Critique of Civil Society* (New York: Fordham, 2014).

21 Foucault, *Security, Territory, Population*, chaps 2–3.

22 Foucault, *Security, Territory, Population*, chaps 12–13.

bourgeois life-style, but 'safe' enough for a bohemian form of life, a minoritarian life-style. It is a simple application of marginal economics: the surplus comes in tolerating just enough criminality, the right 'margin' of crime. What the 'right' or 'natural' margin is cannot be determined by policy: it depends on how much the environment needs in order to attain a certain equilibrium. Once bohemians have settled the neighbourhood, and have opened their cafés, bars and art spaces, and their children can play in the previously out of bounds public parks, in other words, once their form of life constitutes 'human capital', abstract capital investment ('gentrification' proper) in that territory begins: a new 'market' is opened up. 'Foreign investors' come in to the territory and acquire and remodel housing, bring in upscale food markets, offices, and so on. The cycle is then replicated at a higher level: once middle-class investors buy and move into these neighbourhoods, they need to retain the right 'margin' of bohemians (no longer of crime) in order to maintain the 'value' of the now gentrified 'bohemian' neighbourhood.

Thus, the neoliberal idea of regulation is different from both the sovereign and the disciplinarian ideas of law. Neoliberal regulation is not based on the binary opposition of sovereign law, what is allowed versus what is prohibited, which can either let everything through or can block everything. This feature of classical law does not make for a rational theory of 'flows' (communication) because this kind of law cannot 'securitise' these flows. Such securitisation requires a kind of regulation that lets the right amount of both allowed *and* prohibited things. But neoliberal regulation is also different from the disciplinary conception of normativity in so far as it does not focus on the individual body, on the individual acts, but on their aggregates: a sub-population of 'undisciplined' individuals may just bring about the 'right' or desired outcome, namely, a well-ordered or policed society.

As other interpreters have pointed out, Foucault is clearly attracted by the radical lack of *conformism* and *disciplinary behaviour* that follow from Becker's 'economic approach' to the regulation of social behaviour.[23] The main reason for this attraction is that the 'freak-jurisprudence' inherent in Becker's microeconomic analysis reveals a high degree of 'toleration' towards 'illegalism' that matches Foucault's own distance from the disciplinary conditions of capitalist society previously analysed in *Discipline and Punish*, along with his move to the biopolitical conditions of modern 'governmentality' and the crucial interplay of risk, liberty and security.

For instance, Foucault says that Becker's idea of punishment as a 'tax' on crime makes it possible to pose the following questions: 'what must be tolerated as crime?' or, better, 'what is intolerable not to tolerate?'.[24] Similarly, 'the criminal is

23 See now *Foucault and Neoliberalism*, eds, Daniel Zamora and Michael C. Behrent (London: Polity, 2015).

24 Foucault, *Birth of Biopolitics*, 256. Harcourt repeats Foucault's point when he says that 'the optimal level of enforcement of any particular crime would be that which minimized both the costs associated with the crime and the costs of repressing that crime through prevention and punishment. The central contribution of Becker's model is to pinpoint, given a certain definition of crime, what level of policing and punishment minimizes total

nothing other than absolutely anyone whomsoever. The criminal, any person, is treated as anyone whomsoever who invests in an action, expects a profit from it, and who accepts the risk of a loss'.[25] These formulations are quite striking in so far as they signal a shift from a binary conception of law (legal/illegal) to what can be called a probabilistic conception of law: any given action can be designated as a crime only in a probabilistic sense. Until the action gets 'fixed' from a certain framework of observation, which is always relative, any action is both allowed and prohibited – much like in a quantum world, it is impossible to determine at the same time both speed and location of any particle. In other words, the concept of 'law enforcement' ceases to have an analytic or necessary connection with punishment of transgressions, and thus with sovereign power. Since law is only what justifies punishment of some crime, 'what is law' no longer ultimately depends on the sword of the sovereign.

But on Foucault's reading, Becker's generalised application of the 'economic approach' to society not only calls into question the basis of sovereign power: it also undermines the ground of disciplinary power. Since the fact of being observed changes the behaviour itself of the agents, a probabilistic conception of law also no longer depends on the panopticon of disciplinary power. As Foucault puts it, this 'economic approach' runs counter to an idea of society based on 'a mechanism of general normalization and the exclusion of those who cannot be normalized' because it offers instead 'the image, idea, or theme-program of a society in which there is an optimization of systems of difference, in which the field is left open to fluctuating processes, in which minority individuals and practices are tolerated', as long as they are seen to be rational economical actors.[26]

What Foucault is referring to can be approximated by the kind of economic analysis proposed by 'freakonomics'.[27] This is an extension of Becker's 'economic approach' to territories and populations in which 'rule of law' type of conduct is absent and in which the *eidos* of competition seems not to apply (for example, in marriages and family relations, in addictive or criminal behaviour, etc.). In these para-economic zones, economic actors are 'freaks' or 'outlayers' that maximise utility in ways that are difficult to track (by the state as well as by other economic actors) because the cost-benefit calculus carries with it a series of 'shadow-prices' that are hard to make visible, and which for that very reason need to be

social costs – or as Becker provocatively wrote, "How many offenses should be permitted and how many offenders should go unpunished?" ... Some crimes may be better cost-reducers than others: costly crimes that cost little to deter may be more efficient to prosecute, in contrast to low-cost crimes that are expensive to deter', Harcourt, *The Illusion of Free Markets*, 134.

25 Foucault, *Birth of Biopolitics*, 253.

26 Foucault, *Birth of Biopolitics*, 259.

27 I refer to bestsellers like Steven Levitt and Stephen Dubner, *SuperFreakonomics. Global Cooling, Patriotic Prostitutes and why Suicide Bombers Should Buy Life Insurance* (New York: Harper, 2009). These books are popularisations of Becker's microeconomic theory.

approached with 'toleration'. Thus, the entrepreneurial character of 'illegal' or 'alegal' behaviour is analysed as a 'rational' conduct, and is thereby, at least rhetorically, de-criminalised and positively 'tolerated' if not incentivated.

The hypothesis of this chapter is that Becker's conception of human capital carries with it a shadow jurisprudence – what we can call a 'freak-jurisprudence' – that mirrors the three characteristics of a biopolitical understanding of norms that Foucault addresses through the rubrics of 'security', 'territory' and 'population'. On a biopolitical understanding, one can say that for Becker legal norms are no longer solely or predominantly oriented towards making possible the production and exchange of *commodities*, in other words, oriented towards market transactions, as was still the case for Hayek and Posner (according to Harcourt), but are oriented towards making the individual's *life and labour*, understood as 'human capital', into an enterprise that generates utilities, not all of which are capable of being transacted in 'legally' framed 'free' markets. Norms for Becker become rules that make possible a 'form of life'.[28] The norms that determine the accumulation of *human* capital need to provide for 'security' in a sense that is very different from the idea of security in either sovereign or disciplinary forms of power. These norms are, instead, the 'environmental' regulations that allow minoritarian 'forms of life' to generate a surplus of utility. Foucault points out that in order to maintain the law's 'function' as that of a 'rule of the game',[29] what has to be regulated are the 'environmental' factors open to the opportunities and to the liberties in supply and demand, by which Foucault seems to be referring to considerations such as the elastic or inelastic character of the demand. According to Becker, what had prevented certain territories and behaviours from becoming objects of rational utility calculus, what had kept the 'economic approach' from expanding into those areas, was the belief that changes in behaviour are due to arbitrary changes in the preferences or tastes of economic actors. If one rejects this assumption, if instead one assumes that preferences are 'stable over time' and pretty much the same across cultures, genders, classes, then it is in principle possible to analyse changes of behaviour as a function of changes in costs and benefits, changes in restrictions rather than preferences, which can in turn be 'optimised' by properly regulating incentives.

From the cycle of production to the cycle of consumption: the biopolitics of human capital

Like other interpreters of Becker's concept of human capital, Foucault also believed that this concept made possible the entrance of economic thinking into new areas of human behaviour because it allowed neoclassical economics to break the priority that Smith, Ricardo and Marx assigned, each in their own way, to

28 On this term, see now Giorgio Agamben, *The Highest Poverty. Monastic Rules and Form-of-Life* (Stanford: Stanford University Press, 2013).

29 Foucault, *Birth of Biopolitics*, 260.

production and exchange within the economic cycle, and put considerations of labour and consumption centre stage.[30] But for Foucault this shift in emphasis from production to consumption corresponds to a biopolitical turn taken by economics with the Marginalist revolution. Becker's concept of 'human capital' attempts to account for what happens in markets as a function of what has happened outside markets and before the economic actor enters into the market. In this sense, within neoliberal economics the concept of 'human capital' occupies the same structural position that the concept of 'living labour' occupies within Marx's economics. One can say that Becker's concept of human capital thematises political economy from the dimension that Marx, already in the *Economic-Philosophical Manuscripts*, refers to as 'species-life', the very 'biopolitical' dimension of economics that classical political economy always seemed to leave out of consideration due to their 'Robinsonesque' approach to production, which Marx criticised in the *Grundrisse* on the grounds that it denied the social character of production and thus of value. It is thus not entirely correct to claim that Foucault uses Becker to distance himself from Marxist discourse.[31] It is rather the other way around: Foucault makes sense of Becker by transposing his concepts into Marx's language, which is in turn corrected and amplified from a biopolitical perspective.[32]

Foucault begins his discussion of Becker's human capital by asking why individuals labour at all: 'what does working mean for the person who works?'[33] According to Becker, the answer is not because one wants to produce a good that is to be exchanged on a market. For Becker, labour is not 'work', just as consumption is not 'production'. In order to place the theory of human capital in its

30 Or stated differently, it 'makes it possible to supersede the conception of the economic agent as a mere optant between goods that are given, and he becomes the 'producer' of the commodities which gives him satisfaction', Javier Aranzandi, *Liberalism against Liberalism. Theoretical analysis of the works of Ludwig von Mises and Gary Becker* (London: Routledge, 2006), 121.

31 As claimed in Behrent, 'Liberalism Without Humanism', 547. Conversely, in Negri and Hardt there is an attempt to reappropriate the idea of human capital into their post-Marxists analyses of living labour, see Michael Hardt and Antonio Negri, *Commonwealth* (Cambridge: Harvard University Press, 2009). There are deep affinities between Negri's idea of 'immaterial labour' and Becker's 'human capital' since in Negri the 'immateriality' of labour refers to the fact that living labour, properly speaking, is not a function of the external product or commodity: it externalises or objectifies itself not in the form of a commodity but as affects and thoughts that allow for a communal reproduction of species-life. Living labour is really life understood as a function of exchange of information and communication, hence, as 'immaterial'. One should also not forget that Negri was lecturing on the *Grundrisse* in Paris (later published as *Marx beyond Marx*) at the same time that Foucault was lecturing on biopolitics. Negri refers in passing to this coincidence within his lectures.

32 Foucault, *Birth of Biopolitics*, 220–221.

33 Foucault, *Birth of Biopolitics*, 223. Here the translator uses labour and work as synonymous. This is a problem for reasons explained below. Human capital has nothing to do with work, but is a theory of labour.

proper context, it is perhaps useful to adopt the analytical distinction between labour and work that Arendt established in *The Human Condition* in view, precisely, of identifying what distinguishes the *homo laborans* of modern civil society. As Arendt argues, one labours as part of a 'circle' of consumption (not of production), whose end result is the increase of pleasure (utility) and the decrease of pain. But whereas for Arendt the circle of consumption is negatively connoted because it keeps the subject tied to the sphere of animal life, *zoe*, and makes the subject unable to distinguish itself through a proper or autonomous *bios*, from Becker's standpoint things look entirely different: the circle of labour and consumption reaches equilibrium and stabilises into a 'form of life' (what Foucault calls an 'enterprise') that maximises utility. In turn, it is this 'form of life' that actually explains the preferences of the individual, and not the 'existential choices' that are traditionally associated with the idea of a free and autonomous *bios*.

From this point of view, classical economics makes the mistake of thinking about labour in a teleological fashion, starting from what it took to be its end-product, namely, the commodity that is produced. Classical economics confuses labour with production: it collapses labour into work. Whereas 'work' (what Marx calls labour force) is exchanged (Marx would say 'alienated') for a salary, this is not the case of labour as a biopolitical power or capacity, as the output of human capital.[34] Becker's intuition is that one cannot 'live' for a salary (this is, after all, what Marx calls the 'alienation' of the human species; the reification of a form of life). In this sense, his economics can be said to pursue the Marxist ideal of a social life without work.[35] In neoliberal parlance, everyone should be able to live without 'working' a single day of one's life because one's labour would be entirely subsumed by that form or style of life that generates a maximum of utilities (pleasure, *joie de vivre*, well-being, meaning, etc.).[36] For Becker one has to think about labour starting from the consumption of goods that (re)produces 'living' labour in a certain 'form' (from which one can read out the real preferences of the labourers), rather than from the 'product' of the labour once it has been 'sold' for

34 For this reason, it is better to think of labour not as a 'force' but as a form of power (in a Foucaultian sense of the term, that is, as a form of subjectivation), and perhaps the best term for this is none other than the idea of 'capability'. The relation between Sen's and Becker's economic theories must be left for another work.

35 This is what Agamben refers to as inoperability, i.e. an inherent lack of work/product in human praxis.

36 Cooper shows the dark side of this neoliberal ideal: 'It is not only the case, then, that post-Fordism undermines the distinction between the "time of life" and the "time of work", but it also dismantles the standard metric of the Fordist/Taylorist labour contract. As the standard working day and week are supplanted by intermittent call work, night work, overtime, nine-day fortnights, weekend shifts, and annualized work times, a plethora of new contractual forms have emerged to constrain workers to the contingencies of flexible labour market', Melinda Cooper, 'Workfare, Familyfare, Godfare: Transforming Contingency into Necessity', *The South Atlantic Quarterly* 111 (2012): 645–646.

a salary. For, in any case, the product is not of living labour itself, but of fixed capital plus living labour operating in certain relations of production.

Thus, Beckerian human capital deconstructs Marx's thesis concerning alienated labour, even while it preserves the basic Marxist aim of rejecting what it takes to be unfree (forced or extorted) labour. For the early Marx, the true vocation of humanity is the free use of living labour; this vocation is alienated in capitalist relations of production where one is led to believe that one's 'authentic life' is to be found in a passive 'animal-like' existence of consumption, rather than in an active life of cooperative production. Becker turns this around and says: 'animal-like' consumption is in reality 'productive' of utility at the species-life level. My *bios* (the kinds of roles that I 'choose') may give the impression that I am 'alienated' from my labour, but, so says Becker, if I persevere in my preferences as expressed in my form of life (*zoe*), it is because I am making a profit that may be invisible to you and others.

One sees this kind of reasoning employed in the neoliberal critiques of the 'gender wage gap'. From the human capital perspective, the gap is not a consequence of wage discrimination between men and women in the marketplace. Rather, the gap is explained as a function of the different 'life-choices' made by women and men before they have even entered the market. Thus, on this account, women are said to choose professions that have less risk/reward disparity; they are said to choose professions that pay less or are part-time because they have factored in their utility calculus the need to interrupt their careers at some point to have and to care for children, and so on. Here the idea of a 'form of life' that has 'shadow prices' is already built into the economic rationale. Needless to say, feminist critiques of human capital have already pointed out that the asymmetry in procreative and care duties between men and women is not something that is 'chosen', but rather expresses a relation of domination that frames the rational choices of the members of the family enterprise.[37] In this sense, one can argue that the concept of human capital, although it factors species-life into its economics, nevertheless still considers an 'alienated' conception of species-life.

Unlike Marx, for Becker labour-power does not 'flow' from the living and labouring subject to the product or object, where it 'dies' as living labour and becomes transmuted into 'dead' labour or capital. Rather, the choice for this or that object or product, and so its consumption, is a function of labour-power 'producing' itself as a form of life that is preferred over another. Whereas Marx, in *Grundrisse*, argued that production always already contains consumption, Becker is making the inverse point, namely, that consumption always already contains production. In its consumption, living labour 'flows back' from the goods or

37 'As provisioners of care for others in households … women disproportionately remain the invisible infrastructure for all developing, mature, and worn-out human capital – children, adults, disabled, and elderly. Generally uncoerced, yet essential, this provision and responsibility get theoretically and ideologically tucked into what are assumed as preferences issuing naturally from sexual difference … It is formulated, in short, as an effect of nature, not of power', Brown, *Undoing the Demos*, 105.

products into living labour as an 'income stream' generated by human capital. As Foucault explains, 'an income is quite simply the product or return on a capital' or investment.[38] Human capital is to income as labour power is to wages. On this Beckerian picture, the true salary is actually revenue obtained from the worker's human capital.[39] Since the worker, by definition, has no disposable capital, his or her capital must be indisposable, i.e. human capital that is composed from what it obtained genetically or otherwise passively acquired and what it has invested in during his or her life-time (*bios*), and is now generating fruits or utility for him or her: 'we should think of consumption as an enterprise activity by which the individual, precisely on the basis of the capital he has at his disposal, will produce something that will be his own satisfaction'.[40] Perhaps this formulation can be further specified by adding that the 'man of consumption' is a producer not of any market goods, but of forms of life.

For Marx, wages belong to a circle of production that culminates with the commodity and its exchange in the market for a monetary profit. In this circle of production, living-labour is employable only in a specific time and place, and under conditions (the 'relations of production') that are not at the disposal of the worker. And conversely, the living-labour that is at the disposal of the worker remains structurally unemployable. On the contrary, for Becker income streams are generated from the circle of consumption that begins and ends with the form of life that lies outside the market and is, to a much greater extent, at the disposal of the labourer. Human capital can be 'put to work' all the time and in every place. Thus, from the perspective of human capital, an 'unemployed house wife' can also be thought of as the head of an enterprise in which she is constantly 'investing' in herself, her children, and in her husband in order to maximise utilities. For instance, the everyday activities and routines of this 'unemployed house wife' can be economically analysed as a series of investments in her body ('going to the gym'), in her wardrobe ('shopping'), in her status as a 'good mother' and 'good wife', in order to generate for herself an 'income flow' that ultimately comes only partially from the wages of the husband.

For Becker, if consumption does not close itself into a self-reinforcing cycle, if it does not reach stability, the individual will not remain in that labouring activity for very long, because its life process has not yet attained a form of life. On this picture of labour, the phenomenon of migration (of job, residence, country, etc.) is always seen as an 'investment'.[41] It is part and parcel of Becker's well-known advocacy for contractualising all forms of labour as well as flexibilising labour in time and space. It is not simply that contracts (for example, marriage as a contract) reduce transaction costs in the exchange of goods and services, but, more

38 Foucault, *Birth of Biopolitics*, 224.
39 Foucault, *Birth of Biopolitics*, 226.
40 Foucault, *Birth of Biopolitics*, 226.
41 'Migration is an investment; the migrant is an investor. He is an entrepreneur of himself who incurs expenses by investing to obtain some kind of improvement', Foucault, *Birth of Biopolitics*, 230.

essentially, the contract form minimises exit costs for the labourer in case utilities are not being maximised in the respective enterprise, and thus requires the migration of the labourer to a better 'environment'. The point is that labour-power must be exercised in such a way (in such a time and a place) as to make a 'form of life' possible for the labourer. The contract is no longer solely the jurisprudential medium of an exchange of commodities, but it has become the medium through which the labourer attains the kind of 'upward' (but it can also be 'sideward') mobility that allows the cycle of consumption to find equilibrium in a form of life.

The third and last aspect of Foucault's reading of human capital is the idea that such human capital requires investing in the 'environment' of the producer – this is the 'environmental' logic that Foucault relates to the new jurisprudence of Beckerian neoliberalism, tied to the idea of juridical norms as 'rules of the game'. In this context Foucault employs the idea of *Vitalpolitik*, which connects directly neoliberal economy to one kind of 'biopolitics': 'the enterprise schema involves acting so that the individual ... is not alienated from his work environment, from the time of his life, from his household, his family and from the natural environment'.[42] The production of a 'healthy' environment in which the labourer can carry on his or her enterprise is thus an essential part of investments in human capital: workers must have access to wellness programmes, their life/work balance must be regulated, etc.; in short, the whole gamut of issues falling under 'human resources' (as opposed to 'industrial relations') comes into play here.

Thus, from the standpoint of Becker (and here there is a decisive shift with respect to Hayek), the internal connection between economics and jurisprudence does not reduce itself to the regulation that maintains markets 'free' and 'open' and that therefore finds in 'competition' its ideal form. Rather, the crucial 'regulation' occurs before and outside the market, and it has the task of making it possible for populations to *enter* into these markets with sufficient human capital to start off their self-enterprise. Hence this kind of question: 'In what way this or that type of stimulation, this or that form of life [*forme de vie*], this or that relation with parents, adults, others, in what all of this will be able to crystallize in human capital?'.[43] If there is a Beckerian quasi-jurisprudence, then it is centred on what can be called 'environmental' or perhaps better 'ecological' regulations that provide 'security' to the forms of life of minoritarian communities, which in turn produce a surplus in their own lives, a surplus of utility that is not translatable into market goods.

Foucault concludes his analysis of Becker by pointing out that the theory of human capital is a contribution to the Schumpeterian explanation of why the Marxist fundamental 'law of capital' which postulates the diminishing rate of profit is wrong. Schumpeter's famous answer was 'innovation', the ever renewed production of new market goods that 'creatively' destroy entire areas of economic activity and their fixed capital by creating entire new markets. The Beckerian

42 Foucault, *Birth of Biopolitics*, 242.
43 Foucault, *Birth of Biopolitics*, 230.

answer is that 'innovation' is made possible because of privatised investments in human capital: it may very well be that the rate of profit diminishes in the production of market goods, but it does not diminish in the creation of utilities or satisfactions, i.e. that 'surplus' of life due to the consumption of 'invisible', non-market commodities like love, friendship, education, and so on.

De gustibus non disputandum est: the biopolitics of preferences

In the last part of this chapter, I suggest that underlying Foucault's claim according to which the neoliberal *homo oeconomicus* is no longer the 'man of exchange' but 'an entrepreneur of himself'[44] is Becker's theory of preferences and their stability, the heart of his 'economic approach'. Strangely enough, although Foucault himself says that for Becker neoliberal regulation is about 'modifying the terms of the game, not the players' mentality ... You must consider everyone as a player and only intervene on an environment in which he is able to play', he never discusses the question of the stability of preferences.[45] As Brown points out, Foucault's discussion of neoliberalism concludes on the crucial role played by the idea of 'interests' and their pursuit. Brown argues that an account of behaviour that turns on the pursuit of interests seems to be at odds with the kind of behaviours solicited by neoliberalism in so far as it does not account for the dynamic of:

> responsabilization – forcing the subject to become a responsible self-investor and self-provider ... The notion of individuals naturally pursuing their interests has been replaced with the production through governance of responsibilized citizens who appropriately self-invest in a context of macroeconomic vicissitudes and needs that make all of these investments into practices of speculation.[46]

This description undoubtedly captures a crucial aspect of the neoliberal *homo oeconomicus*. However, it raises the question as to what allowed neoliberalism to detach itself from the master concept of classical economics and classical liberalism, namely, 'interest'. Here I suggest that one possible answer turns on the neoliberal adoption and adaptation of the concept of 'preference'.[47] Thus, an analysis of

44 Foucault, *Birth of Biopolitics*, 225–226.
45 For a discussion of this idea from a purely economic standpoint and defending a Misean approach to economics, see Aranzandi, *Liberalism against Liberalism*, 123–132.
46 Brown, *Undoing the Demos*, 84.
47 In my opinion, much more work needs to be done on a biopolitical approach to preferences. To date, the critical approaches to the theory of preference, and *a fortiori* to their stability – found in Amartya Sen, *Choice, Welfare and Measurement* (Oxford: Basil Blackwell, 1982), Hilary Putnam, *The Collapse of the Fact/Value Dichotomy and Other Essays* (Cambridge: Harvard University Press, 2002) and Philip Pettit, 'Preferences, Deliberation and Satisfaction', in *Preferences and Wellbeing*, ed., Serena Olsaretti (New York: Cambridge University Press, 2006), 131–153 – leave power out of the analysis. But a proper comparative and critical study of how and if Sen's capability theory really displaces neoliberal theory of the stability of preference is required.

Becker's conception of 'preferences' and the postulate of their stability may offer another framework within which to understand the seeming oxymoronic phenomenon of self-investment that is both 'responsible' and 'speculative' to use Brown's terms.

Becker makes it clear that markets in which everyone has perfect information are not assumed by his 'economic approach'. What often happens is that it costs too much to get necessary information, and so actors transact with incomplete information and this may give the appearance that they are 'irrational' or that they are 'gambling' or 'guessing' about what will best satisfy their preferences rather than making a calculated choice, and thus they seem to be incurring in 'too much' risk. But for Becker these actors are actually calculating on the basis of an entirely different set of costs and benefits that give a positive margin, even though operating with incomplete information:

> When an apparently profitable opportunity to a firm, worker or household is not exploited, the economic approach does not take refuge in assertions about irrationality, contentment with wealth already acquired, or convenient ad hoc shifts in values (i.e., preferences). Rather, it postulates the existence of costs, monetary or psychic, of taking advantage of these opportunities that eliminate their profitability – costs that may not be easily 'seen' by outside observers.[48]

Becker argues that the assumption of stable preferences does not lead to a 'bundle of empty tautologies' (of the kind: all profit-making activity generates a profit) because 'the assumption of stable preferences provides a foundation for predicting the responses to various changes'.[49] If Becker's economics is a scientific or 'predictive' economics, it owes this feature to the crucial assumption of stable preferences, which together with the assumption of a maximising attitude, allows for changes in the 'rules of the game' or 'environmental' conditions to exercise human capital that can be predicted, that are also thus falsifiable, and hence that amounts to genuine 'scientific' knowledge. In other words, the 'scientific' or 'value-free' claim of Becker's economics (or of neo-classical economics tout court) seems to rest on his theory of human preferences.

Given the discussion in the previous section, it is not surprising that when Becker has to give an example of the kind of positive scientific results his 'approach' obtains, they tend to centre on biopolitical (even, thanatopolitical) phenomena. Let us take one example of an application of the principle of stable preferences adduced by Becker. If one is a heavy smoker and decides not to quit despite having all the necessary information concerning risks of premature death, one interpretation (corresponding to the maxim *de gustibus non disputandum est*) explains this behaviour by saying that the smoker is sticking to his preferences (or tastes) irrationally because preferences are based on values and one cannot dispute

48 Becker, 'The Economic Approach to Human Behavior', 6.
49 Becker, 'The Economic Approach to Human Behavior', 7.

values or tastes because they are based on will, not on reason (i.e. not on facts).[50] For Becker, it may be the case that the smoker has calculated that 'the life span forfeited is not worth the cost to him of quitting smoking' because the form of life of which smoking is an essential part brings him more utility or satisfaction.[51] This presupposes that there is an 'optimum' life span beyond which the cost of living more brings less utility than if those resources had been used up for other ends.

The point is that if preserving 'mere' life were the highest good, as in Hobbes (where human beings pass from one desire to another), then this smoker would be acting irrationally, but if the point of living is to give and maintain life in a certain form, then the decision not to quit smoking may count as a perfectly rational one. What overrides 'mere life' is a bio-juridical idea of 'form of life' for which death is not the worst of all evils. Indeed, Becker generalises his finding and claims that it is probable that most, if not all, 'natural' deaths are in reality 'suicides' because people could have postponed their deaths had they been willing to invest more resources into this project, but instead prefer to remain in their forms of life or choose to retain their seemingly 'costly' habits. Becker says, tongue in cheek, that his economic approach provides evidence for Freud's hypothesis of a constitutive 'death wish'.[52] I would say, instead, that the *Vitalpolitik* of human capital has a necessary thanatopolitical component: 'bare life' is constantly sacrificed in order to produce the 'surplus of life' that one really seeks to maximise, and which is generated only by considering living itself as the product of an enterprise or form of life.

The example of the smoker suggests that for Becker the kind of environmental regulations conducive to the optimal yield of human capital are all reducible to a logic of addiction or a logic of *habitus*. For classical economics, addicts exemplify irrational behaviour because they are literally willing to pay 'any price' for the satisfaction brought by their addictive substance of choice. The typical analysis of addictive behaviour is to say that one's taste changes due to consumption of addictive substances. Thus Becker discusses Marshall's example of 'the more good

50 The maxim *de gustibus non disputandum est* entails the fact/value distinction: facts are unchanging; but values are always changeable, they are unmotivated or arbitrary, and thus can be arbitrarily changed. This assumption is exactly what Becker questions because it limits economic rationality, which is based on 'facts' not 'values'. In this sense, like Putnam but in an entirely different direction, Becker is also denying the distinction between facts and values when thinking about preferences. For Becker, values or preferences have reasons for being what they are, but they are not 'communicatively' or dialogically developed. Pettit also argues that 'preferences' are not like 'tastes' because, unlike tastes, they are 'susceptible to deliberative connections', Pettit, 'Preferences', 137. But Pettit's distinction between 'tastes' and 'preferences' jumps from 'brute states in which one finds oneself' (e.g. having a taste for x or y) and 'preferences' that can be deliberated about, as one does with moral judgments. Becker's 'economic approach' stands in the middle, and problematises Pettit's distinctions.

51 Becker, 'The Economic Approach to Human Behavior', 9. Notice that Becker is not so distant from Sen's reasoning that to be 'wealthy' does not mean to have more income, but to have more 'capabilities'. But this is not the place to discuss the differences and similarities between Becker's 'human capital' and Sen's 'capability' approaches.

52 Becker, 'The Economic Approach to Human Behavior', 9.

music a man hears, the stronger is his taste for it likely to become' and the more he will want to hear music. This is opposed to Marshall's classic illustration of marginal utility, namely, the child who picks just enough berries to satisfy his taste for berries, but not more because past the point of marginal utility, the cost of picking more berries is higher than the benefit of eating them. However, Marshall's example presupposes that the child is not addicted to berries. In the celebrated essay, 'De Gustibus Non Est Disputandum' Becker and Stigler argue that the phenomenon of addiction can be explained by maintaining tastes invariant. The key idea is that of 'consumption capital', that is, the kind of 'human capital' that one needs to have in order to get utility out of consumption of any commodity. Such 'consumption capital' is accumulated by consuming the substance and thus rationally motivates the addictive behaviour. The utility function of the music consumer is made up of 'music appreciation' produced (which depends on how much time one invested in listening to music and getting to appreciate it) plus the production of other commodities. 'Music appreciation' is a consumption capital – its increase leads to an 'increase in productivity of time spent listening to or devoted in other ways to music'. So, the more I appreciate music (by having trained myself by way of intensive exposure to music), the more pleasure I get out of the listening to music, the more 'addicted' I become. But, also, the less time I need to invest later on in getting this 'high' on music, and so the more time I have to dedicate to other consumption: my music consumption has become 'productive'. The time I dedicated in learning to appreciate music is a shadow cost, but Becker also sees it as an 'investment' I make for my future enjoyment of music. So, with increase in age the 'price' I have to pay to get a 'high' from music is lower, therefore I will want to consume more of it. The rise in my demand for music is not due to a shift in my tastes, a shift in favour of music consumption, but 'because its shadow price falls as skill and experience in the appreciation of music are acquired with exposure'.[53] The addiction to music is thus the result of a rational calculus.

Another example, often portrayed in Hollywood films, might feature a young man, alienated from school, family, and society, who spends all his time playing basketball rather than doing homework, and comes back home to watch more basketball. Parents and educators think that this young person is investing his or her time and energy (living labour) in the wrong pursuits or tastes, manifesting an inordinate preference for physical activity; however, from a Beckerian perspective, the young person's preferences are exactly the same as those of the 'nerd' who spends his or her time 'hitting the books': both are investing in their human capital. This is revealed at the end of the film when the young man makes it to the NBA, only thanks to his apparently 'irrational' initial investment.

Becker's idea is that any 'addiction' to a commodity is 'positive' when in so doing it will cost one less over time to produce the same utility from that

53 Gary Becker and George Stigler, 'De Gustibus Non Est Disputandum', in Febrero and Schwarz, *The Essence of Becker*, 189.

commodity (hence as a rational choice), and it costs one less because one has invested more time and energy in getting the 'consumption capital' that reduces over time the price of the addictive substance. One's enjoyment of music, which seems to be merely consumption of a market good, is actually productive (of 'music capital') and will generate utilities later for the consumer. Indeed, it would seem, given the basic preference of stability of tastes, that it is possible to accumulate human capital only as a function of one's (positive) addictions. Life is given a form that maximises the utility of human capital through positive addictions; the opposite goes for negative addictions; both can be manipulated through incentives and disincentives. However, Becker's more radical point seems to be that the distinction between 'positive' and 'negative' addictions does not reside in the 'qualities' of the commodities that are consumed but solely in whether the consumption patterns stabilise themselves into a form of life that generates a surplus.

One can perhaps see in Becker's bio-juridical logic of preferences the foundation of a new jurisprudence and politics that is ostensibly 'libertarian', but which, at the same time, depends on the most radical reduction of action to behaviour. Becker's economics does away for good with the idea that we 'decide' at some deep level 'who we want to be' and that this 'decision' is never reducible to a choice between commodities, 'that is, between goods whose value to the agent does not depend on whether she herself chooses them, or whether they just "come" to her (by chance, as it might be)'.[54] If the society of discipline and punishment generates what Adorno and Horkheimer called the 'authoritarian personality', then perhaps Becker's economic theory reveals neoliberal or biopolitical society as one ruled by the 'addictive personality'.

54 Putnam, *The Collapse*, 83.

Part II

Constituting neoliberalism

Chapter 4

Constructing 'privatopia'

The role of constitutional law in Chile's radical neoliberal experiment

Javier Couso

I Introduction

As this volume makes clear, it is important to distinguish neoliberalism as an ideology from neoliberalism as a political practice. This distinction is particularly relevant when confronted with the topic of this chapter, which analyzes one of the most radical neoliberal experiments ever attempted, that is to say, the one imposed by General Pinochet's dictatorship in Chile, between 1973 and 1990. As we shall see, this experience suggests that – as opposed to what many defenders of neoliberalism would claim[1] – there is nothing spontaneous about it. Indeed, as we shall see below, neoliberalism was imposed in Chile by an authoritarian regime, and then entrenched in a Constitution especially designed to protect it from democracy.

After a brief account of Chile's political and constitutional history, I describe the main tenets of its neoliberal experience, in order to then analyze the role that law – specifically constitutional law – had in the construction and perpetuation of this peculiar type of '*Privatopia*'.[2]

II Chile's political and constitutional trajectory

Chile has long been considered one of the most stable constitutional regimes of Latin America. Indeed, ever since 1833, when a new Constitution contributed to provide political stability to the country for decades – while most of the region was immersed in civil war or chaotic regimes led by charismatic leaders, the so-called '*caudillos*' – Chile enjoyed political stability, legal order and economic progress.[3]

This historical trajectory was, however, punctuated every forty years or so by sudden irruptions of violence, which transformed the previous constitutional order. Thus, after the Civil War that led to the introduction of the Constitution

1 See F.A. Hayek, 'The Results of Human Action but Not of Human Design', in *Studies in Philosophy: Politics and Economics*, ed., F.A. Hayek (London: Routledge, 1967), 96–105.
2 See Javier Couso, 'Chile: The End of Privatopia?', *Berkeley Review of Latin American Studies* (Fall 2013): 2–9.
3 Simon Collier, *A History of Chile: 1808–1994* (New York: Cambridge University Press, 1995).

of 1833, another one (in 1891) effectively changed the constitutional system, until a military coup (in 1924) paved the way for yet another constitutional charter. Then, in 1973, General Pinochet's coup destroyed again the existing constitutional order.[4]

In spite of these periodic disruptions, Chile managed to build a solid rule of law.[5] This, in a region where – to this day – there are countries still attempting to finish their State-building processes.[6] Much of the credit for this remarkable feat should go to the early acceptance, by the first heads of the executive branch, of the constitutional limits to their time in office – a remarkable attitude, considering that during a large segment of the nineteenth century the President was in control not just of the government, but also of the legislative and judicial branches.[7]

The concentration of power around the executive started to weaken around 1860, triggering a process of legislative empowerment that, eventually, led to a quasi-parliamentarian regime. This system, however, collapsed in 1924 after failing to deliver a minimum degree of social justice, in the context of a massive migration from the countryside to the city and a harsh industrialization process.

The country found stability under the constitutional charter enacted in 1925, despite some episodes of tension, such as when Parliament approved the so-called Law of Permanent Defense of Democracy (1948), which banned the Communist Party for a decade.[8] Aside from this troubling episode, during the lifetime of the Constitution of 1925 Chile was able to build a solid political party system and a stable republican regime, which gradually opened the franchise to previously excluded groups (a process that ended in 1958, when a crucial electoral reform finished the tight control exerted by the Conservative Party over the vote of peasants).

In terms of its economic development, during this period Chile followed a strategy known as 'industrialization by import substitution', which gave an important role to the State in the economy, through governmental subsidies and the establishment of trade barriers aimed at protecting national industry.[9]

4 Paul W. Drake and Iván Jaksić, eds, *The Struggle for Democracy in Chile*, rev. edn (Lincoln, NE: University of Nebraska Press, 1995).
5 Hugo Frühling, 'Law in Society: Social Transformation and the Crisis of Law in Chile, 1830–1970' (PhD diss., Harvard University School of Law, 1984).
6 Marcus J. Kurtz, *Latin American State Building in Comparative Perspective: Social Foundations of Institutional Order* (New York: Cambridge University Press, 2013).
7 Javier A. Couso, 'Judicial Independence in Latin America: The Lessons of History in the Search for an Always Elusive Ideal', in *Institutions & Public Law: Comparative Approaches*, eds, Tom Ginsburg and Robert A. Kagan (New York: Peter Lang, 2005).
8 Carlos Huneeus, 'La guerra fría chilena: Gabriel González Videla y la ley maldita' (debate, Santiago, Chile, 2009); Julio Faúndez, *Democratización, desarrollo y legalidad: Chile, 1831–1973* (Santiago: Ediciones Universidad Diego Portales, 2011).
9 Julio Faúndez, *Marxism and Democracy in Chile: From 1932 to the Fall of Allende* (New Haven, CT: Yale University Press, 1988).

III Dictatorship as the breeding ground for neoliberalism

After decades of political stability, much of the Chilean left became radicalized by the impact of the Cuban Revolution in 1959, a process which led to political polarization and, eventually, to the demise of the Constitution of 1925. This was consummated on September 11, 1973, in a military coup led by General Augusto Pinochet.[10] The violent seizure of power was not originally intended to replace the existing Constitution. In fact, the first statement issued by the military junta claimed that their action had been undertaken in order to 're-establish the broken institutional order'.[11] Nonetheless, it soon became apparent that the military had decided to stay in power. Once this path was adopted, the new authorities started to pay attention to the legal foundations of their rule, and declared that it was in control not just of the government, but also of the constituent power of the nation.[12] Subsequently, they adopted a series of constitutional decrees aimed at providing a juridical basis for their government and – more importantly – to dismantle the entire institutional architecture of the previous constitutional order.

The following account by an acute observer writing at the time is illustrative of the foundational aims of the military regime:

> Congress was dissolved; a state of siege was declared, suspending individual guarantees; municipal authorities were deposed and replaced by municipal authorities designated by the Military Junta … Furthermore, the Constitutional Court was dissolved … all public employees were declared to be interim … with the exception of members of the judiciary and the Comptroller General of the Republic … the political parties declared to be Marxist were dissolved, while the rest were declared to be in recess … the universities were intervened by the Military Junta … the electoral register were declared void, and then incinerated … The government passed a decree law authorizing the expulsion of individual from the national territory on political grounds … elections within unions were suspended, and the government adopted norms allowing it to deprive some political opponents of their Chilean nationality.[13]

As this account makes clear, once the Junta decided to undertake a conservative revolution, it did so relentlessly, showing no moderation in the destruction of the

10 Arturo Valenzuela, *The Breakdown of Democratic Regimes: Chile*, eds, Juan J. Linz and Alfred Stepan (Baltimore, MD: John Hopkins University Press, 1978).

11 See Decree Law No. 1, Acta de Constitución de la Junta de Gobernio, Septiembre 18, 1973, Diaro Oficial [D.O.], transcribed in Carlos Andrade Geywitz, *Génesis de las Constituciones de 1925 y 1980* (Santiago: Ediar-Conosur, 1988).

12 The Junta stated: 'The Military Junta has assumed the constituent, legislative, and executive powers'. See Decree Law No. 128, Noviembre 16, 1973, Diario Oficial [D. O.], interpreting Decree Law No. 1.

13 Genaro Arriagada Herrera, *De la 'vía chilena' a la 'vía insurreccional'* (Santiago, Chile: Editorial del Pacífico, 1974), 38–39.

former political and constitutional order. As another scholar noted decades later, Pinochet and the other military leaders decided to make:

> A clear break with the preceding democratic, constitutional form of the rule of law [which] opened a period of de facto rule in which the validity of the dictatorship's legal acts rested solely upon the force of the military's coercive imposition and the claim that the circumstances provided no alternative but exceptional rule, not some prior positive grant of authority.[14]

As we shall see below, Pinochet and his advisers were extremely successful in re-shaping Chile's previous democratic constitutional trajectory.

Once their will to change the path of the country was firm, the military junta faced the problem of determining the program it wanted to introduce. The only political program available was the so-called 'National Security Doctrine', developed by US military in the context of the Cold War and which then spread across Latin America in the mid-1960s.[15] Yet this doctrine provided little guidance for the military junta other than a loosely anti-communist politics. Its inadequacy was particularly evident in the economic field, leading to contradictory policies during the first year or so of the dictatorship.

Eventually, Pinochet decided to give control over economic policy to the so-called 'Chicago Boys', a group of Chilean graduates from the University of Chicago's Economics Department, who had an almost religious adherence to the monetarist policies of Milton Friedman. As Valdés has documented,[16] the Chicago Boys came into existence thanks to a carefully designed plan by the US State Department, aimed at training market-friendly economists who, it was expected, would counter the influence that left-wing economic thinking (in both its Marxist and Keynesian variants) had in Latin America. The plan started in 1955, when the Eisenhower administration concluded that it was crucial to introduce what it took to be sound economic policies in Latin America, in order to avoid the spread of communism in the region. The initiative included the Economics Department of the University of Chicago and the Catholic University of Chile, and it lasted until 1985, creating a critical mass of dozens of master and doctoral graduates from the University of Chicago (in a country that had no more than thirty economists when the program started).

When the first Chicago Boys started to return to Chile – in the early 1960s – they were completely ignored by the mainstream political system, due to the fact that the country had been for decades under the above-mentioned substitution of imports paradigm (a model entailing a level of State involvement in the economy

14 Robert Barros, *Constitutionalism and Dictatorship: Pinochet, the Junta, and the 1980 Constitution*, Cambridge Studies in the Theory of Democracy (Cambridge: Cambridge University Press, 2002), 12.

15 Carlos Huneeus, *El régimen de Pinochet* (Santiago: Sudamericana, 2000).

16 Juan Gabriel Valdés, *La escuela de Chicago: Operación Chile* (Buenos Aires: Grupo Zeta, 1989).

incompatible with neoliberal orthodoxy). In such a hostile environment, the Chicago Boys took refuge in the private sector and the academy, writing for newspapers, and slowly creating an epistemic community.

The political and cultural isolation of the Chicago Boys only ended when General Pinochet bet on this group in 1975. At that time the economy was in trouble, due to the combined effect of economic mismanagement and the impact of the oil crisis of 1973–1974. After proving themselves in the management of these problems, the Chicago Boys offered the military regime something more ambitious: a plan to completely transform Chile's economy, thus overcoming what they considered its chronic backwardness. They proposed a radical departure from the State interventionism that had characterized Chile's economic policies throughout the twentieth century.[17] Their economic program included the following measures: (a) a strict fiscal responsibility; (b) the minimization of the role of the State in the economy, through the privatization of most State-owned companies and the de-regulation of the economy; (c) the liberalization of prices; (d) the opening of the economy to international markets; (e) the liberalization of the financial market; (f) the de-regulation of the labour market; (g) the strengthening of private property rights; and (h) the end of subsidies to non-competitive industries.

In order to implement their radical program of economic and social transformation, the Chicago Boys were placed by Pinochet in key governmental positions. The recession that affected Chile (in 1983–1984) delayed the process of privatization and of de-regulation, but, soon after the crisis was over, the reforms continued, literally, until the last day of Pinochet's administration.[18]

The core philosophy embraced by the Chicago Boys was thoroughly neoliberal. Valdés describes the fundamental ideas underlying their economic plan in the following terms. First, they thought that the market was the fundamental and most natural organizing principle of social life, the paradigm of liberty itself. Second, they held to a methodological individualism: society is composed solely of self-interested individuals, and social classes are simply intellectual constructs. Third, they saw the State as an intrinsic enemy of liberty: because interest groups always obtain unjustified and economically inefficient rents from the government, thus, the smaller the role of the State, the better. Lastly, they adhered to a monetarist economic policy underpinned by a constitutionally independent central bank, completely autonomous from the pressures of politics.[19]

The program of structural reforms designed by the Chicago Boys was complemented by other equally radical measures, such as the introduction of a new Labor Code which diminished State regulation of the labor market,

17 In fact, the role of the State was so important for Chile's economy that the eminent Bolivian sociologist René Zavaleta once described Chile as the '*Patria del Estado*' ('the forefather of the State'): Gabriel Valdés, *La escuela de Chicago*, 133.

18 For an excellent analysis of the Chicago Boys' ascendance within the military regime, see Huneeus, *El régimen de Pinochet*, chap. 8.

19 This summary of the core social and economic principles animating the Chicago Boys is described in Gabriel Valdés, *La escuela de Chicago*, 84–102.

disempowering unions; a new social security program based on 'individual capitalization' (where a person's pension amounts to what she manages to save during her working life); a privatized health care system; and the de-centralization of government administration.[20]

This profound set of neoliberal reforms caused serious social unrest, because they generated an unprecedented average unemployment rate of 17.3 per cent during the period 1973–1989. In fact, it is plausible to say that they could be implemented only because they were undertaken in the context of a harsh military dictatorship in which fundamental liberties were severely curtailed.

The political outlook of the Chicago Boys was authoritarian and technocratic. They generally despised democratic politics as mere 'demagogy', and were frustrated by the lack of a 'scientific' economic debate in Chile. Their hostility towards democracy was similar to the one exhibited by General Pinochet. Indeed, as Meller has argued,[21] both the military and the Chicago Boys shared a sense of mission.[22] While the military thought they had saved Chile from communism, the Chicago Boys aimed at transforming the country into a developed nation, where, they thought, communism would cease to be a threat any more.[23]

Parallel to implementing the sweeping program of social, economic, and administrative reform outlined above, Pinochet and the Chicago Boys started planning a strategy to make sure that the revolutionary changes they introduced would survive the eventual return of democratic rule to Chile. This led them to turn to constitutional matters, which had hitherto been entrusted to a group of jurists. Evidencing a long-term perspective rare among Latin America's military rulers, Pinochet realized the need to project the authoritarian and neoliberal policies introduced by his rule beyond his personal hold on power. In order to ensure this, it was critical to develop new constitutional instruments in preparation for the eventual transfer of power to the opposition.

IV Neoliberalism and constitutional law

The military regime's interest in introducing a new constitutional order had started early. In fact, soon after the 1973 coup, the military junta organized a small

20 For an analysis of Chile's economic transformations under Pinochet's rule, see Alejandro Foxley, *Latin-American Experiments in Neo-conservative Economics* (Berkeley, CA: University of California Press, 1983); Sebastian Edwards and Alejandra Cox Edwards, *Monetarism and Liberalization: The Chilean Experiment* (Cambridge, MA: Ballinger, 1987); Eugenio Tironi, *Los silencios de la revolución* (Santiago: Puerta Abierta, 1988); Jaime Ruiz-Tagle P., *El sindicalismo chileno después del Plan laboral* (Santiago: Academia de Humanismo Cristiano, 1985).

21 Patricio Meller, *Un siglo de economia politica chilena (1890–1990)* (Santiago: Andrés Bello, 1996).

22 In other words, as Patricio Meller himself points out, both the military and the Chicago Boys considered themselves technocrats who knew scientifically what was best for the country.

23 See Meller, *Siglo de economia politica*, 193.

commission entrusted with drafting a new Constitution, the so-called 'Commission for the Study of a New Constitution' ('*Comisión de Estudios de la Nueva Constitución*', also known as the 'Ortúzar Commission'). The group was composed of a handful of law professors and former congressmen who had supported the military.[24]

In its first months of operation, the Ortúzar Commission devoted most of its time to studying ways to improve the constitutional protection of private property, To do so, they analyzed all the threats to property rights that could be posed by future legal or administrative acts, an exercise which led them to adopt a detailed set of constitutional clauses protecting private property (indeed, one of the most rigorous in comparative constitutional law).

The Ortúzar Commission broadened the scope of its proposals after 1977, when it sought to entrench some of the core elements of the neoliberal economic model in the new constitution. The motivation for this shift came from the military regime's economic team which, by then, was starting to worry about the continuity of their structural reform program. This concern was apparent in Session No. 384 of the Ortúzar Commission (held in June 1978), during which the commissioners listened to a group of Chicago Boys sketch out the content that the new constitutional charter should have in order to prevent the 'regression' to the 'populist' economic policies of the past.

A key player in the use of constitutional law to perpetuate neoliberal economic policy was one of the members of the Ortúzar Commission, Jaime Guzmán. This jurist, a conservative Catholic, soon realized that Chile's long democratic tradition meant that the return to democracy was inevitable. This would place the neoliberal revolution in danger, so he devised a highly sophisticated plan to avoid the future dismantling of the economic changes implemented by the Chicago Boys. The new Constitution should, Guzmán argued, be such that all administrations would be forced to follow the main tenets of the neoliberal model no matter which political group was elected.[25] In his own words, the new Constitution ought to ensure that:

> If the opposition ends up in power, they will be forced to follow a line of action not very different from the one we would desire, because – forgive the metaphor – the range of alternatives that the field imposes upon the players would be so limited that it would be extremely difficult to do otherwise.[26]

As it can be appreciated, Guzmán was extremely candid about the role he assigned the new Constitution: that of a 'retaining wall' protecting the neoliberal model from democratic politics.

24 Lisa Hilbink, *Judges beyond Politics in Democracy and Dictatorship: Lessons from Chile*, Cambridge Studies in Law and Society (New York: Cambridge University Press, 2007).

25 Fernando Atria et al., *El otro modelo: Del orden neoliberal al régimen de lo público* (Santiago: Random House Mondadori, 2013).

26 Jaime Guzmán, 'El camino político', in *Realidad*, 7 (1979), pp. 13–23.

V The Constitution of 1980

As was made clear in the previous section, the Constitution of 1980 was meant to establish a radically new institutional order that would be the formal expression of the nation-building project that Pinochet's regime had implemented since 1975. The new charter aimed to ensure that Chile would not return to the rule of political parties, that is to say, to the 'demagogic' capture of the State by political party elites, and that it would never again be threatened by Marxist-Leninist parties.[27] The idea was to ensure the continuity of their project while giving the regime a certain degree of legitimacy.

Among the political aspects of the 1980 Constitution, the following deserve to be mentioned: (a) a strengthened executive branch; (b) the inclusion of the military as the guarantors of the institutional order; (c) the incorporation of a group of non-elected senators, in order to incorporate 'non-political' actors into the legislative process; and (d) a variety of constitutional norms aimed at achieving a 'protected democracy' ('*democracia protegida*'), that is to say, a set of constitutional norms that made any significant change of the new status quo extremely unlikely.

With regard to the economic sphere, the final text of the 1980 Constitution represented a somewhat watered-down version of the more ambitious 'economic constitution' proposed by the Chicago Boys. Having said this, the charter managed to introduce a 'Public Economic Order' ('*Orden Público Económico*'), which enshrined in the Constitution the basic principles and rules furthering the role of markets in society.

A core idea underlying the economic clauses that were finally introduced in the Constitution of 1980 is the so-called 'principle of subsidiarity' ('*Principio de Subsidariedad*'). This notion entails that the State cannot intervene in the economy unless the private sector is unable to do so. Thus, free markets are the general rule, while State intervention is the exception. In this approach, the State is required to provide only the working conditions for the 'real engine' of economic activity, the market.

The 'principle of subsidiarity' is the foundation of the specific economic precepts of the Constitution. Examples of this specific set of norms are: (a) Article 19, No. 21, which guarantees the right to private entrepreneurial freedom (while requiring super-majority legislative approval for the creation of State-owned companies); (b) Article 19, No. 24, which strengthens the protection of existing private property rights, requiring that the State give up-front cash to any individual being expropriated; and (c) Article 19, No. 23, which, for the first time in Chile's history, guarantees the right to acquire private property of all classes of goods (with a few exceptions). These economic rights and liberties were further entrenched in the Constitution by the following expedient: after enumerating

27 As Carl Bauer has put it: 'The 1980 Constitution thus embodied the ideals of a-politicism, technocratic efficiency, anti-communism and laissez-faire economics that the military regime of Pinochet had already been implementing'. See Carl J. Bauer, *Against the Current: Privatization, Water Markets, and the State in Chile* (New York: Kluwer, 1998), 9.

them in the Bill of Rights, Article 19, No. 26 proclaims that the Constitution guarantees that any law or administrative decision regulating the Bill of Rights cannot affect the 'essence' of those rights, nor limit their free exercise. This precept was explicitly aimed at preventing Congress and/or the President from abusing their powers of implementation of constitutional rights by distorting the 'true' nature of the constitutional rights and liberties.

The framers also created a number of entities, mechanisms, and institutional devices aimed at ensuring that the economic principles established by the Constitution would be upheld. For example, Article 97 established an autonomous Central Bank in charge of fixing the exchange rate and setting monetary policy.

To sum up this section, the introduction of an 'economic' section in the Constitution of 1980 reveals the intention of its drafters to end the political debate concerning economic matters, taking this discussion out of the realm of politics and into the realm of constitutional law. This aspiration was coherent with the political philosophy of the military regime and of the Chicago Boys, which was hostile to democratic politics and which aspired to have 'economic science' organize the life of society in a 'rational' way.

VI The legitimation of the 'economic constitution' in the post-authoritarian era

Although the idea of including the central features of the neoliberal economic approach in the Constitution originated with the Chicago Boys and Jaime Guzmán, it was later accepted by mainstream constitutional scholars. In fact, one of Chile's best known constitutional scholars, José Luis Cea, defended the fact that the Constitution of 1980 included the core elements of the economic model introduced by the regime, stating that this made it a 'full Constitution' ('*Constitución plena*'). To have a full Constitution, argued Cea, represented a crucial improvement that reflected an understanding of the fact that social and economic aspects are intrinsically linked to political and juridical ones. In his own words:

> Nobody doubts that the Constitution has to contain the rules of the game of politics. If this is so, and [the Constitution] has to include the essential elements of a social order, why then forget economic and social rules that are so intimately connected with the political aspects?[28]

In a world in which most of human activity is economic, continued Cea, it was impossible for the Constitution to remain neutral with regard to that sphere. It is not a question of constitutionalizing a specific economic model, he argued, but instead giving constitutional protection to the 'basic elements' of what he called the 'Economic Public Order':

28 See José Luis Cea Egaña, *Tratado de la Constitución de 1980* (Santiago: Editorial Jurídica de Chile, 1988), 16 (my translation).

> What we argue for is that the characteristic principles of such [economic] models to be included explicitly and unequivocally in the Fundamental Law … What is the economic model and its social counterpart? The framers of the Constitution have to answer these questions and not take the easy but ultimately dangerous path of value-system neutrality.[29]

As the reader will appreciate, Cea Egaña's attempts to argue that the Constitution should not constitutionalize the specifics of a particular economic model, but only its 'principles', is utterly futile. In the end, he clearly sides against the economic 'neutrality' of the Constitution which, in the case of Chile, means a defense of the constitutionalization of the Neoliberal model imposed by the military regime.

VII The impact of a neoliberal constitution

On March 11, 1990, Pinochet's dictatorship finally came to an end, and a new democratic government initiated what has been generally considered a successful transition to democracy.[30] This process was the result of a pact between the military regime and their opponents, and was implemented under the rules set by 1980 Constitution.[31]

Since 1989, there have been numerous constitutional amendments.[32] Having said this, due to the existence of what Garretón calls the 'authoritarian enclaves' of the 1980 Constitution, not one of those amendments was approved without the consent of the 'political heirs' of the military regime: the right-wing parties Unión Demócrata Independiente and Renovación Nacional.[33] Due to this, a quarter of a century after the end of the military regime, the Constitution of 1980 continues to be considered illegitimate by a large segment of the population, both because of its authoritarian origins,[34] and because it still exhibits authoritarian features, such as the requirement of super-majority quorums to amend some of the core legislation set up by the dictatorship.[35] The harsh constraints imposed on majority rule by the Constitution of 1980 have precluded a fundamental change of the core

29 Ibid.

30 Paul Drake and Iván Jaksic, *El modelo chileno: Democracia y desarrollo en los noventa* (Santiago: LOM Ediciones, 1999).

31 Manuel Antonio Garretón, *Hacia una nueva era política: Estudio sobre las democratizaciones*, Sección de obras de sociología (Mexico City: Fondo de Cultura Económica, 1995).

32 Claudio Fuentes Saavedra, *El pacto: Poder, constitución y prácticas políticas 1990–2010* (Santiago: Ediciones Universidad Diego Portales, 2012).

33 See Fernando Atria Lemaitre, *La Constitución tramposa* (Santiago: LOM Ediciones, 2013); Javier Couso and Alberto Coddou, 'Las asignaturas pendientes de la reforma constitucional chilena', in *En nombre del Pueblo: Debate sobre el cambio constitucional en Chile*, ed., Claudio Fuentes (Santiago: Instituto de Investigación en Ciencias Sociales, 2010).

34 Claudio Fuentes, *El fraude: Crónica sobre el plebiscito de la Constitución de 1980* (Santiago: Hueders, 2013).

35 Atria et al., *El otro modelo*.

features of the neoliberal model introduced by the Chicago Boys in the 1970s and 1980s.[36]

If one were to characterize, in just one word, the political culture created by this constitutional design, it would be 'compromise'. Indeed, over the last two decades, Chile has experienced a political system in which there is constant need to engage in negotiation, understood not as the free consensus reached between political groups placed on an equal footing, but instead as the attempt by democratic forces to obtain concessions from the political heirs of the military regime who, thanks to the structure of the 1980 Constitution, enjoy an effective veto power – which they have used to block any significant change of the core elements of Chile's neoliberal model.

What is more uncanny is that over the years the constant need to negotiate from a position of constitutional weakness has led some of the groups that used to oppose the neoliberal model to start accepting it, due to the impulse to 'get things done'. Indeed, the cultural penetration of neoliberal thinking in Chile has in fact been so strong (particularly among the policy-making elites of most political parties) that even the center-left coalition that ruled the country between 1990 and 2010 came to the conclusion that it was inappropriate to introduce public companies to provide public transportation. This led to the absurd situation that one of the main tasks of the Minister of Transportation is the regulatory 'nightmare' of constantly negotiating (and re-negotiating) contracts with the private companies in charge of delivering public transportation. Another example of the penetration of the neoliberal model in Chile was the decision, by the same center-left government, to give control of prisons to private companies. This led to such inhuman prison conditions that even the conservative journal *The Economist* felt obliged to criticize the policy:

> In Chile, after the San Miguel fire, the conservative government announced a sweeping prison-reform plan, to improve conditions, build four new prisons (at a cost of $410m), recruit 5,000 more prison warders, segregate prisoners by the severity of their offence, and cut prison demand by requiring more offenders to do community service. The aim is to cut overcrowding, from 60% to 15% by 2014. A previous centre-left government turned to the private sector to build and run seven new jails. But the new prisons will be state run.[37]

Note the irony with which *The Economist* points out that the private management of prisons was actually ended by the right-wing government of Sebastián Piñera (2010–2014).

As a consequence of the constitutional structure inherited from the authoritarian era – and the political culture it helped create – the economic system currently in place in Chile is still characterized by the privileged role given to the market in the

36 Carlos Huneeus, *La democracia semisoberana: Chile después de Pinochet* (Santiago: Taurus, 2014).

37 'Prisons in Latin America: A Journey into Hell', *The Economist*, 22 September 2012, 44–46.

delivery of even the most essential public goods and services (such as health care; the pension system; the educational system; transportation and so on), very much in accordance with the Chicago Boys' motto of 'private solutions to public problems'.

While the above-mentioned examples illustrate the cultural force that Chile's radical version of neoliberalism still has in policy circles, this is just one side of the coin. The United Nations Development Program (UNDP) has consistently detected a widespread malaise with the economic model among a sizable portion of the population.[38] This dissatisfaction eventually led to a series of massive social movements (in 2006, and then again in 2011–2012) that have explicitly linked the neoliberal model with the existence of an illegitimate and semi-authoritarian Constitution.[39] This approach was eventually adopted by President Michelle Bachelet who, in October 2015, started a process aimed at introducing a new Constitution. At the time of the writing this chapter, however, the success of this process is in doubt, since its depends on the support of the right-wing political parties that – due to the very character of the 1980 Constitution – still hold the key to allow Chileans to elaborate a Constitution debated in democracy.

VIII Conclusion

This chapter has analyzed the role that law – specifically, constitutional law – has had in the perpetuation of one of the worlds' most radical experiments in neoliberalism: the one imposed in Chile by the military regime led by General Augusto Pinochet. As we have seen, the introduction of a neoliberal regime there required not just a brutal dictatorship, but also a new Constitution aimed at entrenching this economic model. In order to do so, the latter needed to constrain majorities in order to insulate neoliberalism from democracy. A quarter of a century after the end of the authoritarian regime, it is possible to ascertain that the constitutional design introduced by the economists and jurists working for Pinochet worked almost exactly as planned. In fact, it was not only able to prevent the dismantling of the core elements of the Chilean neoliberal model, but also contributed to 'naturalizing' it among most policy-making circles.

What can we learn about the relationship between neoliberalism and law from Chile's experience? In my view, the most important lesson is that the antagonism between democracy and neoliberalism is not limited to the eventual need of an authoritarian regime to introduce it, but that neoliberalism might be more fundamentally in contradiction with democracy, due to its hostility to majority rule, its reliance on technocratic reason over democratic deliberation, and its minimalist understanding of citizenship.

38 See *Desarrollo humano en Chile 2015: Los tiempos de la politización* (Santiago: United Nations Development Programme, 2015).

39 Alberto Mayol, *El derrumbe del modelo: La crisis de la economía de mercado en el Chile contemporáneo* (Santiago: LOM Ediciones, 2012).

Chapter 5

The rise of juridical neoliberalism

Thomas Biebricher

Introduction

This chapter seeks to elucidate the significance of law for both neoliberal theory and practice; or, what might be referred to tentatively as juridical neoliberalism. Conventionally, neoliberalism is understood as a set of economic doctrines that give rise to the unfettered dominance of markets in social life. Accordingly, it may seem doubtful that there is a legal dimension to neoliberal theory and practice that is of any significance. Still, I will argue that neoliberal theory is a body of *politico-economic* thought that does not confine itself to purely economic reflections but is also – necessarily – interested in broadly political themes, among which law is particularly prominent. Furthermore, I will argue that the significance of law is not just a matter of neoliberal theory; juridical norms are a key instrument used in the neoliberal restructuring of economic governance.

The argument is structured in the following way. The preface to any engagement with questions related to neoliberalism has to be a clarification of what is to be understood by the term – not least because one of the few things commentators can agree on is the highly contested nature of neoliberalism. My starting point in developing a working definition of neoliberalism will be a reconstruction of the context of the emergence of the term and the intellectual current it refers to. The next step is an examination of the significance of law in neoliberal thought, which is not a homogeneous current despite considerable commonalities between the various thinkers. Given this undeniable heterogeneity it is useful to distinguish varieties of neoliberal thought and a more encompassing analysis of juridical neoliberalism would require an examination of all those varieties and the respective role(s) that law plays in each of them. Restrictions of space do not permit such a comprehensive analysis here, so I will mostly focus on one particular thinker, namely James Buchanan, who represents a variety of neoliberal thought that draws heavily on public choice theory and is often referred to as constitutional economics, which is already a clear indication of the importance of (constitutional) law for its agenda. It is not possible to do justice to Buchanan's immense oeuvre in its entirety and the various ways in which juridical norms figure in it, so once more I will focus my discussion on one particular aspect that I deem crucial to the normative dimension of constitutional economics, i.e. the call for a constitutional balanced-budget amendment (BBA) that would require state expenditures to be matched by state revenue. This will be the pivot to explore 'actually existing neoliberalism' in the context of the aftermath of the financial crisis in Europe. In response to the sovereign debt crisis that was triggered by the original financial crisis the European Union (EU) has passed a series of reforms to curtail potentially unsustainable economic/fiscal policies pursued by member states. Among them is the Treaty on Stability, Coordination and Governance (TSCG) dubbed the 'Fiscal Compact' in public discourse that can be considered the equivalent of Buchanan's BBA. My discussion and critique of the TSCG will make reference to some of the theoretical concerns raised in the preceding sections and also place the Treaty in the context of Stephen Gill's widely discussed criticisms of what one might consider an earlier incarnation of the TSCG, namely the Stability and Growth Pact (SGP) from 1997 that Gill considered to be an integral part of what he calls the 'New Constitutionalism'. The chapter closes with some reflections on the role of juridical neoliberalism in Europe at the current conjuncture, which is characterized by a somewhat contradictory constellation. On the one hand, we witness what I consider a moralization of juridical norms regarding economic/fiscal policy that is supposed to buttress their legal facticity, i.e. breaking these rules would not only be illegal but also immoral. On the other hand, this fixation on rules that must never be broken exists in an overall context of legal insecurity with regard to EU law; or, more specifically, what commentators refer to as the EU's economic constitution. Almost every aspect of the politics of the sovereign debt crisis from the Fiscal Compact to the European Stability Mechanism (ESM) and the Outright Monetary Transactions program by the European Central Bank (ECB) remains contested with regard to their legal validity. Thus, the overall picture is almost paradoxical. Juridical norms are morally charged to make them almost sacrosanct, but they have been developed in an extra-legal state of emergency. As will become clear in the final section of this chapter, this picture differs in some respects from the diagnosis Wendy Brown submitted about one-and-a-half decades ago with regard to the transformation of law under neoliberalism in the United States: while she detected a growing tacticalization of law, the European developments could be seen to point into the opposite direction.

What is neoliberalism?

Terms used to group together intellectual traditions that also entail political positions are inherently difficult to define. This is not only due to the difficulties involved in trying to pin down the 'essence' or the 'core' of any tradition that supposedly includes a sometimes perplexing variety of thinkers (either because they are considered to be a part of this tradition by others and/or they themselves located their work within it), but also because of the political stakes involved in defining a tradition as including certain elements and thinkers, and, conversely, excluding others. The question of what constitutes conservatism, to choose but one example, and who can or should count as a legitimate representative of this intellectual current, is obviously far from purely academic. Referring to someone as conservative – or socialist, for that matter – is a highly political act of signification. The ensuing difficulties rise exponentially in the case of the intellectual tradition of neoliberalism. Not only is liberalism a notoriously diverse tradition, at least in political discourse being a liberal in Europe has come to mean almost the complete opposite of being a liberal in North America. This is one of the reasons why neoliberalism is almost absent from political discourse in the United States (libertarianism is more prevalent, which, conversely, is rarely even mentioned in political discourse in Europe), although it shows no sign of disappearing from academic discourse. But even in European political discourse – and to some degree academic discourse – the term has become somewhat toxic because it is hardly ever put to non-polemical use. This means that no one refers to themselves as neoliberal and it also means that characterizing a position as neoliberal immediately raises the suspicion that this is just an oblique way of trying to discredit that position in contrast to engaging it substantively. Thus, there is a reluctance to apply the term to others' position because doing so may disqualify one's own position.

Given these inconveniences of the term and its heavy political charge (at least in certain geographical areas), I argue that the most promising way to give it some content is to reconstruct the context of its emergence and the project it referred to by those who actually referred to themselves as neoliberals.[1] This means going back to the interwar years of the last century, and more precisely, the so-called *Colloquium Walter Lippmann* that took place in Paris in 1938. In the records of this meeting, in which a number of first generation neoliberals participated, the term is used for the first time as the label of a common intellectual and political project.[2] The context, from which this project arose, was what appeared to the participants – as well as many other observers at the time – as an existential crisis of liberalism, which manifested itself in phenomena ranging from the Great Depression and the ascent of Keynesianism to the rise of deeply illiberal political forces from Soviet communism, to fascism and National Socialism.

Neoliberalism has to be understood as a response to this crisis, the underlying roots of which the early neoliberals detected in the self-incurred decline of liberalism dating to the second half of the nineteenth century. According to the neoliberal diagnosis, liberalism unraveled into a quasi-social democratic strand on the one hand and a quasi-libertarian one on the other.[3] The neoliberal project, thus, can be summed up in the following formula. It obviously aims to revive

1 See Jamie Peck, 'Remaking Laissez-Faire', *Progress in Human Geography* 32, no. 1 (2008): 3–43; Ben Jackson, 'At the Origins of Neo-liberalism: The Free Economy and the Strong State', *Historical Journal* 53, no. 1 (2010): 129–151.

2 Jamie Peck, *Constructions of Neoliberal Reason* (Oxford: Oxford University Press 2010), 51.

3 See Friedrich August Hayek, 'Liberalismus' (1973) in *Grundsätze einer liberalen Gesellschaftsordnung: Aufsätze zur Politischen Philosophie und Theorie*, ed., Friedrich August Hayek (Tübingen: Mohr Siebeck, 2002), 88–119.

liberal ideas against the illiberal *zeitgeist*, but the precondition for achieving this goal is a critical revision of the liberal agenda that would clear it of both overly social democratic and libertarian elements – the twin legacies of the nineteenth century, so to speak. Of course, neoliberalism is opposed to the merger of liberalism and progressivism but it is also adamant about the fallacies of a simplistic call for *laissez-faire*.[4] Still, while these and many other views are shared among virtually all neoliberals (among them Friedrich August von Hayek, James Buchanan, Milton Friedman, Walter Eucken and Wilhelm Röpke), this group does not form a homogeneous intellectual current. The neoliberal 'formula' already implies plenty of potential controversy because from the very beginning the exact combination of revitalizations and revisions remains a matter of dispute. Therefore, I find it useful to introduce the notion of 'varieties' of neoliberal thought in order to capture the irreducible heterogeneity that is built into neoliberalism. Nevertheless, it is possible to sharpen the substantive contours of neoliberalism beyond this rather thin formula. The common denominator among all varieties of neoliberalism can be expressed in the following way. It is uncontroversial that neoliberal thought accords crucial societal importance to the economic sphere; or, more precisely, functioning markets. Importantly, though, it is not a body of *economistic* thought that exhausts itself in exclusively economic reflections implicitly leading to a detachment of the economic sphere from its context. On the contrary, neoliberalism is explicitly concerned with the question of the conditions of possibility of functioning markets. And if *laissez-faire* is no longer considered to be a satisfactory answer to this question then neoliberalism cannot help but delve into questions about how states should be constituted so they can engage in a market-creating or market-maintaining politics; what actions they must abstain from, what public goods they may have to provide and how all of this might be complicated by the democratic character of a state. Neoliberalism is thus a body of thought engaged in *political economy*. It comes as no surprise, then, that an inquiry into the significance of law in all of these matters is part and parcel of the neoliberal agenda, as I will show in more detail in the next section.

Neoliberalism and law: Hayek, Böhm and Buchanan

As mentioned in the introduction, I will mostly focus on a particular argument, i.e. a core demand of James Buchanan's constitutional economics, but let me begin this section with a quick look at two other neoliberal thinkers and the role that law plays in their approaches: Franz Böhm was a law professor in Freiburg and the inventor of a crucial element in ordoliberal thought, namely the 'economic constitution' that would provide the fundamental legal framework for the economy; Friedrich August von Hayek not only held a doctorate in law, but

4 Friedrich August Hayek, *The Road to Serfdom* (1944; repr., London: Routledge, 2008), 18; James M. Buchanan and Richard A. Musgrave, *Public Finance and Public Choice: Two Contrasting Visions of the State* (Cambridge, MA: MIT Press, 1999), 83.

also his politico-economic thought revolves around the principles and institutions of the rule of law. To begin with, then, there is Franz Böhm, who together with Walter Eucken and Hans Grossmann-Doerth formed the core of the so-called Freiburg School that, in turn, constituted the nucleus of a variety of neoliberalism, namely ordoliberalism, which also included thinkers such as Wilhelm Röpke and Alexander Rüstow. The crucial importance of legal thought is already on display in the so-called *Ordo Manifesto* authored by Böhm, Eucken and Grossmann-Doerth that entails something like a mission statement for ordoliberalism. The authors deplore the decline of the societal influence of both jurisprudence and political economy and set themselves the task of reversing this trend: 'it is true that in Germany these two sciences no longer exercise any appreciable influence on fundamental decisions of a politico-legal and economic nature.' 'Accordingly, the authors consider that the most urgent task for the representatives of law and political economy, is to work together in an effort to ensure that both disciplines regain their proper place in the life of the nation'.[5] But what exactly would be the task of lawyers and political economists? 'Men of science, by virtue of their profession and position being independent of economic interests, are the only objective, independent advisers capable of providing true insight into the intricate interrelationships of economic activity and therefore also providing the basis upon which economic judgments can be made'.[6] So law and political economy are to provide scientific policy advice for political decision-makers and the core project that they should be engaged in is the constitution of a market system: 'we wish to bring scientific reasoning, as displayed in jurisprudence and political economy, into effect for the purpose of constructing and reorganizing the economic system'.[7] In other words, at the heart of the ordoliberal variety of neoliberal thought lies the assumption that the economic sphere in general and markets more specifically are constituted through law, and the most fundamental and encompassing set of regal rules in this regard is called the economic constitution: 'The treatment of all practical politico-legal and politico-economic questions must be keyed to the idea of the economic constitution'.[8] It entails 'a general political decision as to how the economic life of the nation is to be structured'.[9] One aspect of the economic order to which the ordoliberals must pay close attention (because of their specific answer to the question of what the characteristics of a functioning market are) is competition law. Functioning markets are characterized by effective competition and since market actors have an incentive to circumvent the respective pressures, it falls upon competition law as part of the economic order enforced by the state to prevent this from happening and thus ensure 'favorable conditions for the

5 Franz Böhm, Walter Eucken and Hans Grossmann-Doerth, 'The Ordo Manifesto of 1936', in *Germany's Social Market Economy: Origins and Evolution*, eds, Alan Peacock and Joachim Willgerodt (Basingstoke: Macmillan, 1989), 15–16.
6 Ibid.
7 Ibid., 23.
8 Ibid.
9 Ibid.

emergence of effective competition'.[10] Especially in the later texts of Böhm, the benefits of effective competition that are to be safeguarded through a legal 'competitive order' are not only to be found in the minimization of economic power based on monopolies, etc.[11] leading to the dependence of some market actors on others, but also in the proper, i.e. undistorted functioning of the price mechanisms. Only on the basis of this mechanism is a non-coercive coordination of societal activities possible, because prices 'coordinate the partial plans of all participants on the basis of decisions which are made by these participants'[12] and this in turn is one of the more important aspects of what Böhm refers to as a 'private law society', i.e. a 'plurality of people who are subject to a uniform order, indeed, to be more precise, a legal order'.[13] Importantly, this legal order, albeit set and enforced by the state, is not one of public but private law.

The preference for private over public law as the medium of the economic sphere of society and the concern over the increasing entanglement of both kinds of law is shared by the neoliberal thinker who, arguably, has the strongest interest in matters of law, namely Friedrich August von Hayek. Again, this will not be an in-depth discussion, but let us just glance at the general thrust of his reflections on legal issues. Hayek assumes that the rule of law, correctly interpreted, is the key factor in ensuring what he called a catallaxy, i.e. a functioning market economy. His position is informed by a narrative of the decline of the principle of the rule of law, the core elements of which are two interrelated notions. First, the separation of power between legislative, executive and the judiciary including the stipulation that the executive use of coercion is bound by the acts of the legislative.[14] Closely related to that is the second element that concerns the criteria that have to be met for a juridical norm to be considered a law in the proper sense. 'Laws in the substantive sense', i.e. adhering to the principle of the rule of law, are 'essentially long-term measures, referring to yet unknown cases and containing no references to particular persons, places, or objects',[15] writes Hayek in his *magnum opus*, aptly titled *The Constitution of Liberty*. Part of the decline of the rule of law, according to Hayek, is a tendency, fueled by radical republican thought and/or legal positivism, to consider legal norms as laws as long as the legislature has passed them, largely irrespective of their form and content. The rationale behind Hayek's reasoning resonates with many other thinkers in the liberal tradition and their concern about a legalized tyranny of the majority, i.e. the possibility to

10 Franz Böhm, 'Rule of Law in a Market Economy', in *Germany's Social Market Economy*, eds, Alan Peacock and Joachim Willgerodt (Basingstoke: Macmillan, 1989), 57.
11 Franz Böhm, 'Das Problem der privaten Macht: Ein Beitrag zur Monopolfrage' (1928) in Franz Böhm, *Grundtexte zur Freiburger Tradition der Ordnungsökonomik*, eds, Nils Goldschmidt and Michael Wohlgemuth (Tübingen: Mohr Siebeck, 2002), 49–67.
12 Böhm, 'Rule of Law in a Market Economy', 53.
13 Ibid., 49.
14 Friedrich August Hayek, *The Constitution of Liberty* (1960; rep., London: Routledge, 2009), 185.
15 Ibid., 182.

discriminate legally against minorities. To be sure, Hayek is particularly worried about the interventionist potential that the erosion of the rule of law has opened up with regard to the economic sphere. We must keep in mind that Hayek is a *neo*liberal thinker, meaning that the restoration of the rule of law in both of its key aspects, the separation of powers and the generality of law, is not aimed at establishing a system of *laissez-faire*, but at limiting economic policy to a certain quality or kind of action, i.e. it is to be bound by law properly understood. 'The range and variety of government action that is, at least in principle, reconcilable with a free system is thus considerable. The old formulae of *laissez-faire* or non-intervention do not provide us with an adequate criterion for distinguishing between what is and what is not permissible in a free system'.[16] I will not go deeper into the thorny issues that loom large here because Hayek has been famously unclear as to how strictly the generality of law must be interpreted. Just consider the fact that liberal democracies routinely and in line with most of our moral intuitions discriminate between persons of a certain age, for example, when it comes to political rights. Would Hayek be opposed to this? On the other hand, would a regulation that requires all car makers to meet certain exhaust standards be discriminatory because based on the respective products and technologies, given that some will find it much costlier than others to comply with the regulation? If this was the case, states would be bereft of almost any steering capacity – economic or otherwise. Hayek, however, was clear enough about what would definitely be impossible under the proper rule of law, namely any social policy that would aim at equality of opportunity and practically all other variants of social justice: 'those who pursue distributive justice will in practice find themselves obstructed at every move by the rule of law'.[17]

Just as there are parallels and overlaps between Hayek and Böhm, so too are there shared understandings regarding the significance of (the rule of) law between Hayek and Buchanan.[18] But just as Hayek and Böhm differ in some important respects (for example, with regard to the way an economic constitution should be spelt out in detail as well as their respective faith in the expertise of jurisprudence and political economy in advising political decision-makers in this matter), Buchanan and Hayek ultimately part ways, for example when it comes to some of the interconnections of law and politics that I will return to further below. Buchanan could certainly agree with Hayek on the general importance of

16 Ibid., 202.
17 Ibid., 203.
18 James Buchanan is a particularly interesting neoliberal thinker because of the unique combination of ingredients to his thought. He was trained as an economist at the University of Chicago, but then went on to pursue an original research agenda that contributed to the establishment of public choice theory as well as constitutional economics, both of which are key influences for some contemporary varieties of neoliberal thought. In the present context, his significance derives from his focus on public finance and his specific approach to reining in fiscally undisciplined states/governments.

non-discrimination for a meaningful rule of law, but his approach to avoiding a potential tyranny of the majority does not view the reconstruction of a proper understanding of law as the crucial lever in this endeavor. Instead, Buchanan focuses on constitutions that he views as the basic legal framework of a society and analyzes the differing effects that various constitutional arrangements would have – especially on economic matters. The shift to constitutions enables Buchanan, among other things, to reformulate the problem of a tyranny of the majority as a matter of constitutional consent, i.e. to the degree that the level of required consent to constitutional rules (not regular law) approximates unanimity the danger of tyrannical majorities may be averted. But more generally, and more importantly for the present context, is the basic shift away from questions of particular policy choices regarding economic or other matters towards a broadly contractarian perspective that emphasizes the way that basic and institutionally ingrained legal rules – constitutions – frame and structure the possibilities open to ordinary politics.

As mentioned in the introduction, a thorough examination of Buchanan's overall project as I have just described it by far exceeds the scope of this chapter. Therefore, in the following pages I will limit myself to a critical discussion of what is arguably the central but definitely the best-known demand voiced by Buchanan, namely the BBA. Let me begin by reconstructing the argumentative thread that leads Buchanan to the conclusion that the BBA is a concrete constitutional amendment worth pursuing.[19]

Buchanan has highlighted three core assumptions that underlie and inform his research agenda: normative individualism, *homo oeconomicus* and politics-as-exchange.[20] In themselves, these appear not particularly original; only by extending the behavioral assumptions of *homo oeconomicus* beyond the economic sphere to politics and bureaucracy did the approach gain its unique and innovative edge. Accordingly, political actors and among them democratically elected representatives are not considered to be exclusively devoted to realizing what is best for a political community as a whole, i.e. some kind of general interest or general welfare. With this theoretical move, Buchanan puts some distance between this so-called public choice approach and not only welfare economics and its attempt to construct a social welfare function that was supposed to guide well-meaning

19 Two prominent examples of countries, in which such amendments have been introduced, are Germany and Switzerland. The technical specifics differ in both cases. In Germany, the crucial parameter is net borrowing, which must remain below 0.35 per cent of gross domestic product (GDP). In Switzerland, revenue and expenditure have to be kept in balance. Buchanan seems to have in mind the latter version: 'With a balanced budget rule, any proposal for expenditure must be coupled with a proposal for taxation.' James Buchanan and Richard Wagner, 'The Political Biases of Keynesian Economics', in *Fiscal Responsibility in Constitutional Democracy*, eds, James Buchanan and Richard Wagner (Leiden/Boston: Martinus Nijhoff Social Sciences Division, 1978), 79–100, 89.

20 James Buchanan, 'The Constitution of Economic Policy', *American Economic Review* 77, no. 3 (1987): 243–250. See Hayek, 'Liberalismus', 88–119.

politicians but also the ordoliberal trust in the willingness of decision-makers to be informed by scientific expertise from jurisprudence and political economy. Buchanan assumes that individual and collective actors from society will regularly approach their elected representatives and ask for some kind of special treatment, whether it be the recognition of special rights, some form of economic protectionism or some other form of what public choice theorists refer to as 'rent-seeking'. What the extension of the *homo oeconomicus* model to politics yields is the assumption that in the democratic market for rents there is not just demand but also supply. After all, if politicians value their reelection – not necessarily over everything else but enough to consider factors that may play a role in this regard and act on it – it can reasonably be assumed that they have an incentive to participate in the rent-seeking interaction if they can hope to secure the support of the particular actor/group in question as part of a winning alliance at the next election. It is worth keeping in mind that the charge against rent-seeking per se is not exactly that it is an undemocratic practice, which it only is under certain assumptions about the generality of the practice and what it means to represent a constituency and how encompassing this constituency is. Still, Buchanan argues that rent-seeking as a generalized practice has adverse effects that make it imperative to rein it in. And let us note, as an aside, that the uneasiness about undue influence of some societal actors on the democratic political process through lobbying or financial donations particularly in the United States is a cause of uneasiness among observers with widely varying ideological backgrounds. Buchanan's diagnosis continues as follows. Rent-seeking as a generalized practice is a self-defeating endeavor because rents can be considered positional goods, i.e. they are only of value if not everybody can attain them. Any actor that strives to achieve some kind of improvement of their own position vis-à-vis others through the means of political action has to assume that others (if they heed the maxims of *homo oeconomicus*) will try the same, which means that on balance any actor is likely to experience even a worsening of their position relative to others. More importantly for Buchanan, though, is that rents typically incur costs, at least in the realm of economic policy. A decrease in tax rates for home owners, to choose a random example, must be financed somehow. There are in principle three ways of doing this, namely to increase revenue, to decrease expenditures or to run deficits, possibly in combination with a dosage of inflation. The first two are inauspicious from a rational/public choice perspective – at least under many if not most imaginable circumstances. Financing a rent given to one group by burdening the entire electorate through a tax makes little sense and, even if it is possible to finance the costs through the burdening of one particular other group, unless one can be sure that there is no electoral retaliation from that group to fear, this does not appear a winning strategy. Similarly, cutting certain benefits for particular groups or the measures that would affect the entire electorate and thus decrease expenditure also threaten to offset the electoral advantage that politicians may hope to gain through compliance with rent-seeking demands – at least in the world of rational choice, whereas the real world of widespread austerity conveys a very different image. By far the most appealing option and virtually the only one left on the table of political strategies turns out to be running deficits. After all, under most circumstances public debt is politically somewhat intangible and typically only becomes an issue when it has to be paid off, which is supposedly in the distant future and thus running deficits, according to Buchanan, amounts to an externalization of costs onto people who cannot vote at the moment and who may not even be born yet. And the chances are that those who are currently running deficit after deficit will no longer be in office when the accumulated debt inevitably forces governments to resort to either, or even both, of the first two strategies so as to avoid insolvency. Given that future generations have no way of having their voices heard in this regard, let alone to exercise any countervailing influence on political decision-makers, the only effective way of curtailing the inherent tendency of democracies to run permanent deficits and accumulate debt (that they can no longer unilaterally shrink through deliberately inflationary politics because of fiercely independent central banks, which reign supreme in monetary matters, at least in the Western world) is to introduce the BBA.

Let us scrutinize this demand in more detail, especially with regard to two sets of questions. The first set concerns matters of popular sovereignty and representation. Advocates of the BBA could put forward two arguments here. First, the BBA provides a more encompassing form of representation than democratic politics. Without the BBA, there appears to be a short-term bias to democratic politics that fails to give due consideration to the presumed interests of future generations.[21] This case could not only be made with reference to public debt, but also environmental issues such as the politics of climate change. Ensuring fiscal discipline through the BBA would preclude the possibility of future generations having to pick up the tab for the profligacy of the current cohort. It could thus be understood as a device that helps to give advocatory representation to those yet unborn, assuming that they have an interest not to be born into a political landscape in which servicing the public debt, for which they are not responsible whatsoever, crowds out most other political options. The second argument that advocates could make in favor of the BBA refers to the restoration or maintenance of popular sovereignty. A country that accumulates unsustainable levels of public debt *de facto* loses its sovereignty because it is no longer capable of pursuing certain political projects even if a majority of the population were in favor of it, simply because it does not have the financial resources. At some point, servicing the interest of the debt will take up more and more resources and financial markets will require ever higher risk premiums for lending money to such a country. Conversely, only a fiscally disciplined country is really in a position to take on even financially ambitious political projects that a majority of the population might be in favor of. Lastly, Buchanan would probably add a point reminiscent of Rousseau, which we will revisit later. No matter what specific policies we favor as

21 James Buchanan, *Liberty, Market and State: Political Economy in the 1980s* (Sussex: Harvester Press, 1986), 217.

private persons or *bourgeois*, as *citoyens* faced with a constitutional choice we cannot but want to avoid ever rising levels of public debt.[22]

Opponents of the BBA could offer the following rebuttals. The core problem with representing not yet existing persons is that attributing interests to them remains highly conjectural. Of course, it does not seem implausible to assume that future generations will prefer a low public debt over high public debt as a condition they are born into, but this is only uncontroversial if it is *ceteris paribus*. What if fiscal discipline in the present means that investment into public infrastructures – from bridges and roads to schools and water supply works – is put off? Is it not plausible to assume that future generations do not just have one overriding interest in fiscal prudence, but a mix of interests that includes a vital one in investment in public infrastructure even if it means running deficits for this? And as an aside it should be noted that debt is a strictly relational concept. For someone to owe money, somebody else must own the respective obligation. In other words, if we assume a closed economy (and even if not, as the examples of Germany or Japan show), the public debt that has to be repaid at some point by future generations is being held by members of that same generation, which complicates the picture considerably.

Engaging the second argument of BBA proponents takes us to what I consider the normative core of the issue of juridical neoliberalism. Again, there is something intuitively appealing to real and not just *de jure* (popular) sovereignty of a country that is supposedly restored through the BBA. However, it remains questionable whether this is not a highly chimerical goal to be pursued. After all, national sovereignty – and let alone popular sovereignty – has always been as much fiction as it was fact, notwithstanding that it is a powerful fiction that has captured and inspired political passions. Today, at a time when commentators speak of a post-Westphalian world, it seems more fictional than ever despite all the qualifications that need to be added depending on the country and the policy field in question. The effects of globalization have significantly reduced national sovereignty in many aspects of economic policy, the loss of 'boundary control'[23] has been immense and in an increasingly interdependent world the option of 'going it alone' economically, politically and militarily, is highly circumscribed. Lastly, even intergovernmentalist scholars of European integration who insist that sovereignty has only been delegated and not transferred to the supranational level of the EU would acknowledge that the only realistic scenarios for the regaining of *national* sovereignty are either the withdrawal from the Union or the latter's collapse.

22 As an aside we may note that the formulation of a constitutional choice designates the dividing line between Buchanan and Hayek on the link between politics and law. The legal evolutionist Hayek would have held strong reservations against such 'rationalist constructivism' and the critique vice versa can be found in James Buchanan, *The Limits of Liberty: Between Anarchy and Leviathan* (Chicago: University of Chicago Press, 1975), 167.

23 Fritz W. Scharpf, *Governing in Europe: Effective and Democratic?* (Oxford: Oxford University Press, 1999), 121.

Whether *factual* sovereignty would really increase in any of these scenarios must be viewed with great skepticism.

These considerations aside, the more important issue at stake here is whether the BBA can legitimately be portrayed to aim at a restoration of popular sovereignty or whether it is not designed and at any rate bound to achieve the very opposite. After all, a radical republican position would have to be weary of the will of the sovereign being tied down to rules of strict fiscal discipline. This is in effect a circumscription of possibilities in economic policy, i.e. some options are taken off the political table irrespective of the considerable support they might enjoy in some segments of the electorate. I will not delve into the paradoxes of self-binding rules for sovereigns that are often spelt out with reference to Odysseus having himself tied to the mast of his ship so he could listen to the Sirens' song – and still survive.[24] My point here is not that a sovereign can never effectively tie itself, nor is it that sovereignty must not be circumscribed in any way juridically. The concern is rather that the nature of this rule is such that it should not be written into a constitution. Whether fiscal prudence or deficit-financed investment is the better political strategy in a given conjuncture should not be a matter of constitutional fiat because the choices and trade-offs included in this question are inherently political in the sense that they have inevitably redistributive effects and through this reshifting of burdens produce winners and losers. In a widely-discussed argument for the legitimacy of delegating certain tasks to regulatory authorities, Giandomenico Majone builds most of his case on the distinction between the political modes of regulation in contrast to redistribution.[25] Regulation is aimed at the realization of Pareto-efficiency, which benefits at least one of those affected by the regulation and does not put anyone at a disadvantage. Therefore, the requirements of democratic accountability/legitimation can and should be relaxed for these regulatory authorities. Or, to put it more strongly: some matters are better kept out of the hands of parliamentary majorities. Aside from the fact that critics have rightly stressed that few examples really fit this description of regulatory politics,[26] the effects of BBA can hardly be described in terms of Pareto-efficiency. I therefore assume that Majone would be opposed to leaving this matter to a regulatory authority[27] and, by analogy, I would argue that such a *political* issue – after all, the requirements of the BBA may trigger a politics of austerity – should not be a matter of constitutional rules. Despite the concerns one must have about the lack of a long-term sense of responsibility on behalf of elected politicians, it is for them and the public at large to debate these issues and for parliament to decide on it. The

24 See Thomas Biebricher, 'Sovereignty, Norms, and Exception in Neoliberalism', *Qui Parle* 23, no. 1 (2014): 77–107 for some reflections on the paradox of sovereignty.

25 Giandomenico Majone, 'The Rise of the Regulatory State in Europe', *West European Politics* 17, no. 3 (1994): 77–101.

26 Andreas Follesdal and Simon Hix, 'Why There Is a Democratic Deficit in the EU: A Response to Majone and Mravcsik', *Journal of Common Market Studies* 44, no. 3 (2006): 533–562.

27 See Giandomenico Majone, 'From Regulatory State to a Democratic Default', *Journal of Common Market Studies* 52, no. 6 (2014): 1216–1223, 1222.

pernicious effect of juridical neoliberalism lies in precluding the possibility of this debate and a more or less informed choice that results from it.

Let us move to the second set of questions I want to address with regard to the BBA. Here it is not so much its normative justifiability that is at stake, but rather whether Buchanan's theory can consistently explain how it might ever be passed. The point I want to make is not particularly original – even Buchanan himself has acknowledged the theoretical difficulties. Still, the implications are worth considering. Recall that politicians are supposedly rational utility-maximizers (or at least satisfiers/optimizers). Therefore, securing their re-election looms large in their considerations and the ability to grant rents to groups/individuals supposedly conduces to this goal. If this is an adequate way of describing the incentive structure of the situation then it is highly improbable to assume that these politicians will pass a BBA and thus deprive themselves of one crucial strategy of shoring up their chances of re-election. This is inconvenient for Buchanan's brand of neoliberalism because there is no easy way to get out of the theoretical corner he has backed himself into with the extension of the *homo oeconomicus* assumption. Buchanan's call for a 'constitutional revolution', it seems, founders on the lack of a revolutionary subject. Let me briefly explore three arguments that have been introduced to overcome this impasse in Buchanan's agenda. First, there is the appeal to a 'veil of uncertainty' reminiscent of Rawls' veil of ignorance. Due to their general and abstract nature, the impact of constitutional norms for a given individual or group over time is difficult to ascertain. Whether it is overall beneficial or detrimental to the pursuit of someone's plans cannot be determined *a priori*.[28] While this may mitigate the problems of explaining constitutional reform in general, it is less convincing in the case of the BBA. The effect the latter has on politicians who do not want to be deprived of the possibility of offering costly rents seems straightforward enough. Second, what if politicians could be assumed to acquire a truly constitutional mindset? What this is can be inferred *ex negativo* from Buchanan's characterization of those who are constitutionally 'illiterate': 'It becomes impossible to ask such persons to think of their long-term interest, and certainly it remains folly to ask them to think of the interests of the more inclusive community'.[29] But if politicians could be assumed to broaden their considerations and inculcate the presumed interests of the more inclusive community, including future generations, why could they not be trusted to pursue a prudential fiscal policy without the BBA? Lastly, Buchanan has himself gestured toward the possibility of passing the BBA by circumventing the 'cartel' of elected politicians through direct democratic channels, i.e. a citizens' initiative along the lines of the famous 'tax revolts' that would mandate the BBA.[30] But it seems that this way out

28 Geoffrey Brennan and James Buchanan, *The Reason of Rules: Constitutional Political Economy* (Cambridge: Cambridge University Press 1985), 140.

29 Buchanan, *Liberty, Market and State*, 56.

30 James Buchanan, 'The Potential of Taxpayer Revolt in American Democracy', *Social Science Quarterly* 59 (1979): 691–696.

is blocked as well. If citizens were more constitutional and future-oriented in their mindset then simply pursuing a frugal fiscal policy would be a winning electoral ticket, but most public choice theorizing suggests the contrary, hence the need for the BBA: 'Fiscal prudence simply cannot be made to pay off in democracy'.[31] Furthermore, Buchanan himself has conceded that ordinary citizens do not systematically differ from elected politicians in their being torn between constitutional considerations and the incentive to engage in rent-seeking.[32] Consequently, Buchanan has to confine himself to the expression of hope that something might happen that his own theoretical assumptions suggest could never happen: 'To hold out hope for reform in the basic rules describing the sociopolitical game, we must introduce elements that violate the self-interest postulate'.[33] Rather than pursuing the eschatological motives of a *deus ex machina* underpinning this statement, at this point, it is time to explore one more option that will offer a good segue to the next section. After all, the explanatory difficulties of public choice neoliberalism just mentioned notwithstanding, the empirical fact remains that various versions of a BBA *have* been passed.[34] The only explanation available for this seems to be that the rule may have been passed but that it will be watered down or even ignored whenever political expediency necessitates it. This brings us to the fate of the SGP and what Stephen Gill has called the 'new constitutionalism'.

Juridical neoliberalism in practice: from the Stability and Growth Pact to the Treaty on Stability, Coordination and Governance

If someone unfamiliar with Stephen Gill's widely cited article on 'European Governance and New Constitutionalism' read it today they would probably be surprised that it was published as long ago as 1998. This tells us two things. First we must be careful not to overstate the uniqueness of the present transformations of EU governance, significant as they are; and, second, we must not overstate the originality of the diagnosis to follow. All existing differences notwithstanding, the aspects and effects of juridical neoliberalism I will examine in the following are not entirely dissimilar from what Gill had attributed to the 'new constitutionalism'.

The latter is defined in the following way:

> New constitutionalism is an international governance framework. It seeks to separate economic policies from broad political accountability in order to make governments more responsive to the discipline of market forces and correspondingly less responsive to popular-democratic forces and processes.

31 Buchanan, *Liberty, Market and State*, 217.
32 Buchanan and Musgrave, *Public Finance and Public Choice*, 126.
33 Brennan and Buchanan, *The Reason of Rules*, 146.
34 See note 19.

> New constitutionalism is the politico-legal dimension of the wider discourse of disciplinary neoliberalism.[35]

Gill's prime example of this new constitutionalism is the European Economic and Monetary Union as well as the SGP passed in 1997. What they aim at certainly sounds familiar to contemporary ears: 'They seek to institutionalize the new currency and mandate a strict fiscal discipline as part of new practices of economic governance that will give credibility to governments and confidence to investors'.[36] The four main aspects of the new constitutionalism are listed as a monetary policy of sound money, i.e. low inflation with the ECB as the sole guardian, debt sustainability to keep the euro stable and preclude speculation against it, surveillance mechanisms to ensure that member states honor their fiscal commitments in this regard and, finally, the attenuation of democracy as a consequence.[37] However, a skeptic might argue that this was a premature and overly alarmist account of the governance restructuring taking place over the course of the introduction of the euro. After all, the SGP undoubtedly served to discipline Eurozone member states and aspiring candidates to a certain degree but when push came to shove the new constitutionalism turned out to be a 'paper tiger'. In the early 2000s both France and Germany, the economic and political heavyweights of the Eurozone, ran deficits in violation of the 3 per cent of the GDP rule of the SGP for consecutive years. The European Commission in charge of implementing and enforcing the SGP wanted to sanction both countries according to the procedures of the SGP but ECOFIN, the Council of European Economic and Finance Ministers, voted against it. The European Court of Justice confirmed the legality of that vote when it was challenged by the Commission. In other words, what happened was exactly what the theoretical discussion in the preceding section suggested. In the somewhat unlikely case that rules prohibiting 'excessive' deficits and debt are passed, they are bound to be disregarded at least by their more powerful addressees whenever they find it to be necessary. This is an important part of the prelude to the reforms of 2011–2013 that are aimed at tightening the SGP in a number of ways as a response to the sovereign debt crisis that followed the financial one.

The reforms in question are the so-called 'Six-Pack' (2011), the 'Two-Pack' (2013) and the already mentioned TSCG (2012).[38] They aim to ensure that Eurozone member states achieve balanced budgets, avoid excessive deficits and prevent/correct macroeconomic imbalances. The instruments range from

35 Stephen Gill, 'European Governance and New Constitutionalism Economic and Monetary Union and Alternatives to Disciplinary Neoliberalism in Europe', *New Political Economy* 3, no. 1 (1998): 5–26.

36 Ibid., 8.

37 Ibid., 15–17.

38 For concise explanations of the rationale and functioning of these reform measures, see http://ec.europa.eu/economy_finance/articles/governance/2012-03-14_six_pack_en.htm

preventive ones (for example, states have to submit draft budgets to the Commission before national parliaments even deliberate over them) to corrective ones. In the case of excessive deficits or macroeconomic imbalances the Commission issues recommendations to rectify the situation that become binding unless there is a qualified majority *against* it in ECOFIN, and if states do not comply in due time they can be fined up to 0.1 per cent of GDP. The core of these measures is the Fiscal Pact that I would also like to highlight here because it is almost the exact equivalent of the BBA demanded by Buchanan and others in that it stipulates that signees (25 EU countries excluding the UK and the Czech Republic) pass such an amendment at the national level, preferably at the level of constitutional law. So in a way what I consider the prime manifestation of juridical neoliberalism in practice, i.e. the various reforms passed in recent years, amounts to new constitutionalism with a vengeance, similar in its aims but tightened in its implementation and enforcement procedures, which leads to an even greater attenuation of democracy – at least at the nation-state level. After all, the Commission and ECOFIN now wield considerable influence over what used to be considered a core competence of parliaments, namely fiscal policy. And while intergovernmentalists are quick to point out the democratic legitimation of ECOFIN as members of national governments, it is worth pointing out that the Commission has seen a remarkable increase in its power vis-à-vis ECOFIN, not least through the already mentioned reverse majority principle.[39] It is not particularly likely that a qualified majority of ECOFIN, which would have to include countries that might have to act as creditors for indebted countries, will form a majority against the recommendations by the Commission. Needless to say, the fate of the SGP should caution us against overly alarmist diagnoses. These are relatively new rules and as the recent entanglement between the Commission and France over the draft budget has shown, while many may hope that the rules passed trigger quasi-automatically certain procedures and are enforced uniformly, there is obviously some political leeway left. This brings us to some final reflections on the current state of juridical neoliberalism in Europe.

Concluding thoughts

Let me conclude this chapter with three diagnostic observations concerning juridical neoliberalism as it is on display in the reformed governance structures of the EU. First, I would argue that an overarching aim of the introduction of various legal rules and regulations that circumscribe the more or less discretionary decision-making space in economic policy for national governments is to *depoliticize* the respective policy domains to a certain degree. Once a BBA has been passed as stipulated in the Fiscal Compact, the question of whether it may be *expedient* or *reasonable* to run a

39 Michael Bauer and Stefan Becker, 'From the Front Line to the Back Stage: How the Financial Crisis Has Quietly Strengthened the European Commission', *Public Money & Management* 34, no. 3 (2014): 161–163.

deficit of 4 per cent to fund an anti-cyclical economic policy along Keynesian lines, to choose one possible example, is largely off the table because it is simply *illegal*.[40] Still, I expect that this attempt at depoliticizing fiscal policy is likely to fail although it is a matter of speculation how exactly this will manifest itself. The reason is that the matters that are to be depoliticized are inherently political in a double sense. Not only is there no scientific consensus over the causal connection between austerity, inflation and economic growth, to name only the more important variables underpinning the BBA, which makes it seem problematic to treat these questions as purely technical ones to be decided exclusively based on scientific expertise. Second, and relatedly, these rules produce more or less clearly identifiable winners and losers, and in this respect they are the opposite of the regulatory politics that commentators such as Majone considered appropriate for delegation to independent regulatory agencies. Majone himself has written that 'the risk of a complete normative failure – a default rather than a simple deficit of democracy at the European level – is by now quite concrete'.[41] Given this emphatically political nature of the matters at hand, just speaking from a purely functional perspective, it remains doubtful whether juridical norms can sustainably succeed in depoliticizing them. Repoliticizations from the rise of Syriza and Podemos in Greece and Spain to the confrontations between member states and the Commission (e.g. the case of France) are likely to occur and, I would add, are also normatively desirable to avoid an increasingly technocratic form of rule at the European level. Needless to say, the situation particularly in Greece remains somewhat unpredictable, as is the fate of Syriza after the referendum of July 2015 and the ensuing internal strife within Syriza. Still, whether it is Syriza or alternative political forces – be they on the left or the right of the political spectrum, one should add – repoliticizations are bound to continue to challenge the status quo. This is all the more likely since the European refugee crisis has led to some significant changes in European power relationships. With regard to Greece, its geopolitical position as a key entry point to Schengenland has given it new leverage in negotiations with the EU. The brief episode of German hegemony within the EU may already start to fade.

My second observation has to be prefaced with a very quick look at the characterization of the permutations of law under neoliberalism coming from Wendy Brown, albeit in the context of the United States around 2005.[42] Brown analyzes the interplay between neoliberalism and neoconservatism and writes: 'And, as law is tacticalized or instrumentalized, it is radically desacralized, producing the conditions of its routine suspension or abrogation, and paving the ground for what Agamben, drawing on Schmitt, has formulated as sovereignty in the form of a permanent state of exception'.[43] So my second point is that the overall thrust of the discourse surrounding juridical neoliberalism in Europe about ten years after

40 To be precise, it is not entirely off the table because in cases of natural disasters or grave recessions exceptions to the BBA can be made.

41 Majone, 'Regulatory State to Democratic Default', 1221–1222.

42 For the following, see also Biebricher, 'Sovereignty, Norms, and Exception'.

43 Wendy Brown, 'American Nightmare: Neoliberalism, Neoconservatism, and De-Democratization', *Political Theory* 34, no. 6 (2006): 690–714, 696.

Brown's assessment points in the opposite direction.[44] Brown describes the desacralization of law and its bending for tactical purposes, whereas the official discourse in Europe rather aims at what I would consider maybe not a resacralization of law in a strictly religious sense but certainly a moralization that aims to immunize law against critique of its contents and to further deter potential violators. Not only will those breaking the law have to reckon with being sanctioned quite stringently according to the various procedural mechanisms but they also have to bear the moral burden of having shown a lack of solidarity vis-à-vis other EU countries, which might eventually have to pay for bailouts through the ESM or other channels. Moreover, if one subscribes to the necessary link between the common currency and the EU as political project (as Angela Merkel remarked in a speech given to the German parliament on May 19, 2010: 'If the Euro fails, Europe fails') then the moral burden is even more significant. And let us not forget that – aside from solidarity requirements vis-à-vis other countries – it is suggested that a fiscal policy violating the BBA rules is in itself immoral because it is the equivalent of 'living beyond one's means' and burdening future generations with debt; an immoral practice that is rightfully punished with economic calamities by anonymous but – it seems – inherently moral forces: 'We have turned the politics of debt into a morality play', writes Mark Blyth,[45] and even someone as sympathetic to the Eurozone crisis management in general as Mario Monti famously remarked that economics was still considered a branch of moral philosophy in Germany.[46] I do not want to pursue this hint at the role Germany in particular is playing in the moralization of Europe's economic constitution in the (re-)making but rather draw attention to the relation between the two diagnostic theses formulated so far. If the aim of a juridification of economy policy is the latter's depoliticization then what are the respective implications of a moralization of these juridical rules? This is a question that deserves a more thorough treatment then I can offer here, as well as, incidentally, the relation between morality and law more generally. Let me at least note the ambivalence here: of course, one can argue that the moralization of law serves to immunize it even more from challenges, but at the same time this moralization negates the strictly technocratic character of the BBA, etc. which is supposedly just an expression of pure and sober economic reason. Charging these rules with moral implications might inadvertently rekindle and fan the flames of political passions that the strategy of juridification was trying to put out.

44 More recently, Brown has expanded upon her diagnosis with a critique of some landmark Supreme Court rulings, especially the now infamous *Citizens United* case. There, she highlights the neoliberal logic of markets and capital underlying the ruling. Still, the neoliberalization of law she describes in the contemporary American context remains different from the kind of juridical neoliberalism I detect in the European context. See Wendy Brown, *Undoing the Demos: Neoliberalism's Stealth Revolution* (New York: Zone Books, 2015), 151–174.

45 Mark Blyth, *Austerity: The History of a Dangerous Idea* (Oxford: Oxford University Press, 2013), 13.

46 'The Other Moral Hazard: Charlemagne', *The Economist*, September 29, 2012, 61.

My final observation concerns the overall context in which both the depoliticization of fiscal policy and the moralization of the respective juridical rules occur. The EU has been in crisis mode ever since the outbreak of the financial crisis in 2008. However, initially it was mostly the nation-states that dealt with the fallout, i.e. bailing out banks and stimulating faltering economies. This changed with the onset of the sovereign debt crisis that put the common currency in jeopardy and triggered the barrage of reforms mentioned above. What is striking about almost every aspect of the ensuing politics of EU crisis management since 2011 is their ambiguous legal status. To be sure, national and European adjudication so far have confirmed the legality of the measures[47] – although one might suspect that political reasons played a significant role here. Still, from the Six-Pack that is questioned with regard to the possibility of far-reaching recommendations to overcome deficits and imbalances and that can affect policy domains that are exclusive competences of nation states, to the Fiscal Pact's use of the Commission and European Court of Justice for implementation and enforcement – although it is not part of EU law but an international treaty – to the Outright Monetary Transactions program that the ECB launched in 2012, thus seriously pushing the envelope of the bank's mandate to say the least, there is plenty of controversy surrounding European crisis management. Therefore, it has to be noted that Europe is not just faced with an economic and political, but also a legal-constitutional crisis.[48] Of course, this raises specters of extra-legal states of emergency and Wendy Brown's concerns mentioned above come to mind. Nevertheless, at this point I would simply note the contradictory tendencies in the politics of legality in Europe at the current conjuncture. Not only is there a potential tension between the attempt to depoliticize issues through a particular form of juridification and the moralization of the rules in question. But also, the insistence on the inviolability of legal rules that are arguably further immunized by the moralization of their contents stands in stark contradiction to the embattled legal status of these very rules. More encompassing endeavors to critically comprehend the complexities of the politics of legality in the (neoliberal) restructuring of EU governance will have to take these tensions and contradictions into account.

47 When the Portuguese Supreme Court ruled against the implementation of reforms demanded by the Troika, lawmakers responded with a constitutional reform.
48 Michael Wilkinson, 'The Specter of Authoritarian Liberalism: Reflections on the Constitutional Crisis of the European Union', *German Law Journal* 14, no. 5 (2013): 527–560; Christian Joerges, 'Law and Politics in Europe's Crisis: On the History of the Impact of an Unfortunate Configuration', *Constellations* 21, no. 2 (2014): 249–261.

Chapter 6

Neoliberalism as legalism

International economic law and the rise of the judiciary

Ntina Tzouvala

Conceptualising 'neoliberal legality' as a distinct kind of capitalist legality is, arguably, an arduous task. Apart from divergence on what does or does not qualify as neoliberalism, this difficulty derives from the absence of a 'pure' neoliberal legal system – domestic or international. That is because – despite its global triumph – neoliberalism is in a constant symbiotic relationship with other systems of social organisation, such as remnants of traditional liberalism and Keynesianism, pre-capitalist models of legality, or elements of radical forms of social organisation. Hence, analysing neoliberal legality requires a significant degree of abstraction and theorisation.

For this reason, this chapter seeks to make a more modest contribution to debates about neoliberal legality. Instead of inquiring into the 'nature' of neoliberal legality, I will instead focus on the *degree* of legalisation of public affairs and will argue that there is an intrinsic link between an unfolding trend of legalisation and judicialisation of economic governance and the rise of neoliberalism. To do so, this chapter will focus on international trade law as exemplified by the General Agreement on Tariffs and Trade (GATT) system and later the World Trade Organization (WTO) and more specifically on the evolution of its dispute settlement mechanism across the five post-war decades. The central claim is that, despite popular neoliberal slogans for less state and less law, neoliberalism was intrinsically tied to a process of radical enhancement of the judiciary and legalisation of social relations. To substantiate this claim, I am going to examine the historical development of dispute-settlement mechanisms in the context of international trade law, arguing that at least since the 1980s, there has been a distinctive and stable trend of judicialisation and legalisation of the way international trade law is administered. Lastly, I will turn to Nicos Poulantzas' concept of *authoritarian statism*, arguing that the aspiration of neoliberalism to elevate competition into the prevailing principle of social organisation renders the judiciary the ideal repository of law and of economic management, leading to the ongoing legalisation of numerous domains, including international trade law. Furthermore, it will be argued that neoliberalism is intrinsically linked to an effort to reduce the influence of mass politics, organised labour and democratic imperatives on policy-making, and that this trend of judicialisation and internationalisation of economic governance should be understood as part of an 'immunisation' process of the state vis-à-vis popular pressures.

1 From GATT to the WTO: the evolution of international trade law and dispute settlement

While the Second World War was still being fought, Western leaders started planning for post-war international trade arrangements. There were two objectives and sets of principles that guided this process. The first was to avoid economic isolationism and nationalism which, it was thought, contributed to both the deepening of the Great Depression and to the escalation of national antagonisms that in turn led to the Second World War.[1] Second, it was considered crucial to safeguard full employment and general prosperity, as the deterioration of living standards during the Great Depression was thought to have contributed to the rise of Nazism in Germany and authoritarianism across Europe.[2] It is remarkable that this latter motivation is often ignored in contemporary analyses of the development of post-war international trade law.[3] That said, consensus on the goals of the system was not accompanied by consensus on its specifics. The (in)famous conference at Bretton Woods (1944) led to the establishment of the International Monetary Fund and of the International Bank for Reconstruction and Development, but not to the establishment of a specialised trade organisation. Indeed, it was more than a year later (1945) that the United States tabled a proposal for an International Trade Organization (ITO). The final round of the negotiations for the ITO took place at the UN Conference on Trade and Employment in Havana, resulting in the Havana Charter for an International Trade Organization. This organisation probably fell victim to its own ambitiousness, and after the US Congress refused to ratify the agreement, it never became effective.

1 See Gerard Curzon and Victoria Curzon, 'The Management of Trade Relations in the GATT', in *International Economic Relations of the West World, 1959–1971*, ed., Andrew Schonfield, vol. 1, *Politics and Trade* (Oxford: Oxford University Press, 1976), 143–144.

2 Lang has summarised the post-war ideological climate as follows: 'Most importantly, the Depression had entrenched the promotion of full and stable employment as the highest priority of domestic economic policy. While it was recognized that international trade might boost employment in good economic times, the turbulent interwar years had made it clear that, in hard times, trade would have the effect of transmitting economic instability globally.' Andrew Lang, *World Trade Law after Neoliberalism: Re-imagining the Global Economic Order* (Oxford: Oxford University Press, 2011), 26.

3 Amongst many Irwin, Mavroidis and Sykes heavily emphasise the struggle against protectionism almost ignoring the welfarist aspirations of the founders of GATT. See generally Douglas Irwin, Petros C. Mavroidis and Alan O. Sykes, *The Genesis of the GATT* (New York: Cambridge University Press, 2009), 5–8, 12, 96–97. The emphasis on anti-protectionism is common among most relevant writings: 'Following the war, the need for international cooperation to avoid such damaging protectionist policies was widely recognised and played a key role in the negotiations.' Helen Coskeran, Dan Kim and Amrita Narlikar, 'Trade in Manufactures and Agricultural Products: the Dangerous Link?', in *The Oxford Handbook on the World Trade Organization*, eds, Amrita Narlikar, Martin Daunton and Robert M. Stern (Oxford: Oxford University Press, 2012), 346.

Nevertheless, the General Agreement on Tariffs and Trade (GATT) received widespread approval and was 'provisionally' applied for almost five decades. The preamble of GATT states that the contracting parties were 'directed to the substantial reduction of tariffs and other barriers to trade and to the elimination of discriminatory treatment in international commerce'.[4] Henceforth, non-discrimination and reciprocity, especially most-favoured nation treatment, were at the heart of GATT. Importantly, though, full liberalisation of trade was not specified as a goal of GATT and a series of provisions allowed for the use of quantitative restrictions for the realisation of specific domestic goals.[5]

The dispute settlement mechanism of GATT was understandably the object of significant disagreements. Hudec reports that there were two major approaches to this question. On the one hand, the United States advocated for 'hard' legal arrangements,[6] an approach reflected in the early drafts of the Havana Charter, which contained provisions about a formal complaints procedure and access to the International Court of Justice (ICJ). This approach prioritised predictability and certainty over other concerns and was premised on the idea that the standardisation and formalism of a judicial process would best serve these goals. It is nonetheless significant that even this approach did not call for specialised panels, but rather, understood GATT as an integral part of public international law, the court of which would be the ICJ. On the other hand, there was also an opinion, mainly represented by the United Kingdom, that there should be ample space for political negotiations and compromise. A memorandum submitted by the United Kingdom during the Charter negotiations summarises this approach as follows: 'In almost every conceivable case arising under the Charter the issues will of their nature involve the element of economic appraisal and assessment and will not be purely legal in character, and it will be impossible to say where economic judgement ends and legal judgement begins.'[7] This second 'diplomatic' approach eventually (and easily) prevailed in the post-war era until the early 1970s. In fact, even the term 'dispute settlement' was initially avoided for being too confrontational and 'conciliation' was the term usually preferred. This was not a euphemism, since it reflected the fact that the goal of the process was reaching a mutually acceptable solution rather than deciding solely based on law. It is, for example, notable that most individuals involved in the procedures, either as

4 General Agreement on Tariffs and Trade, Preamble, 30 October 1947, 61 Stat. A-11, 55 UNTS 194 (GATT).

5 Ibid., Art. XII, para. 3(d), for example, allowed for quantitative restrictions when 'as a result of domestic policies directed towards the achievement and maintenance of full employment … a contracting party may experience a high level of demand for imports involving a threat to its monetary reserves.'

6 Robert E. Hudec, *Essays on the Nature of International Trade Law* (London: Cameron May, 1999), 39.

7 UN Economic and Social Council, Article 86: Summary of Points Made by Mr Shackle Regarding Interpretation and Settlement of Disputes UN Doc. E/PC/T/C.6/W.77 (14 February 1947).

advocates or as panellists, were diplomats and not lawyers. As such, despite the allegedly 'neutral' character of the panellists, their judgements were more political than legal in terms of their method, vocabulary and objectives.[8]

This reality was also related to the fact that the procedural rules of the GATT dispute settlement were limited to two Articles (XXII and XXIII). According to these provisions, every party 'shall afford adequate opportunity for consultation' about 'any matter affecting the operation of this Agreement' (Article XXII, para. 1). Further, in case of nullification or impairment of any benefit directly or indirectly accruing under the Agreement, the party allegedly affected could make written proposals to the other party. The complaining party could only refer the matter to the contracting parties if it was not satisfactorily resolved. In such a situation the contracting parties were required to investigate the case and make recommendations. Crucially, for the adoption of any recommendation, the unanimous agreement of the parties was required, which politicised the process by enabling bargaining and compromise, rather than making a clear-cut distribution of rights and obligations. The unanimity requirement was, however, criticised by numerous legal commentators for being overly political and for impairing the legalisation of the dispute settlement system. For example, Palmeter and Mavroidis noted that 'the dispute settlement under GATT was handicapped'.[9] Similarly, Jackson identified the veto right of the losing party as 'the most significant defect in the GATT DS process.'[10] Yet this veto occurred on an extremely rare basis: having studied the practice of the states between 1947 and 1992, Hudec concluded that the losing party accepted the outcome of the dispute settlement process in approximately 90 per cent of the cases.[11] This suggests that the later rejection of the provisions stemmed from an opposition to soft, diplomatic methods of administering international trade, rather than from it objectively impairing international trade.

Nonetheless, dissatisfaction with this 'soft' system of dispute settlement grew, paving the way for significant reforms. Even before the Uruguay Round, there was a strong trend towards the standardisation and formalisation of the dispute settlement process. The conclusion of the Tokyo Round in 1979 signalled the adoption of the Understanding on Notification, Consultation, Dispute Settlement and Surveillance, which attempted to put down on paper the customary practice in the field of dispute settlement. This was a first reluctant step towards formalising

8 As Hudec notes, their 'legal rulings were drafted with an elusive diplomatic vagueness'. Robert E. Hudec, *Enforcing International Trade Law: The Evolution of the Modern GATT Legal System* (Salem, NH: Butterworth, 1993), 12.

9 David Palmeter and Petros C. Mavroidis, *Dispute Settlement in the World Trade Organization: Practice and Procedure* (Cambridge: Cambridge University Press, 2004), 9.

10 John H. Jackson, *Sovereignty, the WTO, and Changing Fundamentals of International Law*, Hersch Lauterpacht Memorial Lecturers (Cambridge: Cambridge University Press, 2006), 141.

11 Hudec, *Enforcing International Trade Law*, 278.

the process and transforming it from a political, ad hoc procedure, into a process regulated in detail by law. A Ministerial Conference in 1982 moved a further step towards the WTO system by adding the requirement that the losing party should report within a 'reasonable specified period' on the action taken to implement the recommendations, in order to strengthen and monitor implementation.[12]

The Uruguay Round was, nonetheless, the decisive moment for the future of international trade law. The Round was concluded with the Marrakesh Agreement Establishing the World Trade Organisation, which is broadly considered to be 'the most ambitious and far-reaching international trade agreement ever concluded.'[13] There were numerous novelties introduced by the WTO agreement, which Lang summarises along four major axes: the development of a judicialised dispute settlement system; the expansion of the scope of application of the legal regime to include trade in services and intellectual property; the shift of focus from trade barriers imposed at the border to barriers 'behind the borders'; and, lastly, the development of new jurisprudential styles and techniques.[14] According to Lang, formalisation, technicalisation[15] and a uniquely market-orientated approach to the non-discrimination norm[16] and to the concept of 'like products'[17] marked this new phase of dispute settlement for international trade.

The judicial turn of the dispute settlement mechanism was primarily effected through three elements of the Dispute Settlement Understanding. First, the mechanism acquired the monopolistic and authoritative character of modernist legal systems of dispute settlement, as Article 23 precludes recourse to any alternative dispute settlement system and any kind of unilateral action or 'vigilante justice'.[18] The appellate body (AB) was also elevated to the final arbiter of legality under the WTO, while legality – and not bargaining or compromise – was seen as

12 GATT Doc. BISD 29S/13, 15 (viii).

13 Peter van den Bossche, *The Law and Policy of the World Trade Organization: Texts, Cases and Materials*, 2nd edn (Cambridge: Cambridge University Press, 2008), 42–43.

14 Lang, *World Trade Law after Neoliberalism*, 159.

15 To quote Lang: 'Formalization and technicalization went hand in hand, as two sides of a single basic transformation.' Lang, *World Trade Law after Neoliberalism*, 252.

16 '[T]he underlying conceptual move which drove this new jurisprudence (even if it was never quite fully realised) was to equate a discriminatory regulation with any regulation which shifted patterns of domestic consumption away from foreign product and towards their domestic counterparts.' Lang, *World Trade Law after Neoliberalism*, 255.

17 Lang has summarised the relevant jurisprudence as follows: 'While it considered a number of different factors, the most important criterion seems to have been the way that these products were perceived by consumers in the marketplace.' Lang, *World Trade Law after Neoliberalism*, 257.

18 Van den Bossche, *Law and Policy*, 172. Therefore, unilateral practices like those pursued under Section 301 of the 1974 US Trade Act, which authorised the President to take appropriate action to ensure the removal of any act, policy, or practice of a foreign government that violated an international trade agreement or was unjustified, unreasonable, or discriminatory, and that burdened or restricted US commerce, were rendered directly incompatible with WTO law.

the legitimate way of resolving disputes.[19] Second, Article 6, para. 1 guarantees that the request for the establishment of a panel will not be blocked, unless there is a unanimous agreement of the Disputes Settlement Body. This meant that the process lost its discretionary and diplomatic character, since the respondent was no longer able to control the initiation of the proceedings. Third, the establishment of an AB to hear appeals on an exclusively legal basis enhanced the legal understanding of international trade and promoted the rule of law values of predictability, formality and technical expertise to the detriment of more political and pragmatic approaches. This latter development acquired its own dynamics to the extent that, by 2012, 78 out of 125 panel reports had been appealed and 85 per cent of these appeals succeeded,[20] a reality that went beyond the initial intentions of its very designers.[21] Hence, the dispute settlement mechanism was transformed from 'a rudimentary, power-based system for settling disputes through diplomatic negotiations, into an elaborate, rules-based system for settling disputes through adjudication.'[22]

To sum up, international trade law underwent a process of fundamental transformation that was crystallised and deepened with the conclusion of the Uruguay Round. What needs to be noted here is that the process of increasing liberalisation of international trade and the elevation of competitive relations into a central axis of international trade law coincided with the process of legalisation and judicialisation of dispute settlement. In turn, this process of legalisation was explicitly linked to a desire to 'depoliticise' international trade and to delimit the manoeuvring space for states when regulating international trade. The next two sections will show how these three trends (liberalisation, diminishing regulatory spaces for states and judicialisation) were in fact interlinked parts of one, single process: the 'great transformation' of the state after the rise of neoliberalism.

II From Keynes to Hayek: changing paradigms of international economic law

This brief history of international trade law raises an obvious question: why did this legalisation of the dispute mechanism occur? My argument is that the

19 See also Sol Picciotto, 'The WTO's Appellate Body: Legal Formalism as the Legitimisation of Global Governance', *Governance: An International Journal of Policy, Administration, and Institutions* 18: 477–503.

20 Thomas Bernauer, Manfred Elsig and Joost Pauwelyn, 'Dispute Settlement Mechanism: Analysis and Problems', in Narlikar et al., *Oxford Handbook on WTO*, 488.

21 The rapid development of the dispute-settlement mechanism took even its designers by surprise: 'The chair of the DSU negotiations stated, "we thought that things would go on like in the past, evolving around the panel system; nobody expected that the AB would become as active."' Gregory Shaffer, Manfred Elsig and Sergio Puig, 'The Extensive (but Fragile) Authority of the WTO Appellate Body', Arizona Legal Studies Discussion Paper No. 15–17, James E. Rogers College of Law, University of Arizona, March 2015, Tucson, AZ, 14.

22 Van den Bossche, *Law and Policy*, 170.

history of international legal institutions, while relatively autonomous,[23] nonetheless reflects the rise and fall of politically dominant visions of the 'good life' and the role that law plays in achieving this goal. In the case of international trade law, the flexible, diplomatic approach to dispute settlement in the immediate post-war era reflected the Keynesian model of managing international trade, while the increasing legalisation of the process reflects the ideological and political hegemony of neoliberalism.

David Kennedy has concisely summarised the post-war economic orthodoxy: 'Keynes remained a lodestar for thinking about macroeconomic policy, and macroeconomics continued to dominate microeconomics in thinking about what government and law should be about.'[24] At a very basic level, this meant that:

> Despite its imperfections, Keynes believed that capitalism was the best system humans have devised to achieve a civilised economic society. He recognised, however, that capitalism had two major faults: (1) its failure to provide persistent full employment for all those who want to work, and (2) its arbitrary and inequitable distribution of income and wealth.[25]

Hence, the Keynesian model, while in principle supportive of free trade, also involved state intervention in the market in order to safeguard full employment and, crucially, monetary and fiscal stability.

As Lang observes, the experience of the Great Depression instilled in states the idea that 'they needed to maintain some ability to insulate themselves from international sources of instability.'[26] The GATT was, then, largely reflective of the perception that free-market economy principles should be compromised and reconciled with other objectives, but in no case abandoned. As such, it was thought to be legitimate for governments to intervene in the market and act as a counter-force to some of its detrimental social effects. This was facilitated by legal arrangements that enhanced the role of the executive, which became the primary

23 Akbar Rasulov elegantly summarises this methodological position: 'That is to say, the principal epistemological presumption implied by the positivist theoretical outlook must be that, firstly, the course of legal history unfolds quite independently from that of "economic relations", "culture", and "political struggles"; and, secondly, even though it might be over-determined in some exceptional circumstances by the impact of various external forces, the course of legal history is always inscribed *wholly within its own, field-specific, distinctly legal-historical "medium"*.' Akbar Rasulov, 'The Life and Times of the Modern Law of Reservations: The Doctrinal Genealogy of General Comment No. 24', *Austrian Review of International and European Law* 14 (2009): 106 (original emphasis).

24 David Kennedy, 'The "Rule of Law", Political Choices, and Development Common Sense', in *The New Law and Economic Development: A Critical Appraisal*, eds, David M. Trubek and Alvaro Santos (New York: Cambridge University Press, 2006), 98.

25 Paul Davidson, *The Keynes Solution: The Path to Global Economic Prosperity* (New York: Palgrave Macmillan, 2009), 6.

26 Lang, *World Trade Law after Neoliberalism*, 194.

locus for the formation, interpretation, and enforcement of the law (a process that occurred at both domestic and international levels). The law also became more specific, piecemeal and flexible in character, so as to accommodate the specific goals of the executive at both the domestic and the international levels.[27] The flexible, political dispute settlement mechanism of the GATT provided the institutional framework that enabled this interventionist approach to international trade, in a context where 'liberalization was pursued progressively, slowly and selectively'.[28]

Keynesianism was not, however, the only response to the crisis of *laissez-faire* liberalism, which had loomed since the end of the nineteenth century.[29] Since the 1930s, neoliberal thinkers, such as Lippman, Röpke and Hayek, redefined the relationship between the market and the state in an attempt 'to save from liberalism itself what could be salvaged of the capitalist system'.[30] Like the Keynesians, neoliberals of all strands[31] acknowledged the limitations of *laissez-faire* liberalism: in the Walter Lippmann colloquium, which is largely considered the founding moment of neoliberalism,[32] Rougier called for the construction of a 'positive liberalism'.[33] This

27 Writing about the transformation of Western European states on the eve of the crisis of Keynesianism, Poulantzas noted that: 'Indeed, the general and universal laws still enacted by parliament – which are, at bottom, merely framework-laws – are applied only after the Executive has passed them through a process of concretization and particularisation. This is the stage of decrees, judicial interpretation and civil service adjustment.' Nicos Poulantzas, *State, Power, Socialism* (London: Verso, 2000), 219; 'More broadly, law was primarily seen in purposive terms as an instrument of the broader purposes underlying the regime as a whole, rather than just as a mechanism for producing clear rules and therefore predictable behaviour.' Lang, *World Trade Law after Neoliberalism*, 200–201.

28 Lang, *World Trade Law after Neoliberalism*, 40.

29 Dardot and Laval summarised this historical trend as follows: 'From the mid-nineteenth century, and especially after Bismarck's initial reforms in the late 1870s and early [18]80s, Europe witnessed an increasing trend towards the emergence of apparatuses, regulations and laws intended to protect the condition of wage-earners and, as far as possible, prevent them succumbing to the pauperism that haunted the whole nineteenth century.' Pierre Dardot and Christian Laval, *The New Way of the World: On Neo-liberal Society* (London: Verso, 2014), 24.

30 Ibid., 38.

31 The most common distinction, which can be traced back to Foucault, is between German ordo-liberals and American neoliberals: Michel Foucault, *The Birth of Biopolitics: Lectures at the Collège de France 1978–1979*, ed., Michel Senellart, trans., Graham Burchell (Basingstoke: Palgrave Macmillan, 2008), 216–219. Here it is felt that, despite certain marked differences between the two 'schools' of neoliberalism, the points raised by this chapter apply to ordo-liberals and American neoliberals alike. Therefore, the term 'neoliberal' will be used to denote both groups, unless there is a specific reason to differentiate between them.

32 The conference took place in Paris in 1938 bringing together theorists that were to become the most prominent neoliberals, such as Hayek, Rueff, Röpke and Rustow. For further details, see François Denord, 'Aux origines du néo-libéralisme en France: Louis Rougier et le Colloque Walter Lippmann de 1938', *Le Mouvement social 195* (2001): 9–34.

33 Quoted in Foucault, *The Birth of Biopolitics*, 133.

'positive' or 'neo-' liberalism would break with its classical counterpart by acknowledging that the market is not a natural, pre-political order that flourishes if left alone by the state. Rather, as Wilhem Röpke, one of the most prominent ordo-liberals, put it, 'The free market requires an active, an extremely vigilant policy.'[34] However, unlike Keynesians, neoliberals advocated for state intervention, in order to sustain, support and expand the functions of the market, and not in order to limit them. As Foucault has pointed out, if the purpose of Keynesianism was to nullify the anti-social effects of competition through state intervention, the purpose of neoliberal state intervention is to 'nullify the possible anti-competitive mechanisms of society, or at any rate the anti-competitive mechanisms that could arise within society.'[35] Therefore, the elementary differentiation between the 'new' liberals of the New Deal and the 'neoliberals' of Vienna, Chicago or Freiburg was not about the desirability, or even about the degree of state intervention in the economy; rather, it was about the purpose and orientation of interventionism.

Crucially, neoliberal thought conceives competition, rather than free exchange, as the essence of the free market.[36] This has important implications for the relationship between the market and the state. For if one moves away from the simplistic imaginary of free exchange, one need also move away from the simplistic understanding of the state as a minimal entity that solely guarantees public order and property rights necessary for acts of free exchange to occur. Rather, generalised competition is a fragile condition that requires constant state intervention, in order to uphold and solidify its bases. For American neoliberals and German ordo-liberals alike, the market might be 'spontaneous' or a natural 'trend', but it is not a natural phenomenon capable of endogenously sustaining itself. Therefore, unlike their occasional fellow-travellers, libertarians,[37] neoliberals acknowledge the significance of the state in establishing and maintaining a functional market. James Buchanan was clear in stressing the difference between neoliberals and the so-called anarcho-capitalists: 'Among our members, there are some who are able to imagine a viable society without a state ... For most of our members, however, social order without a state is not readily imagined, at least not in any normatively preferred sense.'[38] Indeed, what neoliberalism attempted to do was to both redesign a legitimate agenda for

34 Foucault, *The Birth of Biopolitics*, 133.
35 Ibid., 160.
36 Before the word 'neoliberalism' became a taboo for neoliberals, Friedman summarised the rising intellectual and political project as follows: 'But instead of the 19th century understanding that laissez-faire is the means to achieve this goal, neoliberalism proposes that competition will lead the way.' Milton Friedman, 'Neoliberalism and Its Prospects', *Farmand*, 17 February 1951, 89.
37 Nozick's understanding of a super-minimal, 'night-watchman' state is taken here as indicative of the libertarian school of thought: Robert Nozick, *Anarchy, State, and Utopia*, ed., Thomas Nagel (New York: Basic Books, 2013).
38 James M. Buchanan, 'Man and the State' (MPS Presidential Talk, Mon Pelerin Society, St Vincent, Italy, 31 August 1986), quoted in Philip Mirowski, *Never Let a Serious Crisis Go to Waste: How Neoliberalism Survived the Financial Meltdown* (London: Verso, 2013), 41.

government and re-determine its legitimate modality. In *locus classicus* of neoliberalism, *The Road to Serfdom*, Frederich Hayek states that 'The question whether the state should or should not "act" or "interfere" is a highly ambiguous and misleading description of the principles on which a liberal policy is based.'[39] Hayek's suggestion for resolving this problematic dilemma was the following: 'it is the character rather than the volume of government activity that is important.'[40] For neoliberals, then, rigorous state intervention is both politically legitimate and economically necessary, to the extent that it generates, spreads and sustains functional, competitive markets. As such, despite the common perceptions and slogans amongst its supporters and opponents alike, neoliberalism is not, and never has been, an inherently anti-statist ideology that strives for more restricted legal regulation of the economic realm.

The idea that the competitive market is produced and maintained through state intervention has had significant implications for the global economy. Röpke was very clear in his rejection of the *laissez-faire* conceptualisations of international trade[41] insisting that institutions and laws sustain the economy on a global scale: 'Economic integration, therefore, presupposes a corresponding extra-economic integration (social-political-moral-institutional-legal integration).'[42] This concern was particularly central in the thought and practice of ordoliberals after the war, and informed their sustained efforts for European integration and for the gradual development of international investment law.[43] These initiatives for restructuring the international (legal) order across neoliberal lines was the direct outcome of ordoliberals' conviction that the Keynesian, welfarist state constituted a direct and constant threat to the international order.[44] One of the ways for this perceived

39 F.A. Hayek, *The Road to Serfdom: Text and Documents; The Definitive Edition*, ed., Bruce Caldwell (Chicago: University of Chicago Press, 2007), 118.

40 F.A. Hayek, *The Constitution of Liberty: The Definitive Edition*, ed., Ronald Hamowy (Abingdon: Routledge, 2013), 331.

41 In his own words: 'This belief was triumphant in the period of historical liberalism of the Nineteenth Century whose representatives came dangerously near to the idea that the competitive economic order might be a completely natural order able to stand on its own feet.' Wilhelm Röpke, 'Economic Order and International Law', *Recueil des Cours* 86 (1954): 203–273, 210.

42 Ibid., 211.

43 Röpke was concerned about the disintegration of the international economy and in 1942 he published a book attributing the war directly to the protectionist policies after 1929: Wilhelm Röpke, *International Economic Disintegration* (The Macmillan Co., 1942). For a brief account of the ordoliberal origins of the EU, see Dardot and Laval, *The New Way of the World*, 193–201. For the centrality of ordoliberals in the construction of international investment law after 1945, see Ntina Tzouvala, 'The Ordo-liberal Origins of Modern International Investment Law: Constructing Competition on a Global Scale', *European Yearbook of International Economic Law* (2017, forthcoming).

44 Röpke did not shy away from the fact that his vision for an international legal order was incompatible with redistributive domestic politics: 'we have to make up our minds whether we can go on with certain national economic policies, which, however popular and tempting, are shown to be incompatible with that order.' Röpke, 'Economic Order and International Law', 255.

threat to be eliminated was the development of a comprehensive international legal framework that would restrain the protectionist tendencies of the states and, crucially, the capacity of organised labour to promote such policies.[45] Indeed, the animosity of ordoliberals, and neoliberals more broadly, vis-à-vis organised labour and mass politics is well-documented.[46] The idea that tradeunions constituted a problem to be managed,[47] and that mass politics of the twentieth century constituted a fundamental threat to individual freedom cuts across neoliberal thinking.[48] This indicates some of the inadequacies of examining the legal and institutional changes of international trade law solely as a product of ideational or conceptual disagreements. The neoliberal turn to international law and to judicialisation of economic governance was not simply linked to a conceptual preference for certain political actors over others. Rather, it is a political intervention that aims to weaken the bargaining position of organised labour and, more broadly, of the political Left. To substantiate this claim, and to link these social processes to neoliberalism, we will now turn to the concept of *authoritarian statism* as proposed by Poulantzas and subsequently developed by Andreas Kalyvas.

III International economic law after neoliberalism: the rise of the judiciary

Two trends are observable in the regulation of global economic matters after the global triumph of neoliberalism: those of judicialisation/legalisation and internationalisation. This section of the chapter argues that these developments are the outcome of a systematic crisis of the capitalist state and part of a wider process of redistribution of power to the benefit of international capital that Nicos Poulantzas has described as the emergence of 'authoritarian statism'. This concept has a number of important theoretical virtues in the context of debates around neoliberalism. First, it allows us to avoid the simplistic distinction between

45 'This tendency is furthered by certain policies of trade unions which, in spite of internationalist lip-service, tend to promote national isolation of labour and commodity markets.' Röpke, 'Economic Order and International Law', 233.

46 The work of Ralf Ptak is of paramount importance in documenting the anti-democratic commitments of ordoliberalism: 'Particularly during the early period, we have ample evidence that the emerging ordoliberal camp was not ready to accept public opinion formation under conditions of parliamentarian democracy, with people freely expressing and mediating diverging interests and economic positions.' Ralf Ptak, 'Neoliberalism in Germany: Revisiting the Ordoliberal Foundations of the Social Market Economy', in *The Road from Mont Pèlerin: The Making of the Neoliberal Thought Collective*, eds, Philip Mirowski and Dieter Plehwe (Cambridge/London: Harvard University Press, 2009), 110.

47 For the convergence and divergence between ordoliberals and American neoliberals regarding trade unions, see Yves Steiner 'The Neoliberals Confront the Trade Unions', in Mirowski and Plehwe, *The Road from Mont Pèlerin*.

48 For the irreconcible tension between neoliberalism and (liberal) democracy, see Wendy Brown, *Undoing the Demos: Neoliberalism's Stealth Revolution* (New York: Zone Books, 2015).

'markets' and the state, which characterises liberal thought and which is likewise found in many left critiques of neoliberalism, since it captures the fundamentally important role of the state in constructing and organising neoliberal capitalism. Second, 'authoritarian statism', if understood to include strategies of internationalisation, also enables us to understand the increasingly important role of international law in neoliberalism without losing sight of the state as the primary organiser of power relations.

An exhaustive account of Poulantzas' conceptualisation of the state falls outside the scope of this chapter. Still, it is essential to keep in mind that Poulantzas' theory constitutes a rupture with conceptialisations of the state as a subject (for example, the Schmittian sovereign) or as a 'thing'. This latter version includes the Marxian orthodoxy of Poulantzas' time that conceptualised the state merely as a 'tool' at the hands of the bourgeoisie.[49] Rather, Poulantzas proposed a strategic and relational understanding of state and law in which both are 'determined by, and conditioning, the relations of social antagonism in specific historical conjunctures.'[50] In other words, for Poulantzas the state is essentially a social relation, an articulation and crystallisation of power relations. Importantly, for Poulantzas the state is the outcome of the particular articulation of social dynamics that, at the same time, sets the conditions and the limits of the deployment of this social dynamics – and, given Poulantzas' Marxism, class struggle was the most significant, yet not the only, aspect of these dynamics.

Poulantzas also paid significant attention to atypical forms of capitalist statehood, such as the then collapsing dictatorships of Southern Europe.[51] This theoretical interest, combined with the widespread sense of crisis experienced in Western Europe since the late 1960s, led him to develop the concept of authoritarian statism, through which he tried to describe the transformation of the capitalist state in the aftermath of the Second World War. According to Poulantzas, authoritarian statism was 'a new historical form of the capitalist state'[52] that included, but was not

49 Kalyvas summarises this instrumentalist understanding of the state within Marxism as follows: 'The state, according to this interpretation, was the instrument that the bourgeoisie used to dominate and repress its class opponents, and particularly the working class. As Marx and Engels put it, the capitalist state is nothing else "but a committee for managing the common affairs of the whole bourgeoisie" – the "dictatorship of the bourgeoisie" (Marx and Engels 1978, 475). Thus, although the state was theorized in terms of the topographical metaphor of an epiphenomenon, a reflection of the deeper and more real sphere of the economy, it was recognized as a crucial instrument of class oppression.' Andreas Kalyvas, 'Stateless Theory: Poulantzas's Challenge to Postmodernism', in, *Paradigm Lost: State Theory Reconsidered*, eds, Stanley Aronowitz and Peter Bratsis (Minneapolis/London: University of Minnesota Press, 2002), 109.

50 Christos Boukalas, 'No exceptions: authoritarian statism. Agamben, Poulantzas and homeland security', *Critical Studies on Terrorism* 7 (2014): 112–130, 121.

51 See generally Nicos Poulantzas, *The Crisis of the Dictatorships: Portugal, Greece, Spain* (New Jersey: Humanities Press, 1976); Nicos Poulantzas, *Fascism and Dictatorship* (London: Verso, 1979).

52 Kalyvas, 'The Stateless Theory', 124.

reducible to, the military dictatorships of Southern Europe at the time. More specifically, during the first three post-war decades it became evident that the traditional, liberal form of legality structured around generally-applicable laws promulgated by national parliaments was no longer representative of reality. For Poulantzas, this transformation of the capitalist state was generally attributable to the peculiar and unstable balance of social powers that gave rise to the Keynesian state. Western European states were confronted by militant workers' movements and by strong parties of the Left. As a result, the ability of the power bloc – that is, the fractions of capital with the greatest influence on the state – to present a hegemonic plan for social organisation was destabilised. Moreover, the alleged dominance of monopolies over other fractions of capital and, importantly, the challenges posed to the Western capitalist state by the rise of wefarism, rendered the 'typical' forms of capitalist statehood and legality unable to safeguard the long-term sustainability of capitalist accumulation. This triggered a long and complicated process of transformation of Western capitalist states that manifested one or more of the following attributes: 'the subordination of the legislative branch to the executive (usually plebiscitarian in character), the abolition of separation of powers, the rise of the administrative-bureaucratic state, the crisis of the rule of law, where general, abstract, and universal laws are replaced by discretionary and arbitrary decrees'.[53] We can see, then, that Poulantzas stresses the importance of this transformation of the state for the form and function of law, with the increasing domination of the executive over the legislative branch of the state marking the end of 'the preponderance of parliament as the sanctuary of law'.[54] While there were several factors that dictated this transformation, what is of particular relevance to us is that it was the direct consequence of the rise of popular struggles in the 1970s.[55] The weakening of the representatives of the people corresponded to a transfer to a branch of the state (administration) that is not directly subject to popular pressures, and which is staffed by officeholders who, being more remote from the general public, are subject to values like internal hierarchy and obedience to the state, rather than democratic representation and political confrontation.

Poulantzas developed his analysis of authoritarian statism in the mid-1970s, just as the Keynesian state was entering into a state of generalised (and largely fatal) crisis. Since then, however, the global economy has been transformed by the impact of neoliberalism. At the same time, the dominant state form in the capitalist West has changed, and it is arguable that it no longer has the same characteristics – in particular, the dominance of the national executive – as those noted by Poulantzas in the mid-1970s. Yet the relevance of Poulantzas' analysis does not depend upon the specifics of the conjuncture he confronted, but rather, in his attempt to theorise the political dynamics he observed in the context of the economic developments and political struggles of the time. It needs to be stressed here that the concept of

53 Kalyvas, 'The Stateless Theory', 124.
54 Poulantzas, *State, Power, Socialism*, 218.
55 Ibid.

authoritarian statism attempts to capture the transformations of the state in relation to the requirements of capitalist accumulation. In a nutshell, *authoritarian statism* encapsulates the transformation of the capitalist state in the face of intensified social antagonisms and uncertain conditions for the reproduction of capitalist relations. If we accept this statement to be true, then it follows that *authoritarian statism* is a concept of broader analytical significance, which does not coincide with the specific *form* the capitalist state assumed at the time Poulantzas was writing. If we treat authoritarian statism as an analytical rather than descriptive concept, then it becomes possible to use Poulantzas' insights in order to conceptualise subsequent developments, and more specifically the rise of neoliberal capitalism.

Following this line of argument, Andreas Kalyvas has coined the term 'liberal authoritarian legalism' to describe a transfer of power from the legislative and the executive to the judiciary that has occurred, along with the revival of formal, abstract, general legal rules, since the 1980s. For Kalyvas, the heart of 'liberal authoritarian legalism' lies in 'the depoliticization and neutralization of democratic legitimacy and the divestment of the popular sovereign of its political responsibilities.'[56] This trend arises from the tension between neoliberalism, with its aspiration to spread the discipline of the market across the social spectrum, and democracy, with its egalitarian aspirations. Differently put, the judiciary is the ideal agent for consolidating market discipline. Judges are supposed to be independent from direct political pressures (such as someone picking up the phone and dictating the contents of a ruling). However, they are also insulated from popular demands and struggles through their preference for abstract and general rules and their suspicion of immediate political goals, through which representative government might try to limit the potentially harmful effects of a totalising market society. If this is indeed the case, we need not conclude that the neoliberal transformation of the state means that the concept of authoritarian statism is outdated. Rather, the dominance of the executive that Poulantzas observed has turned out to be only the first stage in 'armouring' the state against popular struggles: this antidemocratic trend has been further deepened and consolidated with the emergence of neoliberalism, which has further weakened parliaments by enhancing the judiciary and internationalising decision-making.

The rise of the judiciary is consistent with the neoliberal suspicion toward the state, which exclusively targets the legislative and executive, while praising courts as the ideal agents to enforce the rule of law. The position of the ordo-liberal Röpke in defence of expansive judicial review is telling: 'It is now advisable, to make courts, more than in the past, organs of the economy and to entrust to their decision tasks that were previously entrusted to administrative authorities.'[57]

As has already been argued, international trade regulation has been moving steadily toward more internationalised and legalised schemes since at least the 1980s:

56 Kalyvas, 'The Stateless Theory', 100.

57 Wilhelm Röpke, *The Social Crisis of Our Time*, trans., Annette and Peter Schiffer Jacobsohn (Chicago: Chicago University Press, 1950), 193.

judges have been given dispute-settlement authority, and dispute settlement has been subjected to the requirements of the (Hayekian) rule of law, which insists that law should be comprised of formal and general rules, which will facilitate predictability vis-à-vis economic decision-making. The gradual judicialisation of the dispute settlement mechanisms from GATT to WTO needs to be seen as symptomatic of the new judicial and legalistic form that authoritarian statism has assumed.

Arguably the WTO is not exceptional in this judicialisation process, even though 'the designers of the WTO have created one of the most legalized interstate dispute settlement systems worldwide.'[58] This evolution of international trade law toward a heavily judicialised model enabled the 'purification' of interpretation and application of the treaties from interventionist policy considerations that determined dispute settlement in the GATT years. In fact, the ongoing legalisation of WTO law is reflected in the fact that even diplomats chosen for *ad hoc* panels are increasingly of a legal background.[59] In this context, judges are explicitly understood as a quasi-constitutional counter-weight to governmental policies, and as Judith Goldstein argues, particularly to democratic governments, which are understood to be biased against trade liberalisation, to the extent that they need to take into consideration popular demands and electoral preferences.[60]

The substantive transformation of international trade law toward neoliberal trade policies and the judicialisation of dispute settlement should be seen as parts of the same process. With decision-making switching to judges the methodology of approaching WTO law changed as well. First, a turn to formalism, even to literalism, can be detected. For example, a 2011 study showed that 70 per cent of the AB's decisions cited dictionaries to support their reasoning.[61] This technical approach constitutes, according to Sol Picciotto, a method of technocratic legitimacy that 'tends to exclude debate about the values involved in the interpretative choices made by the adjudicator.'[62] This avoidance of value-related preoccupations is also hinted at by the insistence of the AB to reach unanimous decisions. Thus far, only six separate and two dissenting opinions have been issued, enhancing the perception that the work of the AB is simply technical. In the words of Shaffer, Elsig and Puig 'By wrapping their rulings in textual and technical reasoning and consensus decision, the AB members enhance their authority as the upholders of

58 Bernauer et al., 'Dispute Settlement Mechanism', 485.

59 José Augusto Fontoura Costa, 'Comparing WTO Panelists and ICSID Arbitrators: The Creation of International Legal Fields', *Onati Socio-Legal Series* 1, no. 4 (2011): 18, http://papers.ssrn.com/sol3/papers.cfm?abstract_id=1832382

60 'This bias towards pro-protection policy is especially evident in democratic regimes. In the absence of institutional mechanism to either diffuse pro-protectionist groups or to overcome the barriers to collective action facing those who would gain from free trade, political factors will make it difficult for politicians to consistently support open borders to trade.' Judith Goldstein, 'Trade Liberalization and Domestic Politics', in Narlikar et al., *Oxford Handbook on WTO*, 64.

61 Gregory Shaffer and Joel Trachtman, 'Interpretation and Institutional Choice at the WTO', *Virginia Journal of International Law* 52: 103–153, 115.

62 Picciotto, 'The WTO's Appellate Body', 480.

the law.'[63] Arguably, the room for policy manoeuvring and deviations from free-trade rules is substantively diminished through this formalist approach, which prioritises faithful application of the agreements over policy considerations.

Nonetheless, this literalist approach has its limits. Since textual indeterminacy remains unavoidable, the authority of the AB is much more complicated than simply enforcing rigorously the pro-liberalisation terms of WTO agreements. Perhaps much more crucially, the AB has exercised positive, constructive power in interpreting indeterminacies according to market-oriented principles. The concept of 'like products' is a good example here, since it is a core requirement of GATT that 'like products' must be treated in a 'non-discriminatory' manner.[64] Here, despite the existence of a series of potential approaches, consumers' choices and perceptions have been elevated into a central criterion. The physical properties, the end uses and the international classification of the products are also criteria adopted by the WTO, but the products being 'directly competitive or substitutable' is the central axis of the judgment whether two projects are 'like'. In turn, '[t]he context of the competitive relationship is necessarily the marketplace since this is the forum where consumers choose between different products.'[65] Hence, the AB has elevated the marketplace to the ultimate arbitrator of 'likeness', giving legal form to the neoliberal idea of a social and legal order constructed around the concept of competition and relegating environment, labour, public health or other considerations to a secondary, if not totally irrelevant position.

The preceding analysis does not exhaust the ways in which the process of judicialisation is linked to substantive alterations of international trade law, and the interaction between process and substance is also a complicated one. We can however, take them as indicators of the changes in international law and governance that have occurred at the same time that neoliberalism has come to dominate economic policy. What we see is a transformation of capitalist law and legality that transfers decision-making power to the juriciary, who are significantly insulated from political struggles, and whose normative commitment to formalism is a welcome quality for those applying and developing international economic law in neoliberal times.

Neoliberal theorists and politicians do not have a consistent view on the relationship between the national and international spheres. The use of international law to insulate the economy from the demands of the *demos* has, however, been a strategy explicitly advocated by neoliberal thinkers. Specifically, Röpke attempted to provide an account of the 'proper' relationship between the economy, the state and international legal order.[66] The ordo-liberal thinker criticised trade unions and socialist thinkers, arguing that even though internationalism has been central to socialist thinking, socialist practice consistently promoted economic policies

63 Shaffer et al., 'The Extensive Authority'.

64 See Marrakesh Agreement Establishing the World Trade Organization, Arts 1 and 3, 15 April 1994, 1867 UNTS 154 (Marrakesh Agreement).

65 Appellate Body Report, *Korea – Taxes on Alcoholic Beverages*, para. 114, WT/DS75/AB/R, WT/DS84/AB/R (18 January 1999).

66 Röpke, 'Economic Order and International Law', 210.

restrained to and dependent on the nation-state.[67] In turn, Röpke maintained that this resulted in the collapse of the nineteenth-century international order, since the 'unimpeachable legal order'[68] of free trade and private property was subjected to what he understood as the arbitrariness and unpredictability of state planning. In turn, the 'politicisation of economic life' was repeatedly identified as the source of the problem.[69] Hence, it is argued that state sovereignty, which through the rise of mass politics was often associated with popular sovereignty, had become excessive and therefore, '[t]o diminish national sovereignty is most emphatically one of the urgent needs of our time.'[70] Hence, for Rökpe internationalisation of economic law and governance was not simply about transferring sovereignty from the state to other actors: rather, internationalisation was seen as an opportunity to abolish altogether the sovereign functions that impeded 'free markets, free competition and a freely working price mechanism'.[71]

Internationalisation thus isolates significant issues from the pressures of the *demos* by transferring decision-making away from the domestic sphere and delegating it to international judges, commissions and bureaucrats, who are not answerable to the public of any state or to 'global civil society'. In the absence of the material conditions and effective political mechanisms that enable popular mobilisation and participation, law-making and governance are relatively immunised from popular pressures. The process of establishing a global, competitive, neoliberal economic order is objectively facilitated by this development in international law, which aspires to provide a homogenised legal and institutional framework that sets the 'rules of the game' on an international scale. In Schneiderman's words, it is democracies' 'capacity to take self-protective measures beyond the status quo that is threatened by the constitution-like features of transnational investment rules regime.'[72]

Extending on Poulantzas' and Kalyvas' line of argument, then, we should see the quantitative expansion and qualitative elaboration of international law as being an aspect of contemporary authoritarian statism, since international arrangements gradually replace domestic ones, further 'immunising' the processes of law-making and dispute-settlement from popular pressures and constructing a global legal order based on market imperatives. The development of international economic law, or in our specific case international trade law, did not simply denote a transfer

67 In Röpke's own words: 'But whenever an attempt was made [...] to present a socialist system in concrete practical terms, the regular and perhaps inevitable result was the blue-print of a planned economy whose geographical framework is the nation and whose political and administrative center is the national government.' Röpke, 'Economic Order and International Law', 216.

68 Ibid., 218.

69 'The logical end of this development is collectivism as a system which involves the complete politisation of the economy.' Ibid., 236.

70 Ibid., 250.

71 Ibid., 213.

72 David Schneiderman, *Constitutionalizing Economic Globalization: Investment Rules and Democracy's Promise* (Cambridge: Cambridge University Press, 2008), 14.

of powers from national to international realms, but rather, a process of reconceptualisation of the appropriate functions of law and a radical redrawing of the line between acceptable and unacceptable forms of state intervention. In turn, the target of this reconceptualisation was the 'politicisation of the economy', which had enabled questioning the centrality of private property, free competition and free price formation in economic and social organisation.

IV Conclusion

By focusing on the transformation of international trade law in the second half of the twentieth century, this chapter has shown that legalism is an important part of the transformation of the state in the age of neoliberalism. Given that neoliberalism has a tense relationship with democracy and other forms of participatory, mass politics formalisation, legalisation and judicialisation of economic governance can be seen as a core characteristic of the rise of a distinctively neoliberal legality, designed to immunise law-making from popular pressures. While international law plays a less central role in neoliberal theory than the idea of the rule of law as such, the chapter has also argued that the unprecedented development of international law is also a constitutive element of neoliberal legality. This is the case to the extent that the development of a nuanced international legal framework was essential for the advancement of a genuinely global neoliberal international economic order. To substantiate this argument, I revisited Poulantzas' arguments about authoritarian statism, as further elaborated by Kalyvas. By doing so, I have argued that the steady internationalisation and judicialisation of trade law need to be conceptualised as integral of a broader transformation of the capitalist state. The crisis of capitalist accumulation and the intensified social conflicted of the 1970s were eventually resolved through a reorganisation of capitalist power. Immunising economic decision-making from popular struggles was of paramount importance in this process, and the emergence of a formal, judicialised regime governing international trade was a crucial step in this direction. Conceptualising neoliberalism as a legalist project helps us to escape the conviction, in all strands of the legal profession, that extending the realm of law and regulation is inherently desirable. Instead, the preceding analysis shows that the quantitative expansion and qualitative refinement of international trade law have been integral to the neoliberal reorganisation of capitalism and, correspondingly, for the perpetuation and further entrenchment of relations of power and exploitation.

Part III

Human rights and neoliberalism

Chapter 7

A powerless companion

Human rights in the age of neoliberalism

Samuel Moyn

I Introduction[1]

It is increasingly common to claim that international human rights law is a neoliberal phenomenon. And certainly their common timing is right. In an important new essay, Marxist international lawyer Susan Marks compares Naomi Klein's *The Shock Doctrine* with my own recent history of international human rights, which emphasizes the 1970s as the moment of breakthrough for their ascent. Both histories, Marks observes, ascribe the newfound visibility of human rights to their promise to transcend formerly attractive political options east and west that seemed inadequate or even dangerous.[2] 'For her too', Marks acknowledges of Klein's treatment, 'the human rights movement as we know it today took shape during the 1970s. And for her too, a defining characteristic of the new movement was its non-political creed'.[3] But for Marks, Klein succeeds by unveiling the neoliberal circumstances of human rights that have permanently defined their trajectory:

> [S]he considers that a rather important aspect of the context for the movement's emergence is one Moyn omits to mention: the rise in that period of the neo-liberal version of 'private' capitalism, with its now familiar policy prescription of privatisation, deregulation and state retreat from social provision. To its influential enthusiasts then and now, *that* is the last utopia ... From

1 I am extremely grateful to Jeremy Kessler for his help in finalizing this chapter, and to the editors of *Law and Contemporary Problems* for their exceptional care in editing. [Eds: This chapter was previously published in *Law and Contemporary Problems* 77 (2014): 147–169.]

2 See Susan Marks, 'Four Human Rights Myths', in *Human Rights: Old Problems, New Possibilities*, eds, David Kinley, Wojciech Sadurski and Kevin Walton (Cheltenham: Edward Elgar, 2013). See also Naomi Klein, *The Shock Doctrine: The Rise of Disaster Capitalism* (New York: Henry Holt, 2007), 11; Samuel Moyn, *The Last Utopia: Human Rights in History* (Cambridge, MA: Harvard University Press, 2010); Samuel Moyn, 'Substance, Scale, and Salience: The Recent Historiography of Human Rights', *Annual Review of Law and Social Science* (2012): 123–40.

3 Marks, 'Four Human Rights Myths', 226.

> Klein's perspective, then, the history of human rights cannot be told in isolation from developments in the history of capitalism.[4]

(At this point Marks notes that Milton Friedman won the Nobel prize for economics in 1976, the year before Amnesty International was given the Nobel peace prize.)

Friedrich Hayek, the guru of neoliberalism, was as impressed a witness of the human rights revolution of the 1970s as anyone else. But it is interesting that, although occasionally an advocate of the constitutionalization of basic liberties like freedom of speech and press, he was in fact an acerbic critic of that revolution. In an interview, he described the spike in talk around human rights associated with Jimmy Carter's election to the American presidency as a strange fad, which (like all fashions) risked excess:

> I'm not sure whether it's an invention of the present administration or whether it's of an older date, but I suppose if you told an eighteen year old that human rights is a new discovery he wouldn't believe it. He would have thought the United States for 200 years has been committed to human rights, which of course would be absurd. The United States discovered human rights two years ago or five years ago. Suddenly it's the main object and leads to a degree of interference with the policy of other countries which, even if I sympathized with the general aim, I don't think it's in the least justified … But it's a dominating belief in the United States now.[5]

All the same, since that moment of modish popularity, the staying power of human rights has led to many more positive visions of the essential harmony – if not identity – of economic liberalism and international human rights. The Marxist left, indeed, is hardly the only source of claims concerning the synergetic relationship between the advancement of market freedoms and human rights.[6] If anything, it is much more common to promote neoliberalism as an agent of the advancement of human rights rather than to link them as malign accomplices.

Perhaps most notably, Ernst-Ulrich Petersmann argues that, although human rights law may exact some costs to efficiency, the general relationship between economic liberty and human rights is productive and strong, so much so that promoting the former and latter are not very different enterprises.[7] He writes:

4 Marks, 'Four Human Rights Myths', 226, n44.

5 Friedrich A. Hayek, interview by Robert Chitester, 1978, http://www.hayek.ufm.edu/index.php?title=Bob_Chitester_part_I&p=video1&b=930&e=1037

6 Admittedly, others nearly always construe 'human rights' as a set of abstract values rather than a set of concrete movements and legal regimes. See, e.g. John C.W. Touchie, *Hayek and Human Rights: Foundations for a Minimalist Approach to Law* (Cheltenham: Edward Elgar, 2005).

7 Ernst-Ulrich Petersmann, 'Time for a United Nations "Global Compact" for Integrating Human Rights in the Law of Worldwide Organizations: Lessons from European Integration', *European Journal of International Law* 13 (2002): 621–622.

> [E]njoyment of human rights require[s] the use of dispersed information and economic resources that can be supplied most efficiently, and most democratically, through the division of labour among free citizens and through liberal trade promoting economic welfare, the freedom of choice and the free flow of scarce goods, services, and information across frontiers in response to supply and demand by citizens.[8]

There is, accordingly, little daylight between economic liberalization and the promotion of international human rights. And though Petersmann's optimism about easy compatibility has certainly drawn their fire, mainstream international human rights lawyers generally envision a large zone of compatibility between free trade and other components of capitalism; they merely insist that the values of international human rights need to be kept separate so as to provide critical purchase on 'globalization' if and when it goes wrong.[9] In the mainstream vision, international human rights can offer a toolbox of legal and other standards to guide, tame, and 'civilize' an era of transnational market liberalization that has generally improved the human condition.[10]

This article argues that it is far too soon – analytically in the one case, and historically in the other – to sign on to either the Marxist or mainstream position about the relationship between human rights and neoliberalism. To the first position, much more analytical clarity is required to prove more than a simple case of conjuncture between the two phenomena that are sometimes too easily conflated. To the second, the record so far suggests that human rights seem fit to provide little, if any, help in remedying (let alone overturning) the development in the history of capitalism that its critics range under the heading 'neoliberalism'. In largest part that is because, although the record of capitalism in our time is highly mixed when it comes to the achievement and violation of basic human rights, its most serious victim is equality (of resources and opportunities alike) both in national and global settings – a value that the Universal Declaration of Human Rights of 1948 and the international human rights movements following in its wake do not even set out to defend.[11] Since globalizing neoliberalism and

See also Ernst-Ulrich Petersmann, 'Human Rights and International Trade Law: Defining and Connecting the Two Fields', in *Human Rights and International Trade*, eds, Frederick M. Abbott, Christine Breining-Kaufmann and Thomas Cottier (Ann Arbor, MI: University of Michigan Press, 2005).

8 Petersmann, 'Time for a United Nations', 629.

9 Philip Alston has famously alleged that Petersmann's goal was 'to hijack, or more appropriately to Hayek, international human rights.' See Philip Alston, 'Resisting the Merger and Acquisition of Human Rights by Trade Law: A Reply to Petersmann', *European Journal of International Law* 13 (2002): 815–844, 816.

10 See, e.g. David Kinley, *Civilising Globalisation: Human Rights and the Global Economy* (Cambridge: Cambridge University Press, 2009), 1–3; Rhoda E. Howard-Hassmann, *Can Globalization Promote Human Rights?* (University Park, PA: Pennsylvania State University Press, 2010).

11 See Universal Declaration of Human Rights, GA Res. 217 (III) A, UN Doc. A/RES/217(III) (Dec. 10, 1948).

international human rights emerged at the same moment and developed in parallel, there are undoubtedly connections to be found. But the interactions between human rights and neoliberalism are more subtle than Marxists so far claim. Indeed, the crucial connection is a missed connection: precisely because the human rights revolution has at its most ambitious dedicated itself to establishing a normative and actual floor for protection, it has failed to respond to – or even allowed for recognizing – neoliberalism's obliteration of the ceiling on inequality.

'Neoliberalism', especially in leftist discourse, often does massive work in diverse settings of argument, coming close through its overuse to functioning as a call for explanation rather than the real thing. And with its moral charge, it is sometimes deployed like holy water, sprinkled liberally for safety's sake to ward off evil. Although its rise as an item of discourse and apotropaic talisman reflects understandable anger, it is also symptomatic of explanatory confusion.[12] Nonetheless, as David Singh Grewal and Jedediah Purdy indicate in their introduction to a recent journal issue on the topic, citing an inadequate shorthand for the complex of individualist thought, market solutions, and state retrenchment both domestically and internationally is better than omitting these topics altogether, as American legal scholarship has so far done to its detriment.[13]

But looking beyond America, the prominence of neoliberalism as a category in scholarship about human rights means that the exact nature of the linkage of the two requires as much attention as the omission of the former from thinking about the latter. 'Human rights, as with power and money, became a means to an end of globalizing neoliberal democracy', Stephen Hopgood remarks in his much noticed recent study, in a commonplace observation.[14] And yet, so far, Marxists such as Wendy Brown, Susan Marks, and others have offered indeterminate and unsubstantiated claims that do not suffice to plausibly elevate the chronological coincidence of human rights and neoliberalism into a factually plausible syndrome. For there is a long way from historical 'coincidence' or companionship – which there certainly has been between neoliberalism and the human rights phenomenon – to actual causality and complicity. 'We would do well to take the measure of whether and how the centrality of human rights discourse might render … other political possibilities more faint', Brown has argued in a classic indictment at the center of the recent commentary.[15] Even this displacement theory, about which Brown explicitly invites further reflection rather than offering a strong

12 See, e.g. Keally McBride, 'Neoliberalism: Its Untimely Life and Timely Death' (paper presented at the American Political Science Association Annual Conference, Chicago, September 2013).

13 David Singh Grewal and Jedediah Purdy, 'Introduction: Law and Neoliberalism', *Law and Contemporary Problems* 77 (2014): 1–23.

14 Stephen Hopgood, *The Endtimes of Human Rights* (Ithaca, NY: Cornell University Press, 2013), 95.

15 Wendy Brown, '"The Most We Can Hope for …": Human Rights and the Politics of Fatalism', *South Atlantic Quarterly* 103 (2004): 461–462.

conclusion, is weak compared to the much stronger accusation of complicity that Brown and others simultaneously offer.[16]

Though it seems likely that some displacement of other schemes of justice has indeed occurred thanks to the rise of human rights, I do not think a much stronger claim is likely to work.[17] To say that human rights were coincident with or part of the context of neoliberal victory is not only not to say more – it is also not to say much. In particular, it is not to say that neoliberalism has *required* human rights to make its way in the world – or vice versa. Picayune an agenda as it might seem to specify how weakly related the ascent of human rights appears to the market fundamentalism of our time, I suggest that the finding of only a tenuous relationship between the two has substantial ramifications for judging human rights and their spectacular rise in the last few decades – and thus for assessing the mainstream position.

Excusing human rights from causally abetting the free market victory of the neoliberal age is, after all, no defense of their prominence today. It is certainly worth considering the possibility that human rights provide some sort of moral leverage against neoliberal developments. However, even if the value of the normative guidance that human rights provide is undoubted, the trouble is that it amounts to little more than a set of mostly rhetorical admonitions. Worse, by focusing on a minimum floor of human protection, human rights norms prove inadequate in facing the reality that neoliberalism has damaged equality locally and globally much more than it has basic human rights outcomes (which, in some cases, it may indeed have advanced). It is hardly less distressing, but, so far, much more justifiable to conclude that human rights have not made enough of a difference in the short timeframe and global space they share with their neoliberal *frère ennemi*. They have been condemned to watch, but have been powerless to deter. Added to the fact that human rights at least as canonically established have nothing to say about the principal value of equality that neoliberalism threatens, it seems hard to conclude that they are a useful resource in response.

If my perspective in between Marxism and the mainstream is adequate, it also follows that there is not much of critical or political value in opposing human rights out of understandable outrage at neoliberalism. Instead, the economic transformations of the current era force a heavy burden on those concerned to formulate or to find a more serious analytical account of economic transformations and to offer more robust political resistance than they have marshaled so far. And

16 See ibid. In the same essay, though tentative about displacement, Brown claims that human rights 'legitimate' neoliberalism in the form of global free trade and engage in 'an old ruse of liberal reformers, in pursuing agendas that have significant effects in excess of the explicit reform, while insist[ing] that all they are doing is a bit of good or holding back the dark.' Ibid., 461.

17 The relationship between human rights and imperial agendas is a separate matter I do not take up here, but my own view is that the case for intermittent causal relation is much stronger, for there is no denying the role of moral claims in creating legitimacy for great powers (as well as other actors).

since human rights idioms, approaches, and movements are unlikely to offer either – and, indeed, do not strive to do so when it comes to inequality – they should stick to their minimalist tasks within and outside the socioeconomic domain, in part to avoid drawing fire for abetting the stronger companion of their historical epoch.

This chapter is structured to reach these conclusions by examining a range of Marxist positions on the relationship between neoliberalism and human rights, beginning with Karl Marx's own theory of rights, both because of its intrinsic importance and its frequent application to current debates. After concluding that this theory offers only initial starting points for analyzing international human rights and the neoliberal era of capitalism alike, the chapter's next section turns to the late twentieth-century history of the companionship of the two, tracking their contemporaneous inceptions to examine their harmony and dissonance. The final section of the chapter stresses that human rights offer a minimum of protection where the real significance of neoliberalism has been to obliterate the previous limitation of inequality. Although human rights idioms, regimes, and movements have valuably formulated one approach to that floor, they have so far done little or nothing to build it, even as they surged discursively across the same era as the ceiling on hierarchy has been simply blown away.

II The Garden of Eden of the Rights of Man

It is worthwhile to begin by establishing how much work would be required – certainly far beyond that done so far – to regard human rights as an apology for 'neoliberal' capitalism, in part because of how much work Karl Marx's own texts leave to be done. And this is so for two overlapping sets of reasons. For one thing, there were the different phases in Marx's own account of rights, which provide an inadvertent reminder of how institutionally new international human rights today are. Second, there is massive distance between the globalizing capitalism to which he bore witness and our world. Even if his own work provides considerable resources for thinking about rights generally, it falls silent when it comes to the specificities of our problem, both because of the 'neoliberal' form of our capitalism as well as the globalizing reformism of our rights movements.

Marx, of course, offers his most famous criticism of 'human rights' in *On the Jewish Question*, where he takes the French Declaration of the Rights of Man and Citizen as an index of the failure of political emancipation compared to the 'human emancipation' for which he calls.[18] Yet in this early text, Marx usefully makes central (even if he fails to effectively theorize) what may have been the central fact of the rights of man for most of their history: they have long been constituted within the state.[19] There is, of course, no doubt that the political

18 See Robert C. Tucker, ed., *The Marx-Engels Reader*, 2nd edn (New York: W.W. Norton, 1978).
19 See ibid., 23–24.

language of natural rights has an elective affinity, perhaps more so with the birth and expansion of capitalist social relations, and Marx eventually understood that their reduction to his original statist framework was misleading.[20] Yet it remains of great interest that, in taking the French Revolution's Declaration of the Rights of Man and Citizen of 1789 as his early prooftext, Marx believed that a moral philosophy of natural rights in its most abstract formulations depends in history on the agency of the state (even nation-state) to be politically operationalized.[21] Marx did not take this alliance as a matter of contingent mistake; to him, it was rather a core feature of the rise of rights. Textually, to put it differently, Marx's critique of human rights is a critique of *political emancipation within the state*. If his critique is seen as going to the formal abstraction of rights, then, it is an abstraction within a (rather institutionally concrete and historically specific) forum of the political citizenship provided by the state.[22]

Marx's insistence on the limits of the state as an agent of emancipation, alongside his lack of interest in the state-making many have prized down through the era of twentieth-century decolonization, should thus not distract from the fact that *his own framing* of the significance of the rights of man in his most classical treatment fails to link them to the workings of global capital. Whether or not Marx's critique transposes easily to the abstractions of rights in moral philosophy, then, it definitely requires significant theoretical work – and ultimately, a changed account from that early essay – to apply it to modern-day international and global human rights politics. When they became a newly prestigious mobilizational and legal option, international human rights politics broke in fundamental ways with the statist framework within which Marx himself worked and the institutionalized rights politics that he observed in the French Revolution. If anything, the centrality of the state to bourgeois order indeed meant that the response of working men had to be itself globalizing, though certainly not in the mode of contemporary human rights activists.

None of this means that the entanglements of 'human rights' and 'modern capitalism' (including 'neoliberalism') do not exist, but it does mean that they are not obvious, even or especially for Marxists, who must build rather than assume an account of them. And as much as Marx's own theoretical evolution after 'On the Jewish Question' provides better grounds for success in this venture, it also leaves

20 The classic argument is C.B. MacPherson, *The Political Theory of Possessive Individualism: Hobbes to Locke* (Oxford: Oxford University Press, 1962).

21 Historians such as Richard Tuck have diagnosed a much deeper causal relationship than Marx himself perceived between the ascendancy of rights in early modern natural law theory and the perfection of modern state as the essential and long-term forum of their political meaning. See Richard Tuck, *The Rights of War and Peace: Political Thought and the International Order from Grotius to Kant* (Oxford: Oxford University Press, 2001). I followed Tuck's general argument somewhat slavishly in my own book in distinguishing international human rights. See Moyn, *The Last Utopia*, chap. 1.

22 That was why the response to a bourgeois regime of rights required the liquidation of the distinction between the state and civil society, and though perhaps not what Engels later called the 'withering away' of the state.

severe obstacles. For one thing, it is also true, as recent research has shown, that Marx himself was by no means above invoking rights as a basis of progressive reform, in spite of his apparently totalistic rejection of them before.[23] Indeed, as Andrew Sartori emphasizes, the constitutive emancipatory promise of liberalism and its rights talk as Marx understood both as much authorized intermittent criticisms of capitalism (and empire) as obfuscated their obvious depredations.[24] But the real challenge is that Marx's ultimate critique of rights is general, going to the relation between the globalization of capital, property ownership, and social abstraction, rather than anything so narrow and particular as an analysis of international human rights regimes and movements (which, if they existed in his time, did not interest him).

When he evolved beyond the juvenilia of *On the Jewish Question*, Marx altered his presentation of bourgeois rights to moderate the statist emphasis of his early account. But these theoretical shifts were really in the service of an account emphasizing how a (potentially) globalizing set of market relations required a set of social abstractions that might comfortably take formal individual rights as its legal form. Hence Marx's claim in *Capital* that the capitalist market is

> a very Eden of the innate rights of man … [There individuals] contract as free persons, who are equal before the law. Their contract is the final result in which their joint will finds a common legal expression … [E]ither in accordance with the pre-established harmony of things, or under the auspices of an omniscient providence, they all work together to their mutual advantage, for the common weal, and in the common interest.[25]

Yet even in the evolved form of Marx's critique, there is a drastic set of differences between that *general* account – which might fit, for example, the modern globalization of markets and the globalization of property rights quite well – and some *specific* account needed to capture the particularity of international human rights regimes and movements in the last several decades.[26]

23 See David Leopold, *The Young Karl Marx: German Philosophy, Modern Politics, and Human Flourishing* (Cambridge: Cambridge University Press, 2009), 150–163; Justine Lacroix and Jean-Yves Pranchère, 'Karl Marx fut-il vraiment un opposant aux droits de l'homme?: Émancipation individuelle et théorie des droits', *Revue française de science politique* 62 (2012): 433–451 (both demonstrating Marx's deployment of rights talk for the sake of emancipation).

24 Andrew Sartori, *Liberalism in Empire: An Alternative History* (Oakland, CA: University of California Press, 2014). I am very grateful to Professor Sartori for assistance with this section of the chapter.

25 Karl Marx, *Capital: A Critique of Political Economy*, trans., Ben Fowkes, 3 vols (Harmondsworth: Penguin Books, 1976), 280.

26 As Marx's own treatments imply, appeal to natural and human rights remained more common in his own era as cited rationales for the protection of free contract and private property. In fact neoliberals today refer much more rarely to the justificatory basis of natural or human rights than their nineteenth-century forebears did in defense

After all, neoliberal capitalism is a specific episode in the history of capitalism that Marx never knew. More important for my purposes here, today, human rights are often self-consciously presented (though not with great plausibility, as I ultimately argue) as a force that can or will moderate or even reverse the evils of the current form of global market relations. Stereotypically, and to some extent really, human rights legal orders and mobilizational politics have lost their associations to the defense of freedom of contract and private property – there are other bodies of law, and other movements, for that purpose. Rather, in human rights regimes from the United Nations processes to treaty mechanisms, and in human rights movements from Amnesty International to global antipoverty campaigns, the goal is to ameliorate the suffering of others or even insist upon the basis for justified, though minimal, redistribution. Whatever one wants to say about human rights as they exist today, in short, must depart radically from Marx's early work, and build substantially on his later work. And though Marx could not have theorized either neoliberalism or human rights as they are now known, he might not have been surprised to learn that the chief objection to the latter is that they share the same historical era as the former, without unsettling it.

III Human rights and neoliberal economics: harmony and dissonance

Although the broad outlines of the emergence of neoliberalism have been and continue to be the subject of an accelerating and exciting literature, in the final analysis the origins are fairly straightforward. As the prospect of state-led growth and redistribution loomed in the middle of the twentieth century, Friedrich Hayek and his initially obscure compatriots, offering a complex revival of nineteenth-century economic liberalism, linked the emergence of the Western welfare state to the communist planned economy (even though, in fact, the leaders of welfare states were about to enter a bitter global struggle with their communist opposite numbers). Thirty years later, in the midst of the 1970s, the neoliberals suddenly and surprisingly found in the economic crisis of the welfarist project an opening for their views.[27] The rest of neoliberalism's history since that breakthrough moment in well-known: the evisceration of the regulatory state in the North Atlantic industrial zone together with an international program towards the global south (as well as, perhaps most spectacularly, formerly communist

of their economic liberalism, presumably because reformists and humanitarians have so successfully captured the language for their cause. Compare Robert Green McCloskey, 'Judicial Conservatism and the Rights of Man', in *American Conservatism in the Age of Enterprise 1865–1910* (Cambridge, MA: Harvard University Press, 1951), chap. 5, with Samuel Moyn, 'Nationalism and Capitalism as Nineteenth-Century Rights Movements', in *Oxford Handbook of Human Rights History*, ed., Devin O. Pendas (Oxford: Oxford University Press, forthcoming) (both demonstrating the popularity of libertarian rights talk in the nineteenth century).

27 See Angus Burgin, *The Great Persuasion: Reinventing Free Markets since the Depression* (Cambridge, MA: Harvard University Press, 2012).

Eastern Europe) to facilitate capital movement to the detriment of opposing forces.[28] Strikingly, this barebones narrative has numerous parallelisms to the history of the emergence of human rights. After all, human rights also revive a version of classical liberalism in new form. Intellectually, international human rights were not new in the 1970s but enjoyed new practical circumstances in the middle of that decade that made them prestigious overnight. And during the 1970s (as well as today), the premier target of international human rights politics was (and continues to be) the postcolonial and developmentalist state. These coincidences seem to be (in the Marxist phrase) 'no accident'.

The most plausible explanation for these facts is that human rights and neoliberalism shared both a predecessor and a target: a developmentalist statism that, while certainly present in the welfarist West and North, found its most famous expressions in Eastern Europe and the global south. Put differently, the paired breakthroughs of human rights and neoliberalism shared common institutional foes and especially negative conditions as those foes lost prestige. A national welfarist commitment found across the North Atlantic, normally defended in collectivist terms, was on the wane just as human rights and neoliberalism began enjoying success, and the same was even more true of the developmentalist vocation of the postcolonial nation-state to prioritize rapid growth, often by pursuing economic autarky. Without their departure, it seems hard to imagine that either international human rights or neoliberal frameworks and policies would have begun their rapid ascent in the mid-1970s, which gave them a kindred trajectory against a shared prior background.

Furthermore, neoliberalism and human rights share key ideological building blocks. Most obviously, they share a commitment to the prime significance of the individual, whose freedoms matter more than collectivist endeavors, even when those are justified on the grounds that they will generally advance the well-being of individuals. More controversially, their shared antipathy towards, or at least suspicion of, the state, and especially the nation-state, also seems plain, since both reject its moral credentials (even as both rely on its agency for enacting policy reform).

28 On intellectual foundations, aside from Burgin, see also Serge Audier, *Néo-libéralisme(s): Une archéologie intellectuelle* (Paris: Grasset, 2012). To date the general histories of neoliberalism are surprisingly intellectual, and nothing comparably synthetic exists on enacted policies of the 1970s and since. But for early pictures and building blocks, see David Harvey, *A Brief History of Neoliberalism* (Oxford: Oxford University Press, 2005); *The Road from Mont Pèlerin: The Making of the Neoliberal Thought Collective*, eds, Diethelm Plehwe and Philip Mirowski (Cambridge, MA: Harvard University Press, 2009); see also Colin Leys, *Market-Driven Politics: Neoliberal Democracy and the Public Interest* (London: Verso, 2003); Johanna Bockman, *Markets in the Name of Socialism: The Left-Wing Origins of Neoliberalism* (Stanford, CA: Stanford University Press, 2011); Jamie Peck, *Constructions of Neoliberal Reason* (Oxford: Oxford University Press, 2013). For the response to recent capitalist setbacks, with heavy emphasis on the economics profession (rather than structural forces), see Philip Mirowski, *Never Let a Serious Crisis Go to Waste: How Neoliberalism Survived the Financial Meltdown* (London: Verso, 2013).

Though clearly neoliberalism and human rights share several negative conditions and ideological building blocks, the question is whether these common traits obscure much more than they reveal about the causal interdependence of the two phenomena – or, more accurately, lack thereof. After all, the general affinities of human rights with market fundamentalism only go so far. To state the obvious, for human rights' many partisans, they are a discourse of hope and reform and have typically been directed at the totalitarian and authoritarian state. That state persists in many places today, in response to which human rights advocates continue to engage in their informational politics without any conscious commitment to a particular scheme of economic relations (or perhaps more accurately, with a conscious though frequently separate commitment to unspecified visions of social justice). The ongoing critique of the atrocity, despotism, and misrule of the state in which the human rights movement overwhelmingly engages hardly amounts to a grim recipe for rollback of the national welfare state and could not possibly entail that rollback on its own.

And so, very quickly in the assessment of how human rights have tracked the emergence of a neoliberal age, one is pushed onto the ground of troubling chronological simultaneity, negative conditions, vague descriptive affinity. All of these perhaps authorize suspicions of weak complicity, but hardly of more dastardly synergy, between neoliberalism and human rights. And in spite of these parallelisms between the two phenomena, it is an altogether different matter whether the moment of success in the 1970s that each enjoyed depended on the success of the other. There are, in fact, many reasons to doubt that this is the case.

With their scalar novelty as global principles informing a transnational political movement, human rights were resurrected under very specific circumstances from their entombment in obscure United Nations documents and procedures (including the Universal Declaration of Human Rights of 1948 itself and the international supervision some envisaged on its basis). There were three great causal factors that led to their dissemination outside the United Nations: (1) the loss of faith in Cold War paradigms of personal engagement (and notably the loss of faith in socialism) in favor of a new and putatively 'antipolitical' sort of movement; (2) the rise of human rights as a language of state legitimacy in the international system, surprisingly sponsored first and foremost by American presidents along with some West European leaders; and (3) the achievement of decolonization, which, from Western capitals, often seemed to cry out for a new form of rights-based international supervision that suddenly seemed relevant.[29]

For one episode that suggests that the coincidence of the parallel breakthrough of neoliberalism with the emergence of international human rights politics may

29 See Moyn, *The Last Utopia*. For even more factors, see also Jan Eckel, 'The Rebirth of Politics from the Spirit of Morality: Explaining the Human Rights Revolution of the 1970s', in *The Breakthrough: Human Rights in the 1970s*, eds, Jan Eckel and Samuel Moyn (Philadelphia, PA: University of Pennsylvania Press, 2013). On the American case, see Barbara J. Keys, *Reclaiming American Virtue: The Human Rights Revolution of the 1970s* (Cambridge, MA: Harvard University Press, 2014), 75–152.

explain little, consider the example of the southern cone of the Americas after 1973. Notoriously, General Augusto Pinochet after his 1973 coup adopted Milton Friedman as an adviser, and the neoliberal Mont Pèlerin Society held meetings in Chile. Indeed, Naomi Klein takes this example as the starting point in her history of neoliberal 'shock'.[30] In a very brief section of her book, the most popular history of neoliberalism ever written, Klein takes up how human rights imposed 'blinders' on the relationship between capitalism and terror.[31] Instead, she rightly says, Amnesty International took a neutral attitude toward structural matters (like the class struggle and ongoing counterrevolution Marxists saw) in order to focus on an informational politics that merely singled out incontestable state abuses.[32] Marks agrees that 'where the effects of neo-liberal reconstruction began to bite, activists confined their criticism to the denunciation of abuses, leaving unchallenged the conditions in which those abuses had become possible'.[33]

But although it is true (indeed, centrally important) that the coalescence of a new sort of transnational-rights movement in response to Latin American misdeeds confined itself to state crimes, it is important to be clear about what is and is not being said. No one asserts that this early instance of a now-familiar sort of informational activism was a cause of either the coups themselves or the disarmament of other sorts of criticism against the misdeeds of Pinochet's government or other new authoritarian regimes.[34] Klein, unlike Marks, registers clearly why, if contributory blame falls on human rights optics, it is really only with regard to the regime's external critics – for, at that point in history, its internal opponents had no choice but to narrow their focus and ignore the political economy of state terror. 'Every facet of the human rights movement was functioning under highly restricted circumstances … Inside the affected countries … they didn't talk about the political or economic agendas behind the disappearances because to do so was to risk being disappeared themselves'.[35] Klein could have added that the coalescence of a transnational human rights movement, for all the price that movement paid in muting structural critique, functioned in coalitional ways quite differently from a more divisive revolutionary politics. But it remains true that the international left was alive and well, and part of the success of human rights in the 1970s was due to the left's own failure either to escape savage repression in a range of countries or to successfully bring together a coalition to denounce dictatorial

30 Klein, *The Shock Doctrine*, 7.
31 Ibid., 118–121.
32 Ibid., 118–119.
33 Marks, 'Four Human Rights Myths', 9.
34 One would need a much more intricate story to make the latter case, of the sort attempted (to my knowledge) only in the case of Uruguayan exiles after the coup in their own country in the summer of 1973; and the substitutional story about their peregrinations towards human rights as opposed to inherited leftism took long into the later decades. See Vania Markarian, *Left in Transformation: Uruguayan Exiles and the Latin American Human Rights Networks, 1967–1984* (New York: Routledge, 2005), 67–106.
35 Klein, *The Shock Doctrine*, 149.

misdeeds with equal success as human rights movements. It is true that Klein concludes that 'the human rights movement also helped the Chicago School ideology to escape from its first bloody laboratory virtually unscathed'.[36] Yet the blame it deserves in this regard seems rather negligible compared to a host of other forces – including failures and mistakes on the left at what remained a very open moment in history. Further, as Klein acknowledges, the human rights 'movement unquestionably played a decisive role in forcing an end to the junta's worst abuses'.[37]

As for the rest of Klein's book, which proceeds through the present, nowhere else does it mention human rights movements (except to rely serially on their information in order to frame her critique). And in any case, much more interesting than a debatable causal linkage between neoliberalism and human rights in the 1970s is the two movements' ongoing companionship as they both entered adolescence in the 1980s and achieved close to full capture of their respective realms of ethical and economic governance, both on national and international scenes, in the 1990s. Even as the transnational left remained alive and well in the 1970s across the world, in the 1980s and 1990s (and indeed, through today) human rights frameworks came and continue to come close to occupying the imagination of reformist-minded individuals and groups the world over – and thus deserve much larger causal association with a range of phenomena. (If there has been 'social resilience' in the face of various neoliberal successes worth emphasizing, the left has not fared as well, in practice and perhaps in theory too.[38])

And yet it remains a completely open research question how exactly to frame the relationship of the human rights explosion with neoliberal victory, in Latin America and especially beyond. Was it the same everywhere and all along? I do not think so, for the allegation that human rights silenced structural and 'political' criticisms of what amounted to a neoliberal era became much more valid and convincing as time went on. But there is still the work to accomplish to say even that much. As Mary Nolan cautiously and insightfully puts it, 'There is no single relationship between human rights and market fundamentalism across countries and types of rights'.[39] The same observation applies across time. The history of the initially distant companionship remains to be written.

36 Klein, *The Shock Doctrine*, 149.
37 Ibid., 147.
38 See *Social Resilience in the Neoliberal Era*, eds, Peter A. Hall and Michèle Lamont (New York: Cambridge University Press, 2013).
39 Mary Nolan, 'Human Rights and Market Fundamentalism in the Long 1970s', in *Towards a New Moral World Order: Menschenrechtspolitik und Völkerrecht seit 1945*, eds, Norbert Frei and Annette Weinke (Göttingen: Wallstein Verlag, 2013), 174. The essay is a promissory note for a major research project that is intended to spell out the relationship in careful detail. See also Mary Nolan, 'Gender and Utopian Visions in a Post-utopian Era: Americanism, Human Rights, Market Fundamentalism', *Central European History* 44 (2011): 13–36.

To me, it already seems clear that a better way to frame the relationship between neoliberalism and human rights, at least based on current research, is in terms of parallel trajectories, with the tragic consequence that (as some of Marks's own brilliant work implies) structural insight into the root causes of social suffering went missing at the time that it was badly needed.[40] Yet this result occurred only in small part because human rights became a more coalitionally successful prism for interpreting and addressing injustice than other imaginable frameworks. It is possible (as I have argued in *The Last Utopia*) for the prestige and prominence of international human rights to be symptomatic of a loss of structural accounts of social relations, without their being causally responsible or morally culpable for it.[41] If such modes of thought have been lacking due to the 'superficiality' of the informational focus of human rights politics, it is not as if those politics are alone or even primarily to blame. The failure of a convincing structuralism and the programmatic aphasia that resulted is the work of many forces, and it is implausible to believe that either has gone missing thanks primarily to human rights hegemony.

If all of the above holds – and one assumes that historical coincidence is not necessarily a causal relationship – then the analysis becomes much less one about blame (or excusal) and much more about the failure of structural modes of thinking and more activist political strategies to retain widespread appeal. Human rights look more like a symptom of a much broader syndrome, and the point of criticizing them changes accordingly. It becomes about convincing their adherents that, although serviceable for some tasks (like singling out state abuses), human rights fail at others, and need to be supplemented by both new frameworks of analysis and new modes of intra- and transnational activism.

IV The failure of human rights in the socioeconomic domain

In his classic *A Brief History of Neoliberalism*, David Harvey is surprisingly generous to the birth of human rights, though he is well positioned to see early on that it coincided with the trajectory of his own object of study. He notes:

> The universalism of rights has been and can be used with progressive aims in minds. The tradition that is most spectacularly represented by Amnesty International, Médecins sans frontières, and others cannot be dismissed as a mere adjunct of neoliberal thinking. The whole history of humanism (both of the Western – classically liberal – and various non-Western versions) is too complicated for that.[42]

40 See Susan Marks, 'Human Rights and Root Causes', *Modern Law Review* 74 (2011): 57–78.
41 See Moyn, *The Last Utopia*.
42 Harvey, *A Brief History*, 178.

And in spite of various criticisms of human rights that are easily made – their limitation to first generation liberties, their cooptation by imperial projects, their nondemocratic credentials even when intervention abroad takes nonmilitary form, or their elitist distance from grassroots politics – Harvey concludes it is a mistake to dismiss them. Instead of 'eschew[ing] all appeal to universals as fatally flawed' and 'abandon[ing] all mention of rights as an untenable imposition of abstract, market-based ethics as a mask for the restoration of class power', in the end it would be 'unfortunate to abandon the field of rights to neoliberal hegemony. There is a battle to be fought, not only over which universals and what rights should be invoked in particular situations but also over how universal principles and conceptions of rights should be constructed'.[43]

However, that hypothetical apology for some version of universalism or even some version of human rights should not lead to complacency. It cannot substitute for an inquiry into how much of a difference that the actual, so-far-enacted forms of universalistic human rights law and policy have made – notably with respect to the economic arrangements that neoliberalism has transformed.[44] In this regard, a harsh and unforgiving verdict on international human rights politics seems necessary in order to stave off sentimental hopes and to promote intellectual commitments and practical mobilization that will do better. If the human rights movement is the weak and subordinate doppelgänger of its neoliberal brother – with whom it is joined in a mysterious common destiny but to be dragged without providing direction – then some other sort of opposition is necessary in both the short and long run.

Recently, empirical political scientists have adopted the goal of verifying whether human rights law makes any difference – that is to say, whether it leads to any positive outcomes. In my view, the language of human rights has worked well in robbing legitimacy from certain extreme regime forms, although it is highly controversial whether human rights law actually played a causal role in the political transformation in the former Soviet bloc, Latin American autocracies, and elsewhere. And, in any event, any study of the uses of human rights law needs to incorporate attention to its misuses. Skeptical of the human rights mobilization across borders, leading empirical analyst Beth Simmons has convincingly argued that where the political and material circumstances of modern citizenship already exist, human rights law allows an additional tool of domestic mobilization, beyond even that made available by constitutional law, at least when it comes to norms like freedom of speech and integrity of the human body.[45] Harvey's optimism about the emancipatory possibilities of rights-claiming is most plausible in these cases. However, empirical political scientists so far provide no case for the

43 Harvey, *A Brief History*, 178–79.

44 See Samuel Moyn, 'Do Human Rights Treaties Make Enough of a Difference?', in *Cambridge Companion to Human Rights Law*, eds, Conor Gearty and Costas Douzinas (Cambridge: Cambridge University Press, 2012).

45 See Beth A. Simmons, *Mobilizing for Human Rights: International Law in Domestic Politics* (New York: Cambridge University Press, 2011), 151–171.

productive uses of human rights norms regarding economic and social entitlements. It is indeed remarkable that Simmons, Kathryn Sikkink, and others who hope to redeem human rights from cynicism about their negligible effects have so far focused exclusively on some rights to the detriment of others – especially rights purporting to afford protections in the socioeconomic domain.

A brief, and therefore necessarily superficial, survey of the shortcomings of human rights norms and movements with the structural transformations of the era of market fundamentalism in mind must start with a basic and rarely-made point: in their legalized forms, human rights do not purport to provide an egalitarian agenda. It is perfectly possible to imagine a fully achieved local and global regime of human rights protection that simultaneously features the worst hierarchy of wealth and other primary goods known to history. Indeed, in some ways, grasping the paradoxical relationship of human rights and so-called neoliberalism amounts to seeing how thorough a disjuncture there is between an agenda of economic and social rights protection and a more ambitious egalitarian agenda.[46] When it comes to the sorts of concerns addressed by the International Covenant for Economic, Social and Cultural Rights, it is not how much they promise but how little that needs to receive more emphasis, since the Covenant strives for a minimum floor of protection in domains like housing, health, and food, rather than a fuller bodied egalitarianism.

It is popular, and understandable, to focus on those episodes (Pinochet's Chile, for example) where neoliberal policies have gone along with state repression – which Klein's indictment of the shock doctrine dramatizes (or sensationalizes). But, in certain ways, it seems much more disturbing to observe that neoliberal victories are perfectly compatible with full respect for not just civil and political liberties, but also for economic and social rights. If one extrapolates the most extreme possible illustration of this point, it is perfectly possible to imagine an alternate reality in which one man personally owns everything, but with all the provisions of the Universal Declaration of Human Rights nonetheless honored (through his subsistence spending). Even the much-ridiculed promise in the Universal Declaration's Article 27 of paid vacations is completely harmonious with a world controlled by a galloping hierarchy of means.[47] Society has indeed headed towards a scenario in the last thirty years where a formerly egalitarian impulse has sometimes successfully been displaced, as inequality has spiked, by an agenda in which a set of protections alleviates the most abject destitution. Generalizing drastically, it is fair to say that the present era of world history is one in which a floor has been partially built to save the wretched of the earth from the worst

46 For a less oppositional view that nonetheless recognizes the different vocations of (canonically established) economic rights and theories of overall social justice, see Jeremy Waldron, 'Socioeconomic Rights and Theories of Justice' (Public Law & Legal Theory Research Paper Series Working Paper No. 10–79, New York University School of Law, New York, 2010), http://papers.ssrn.com/sol3/papers.cfm?abstract_id=1699898

47 See Universal Declaration of Human Rights.

suffering, even as the ceiling for hierarchical wealth concentration has been obliterated.[48]

The conceptual point, in other words, is that an economic and social rights agenda is different – and much more minimalist – than an egalitarian agenda. It is perfectly possible for one to succeed as the other fails. The historical point is that the ends of the first agenda have often been prioritized – and sometimes achieved – across an era during which the ends of the second agenda have been forsaken. But two crucial qualifications are necessary to understand the historically juxtaposed trajectories of the two agendas. For one thing, for all the progress made in saving humanity from the most extreme sorts of immiseration, much remains to be done even to provide a floor of basic protection. No one wants to trivialize social and economic rights protection, even in the name of a plausible indictment of aphasia concerning broader patterns of wealth and income distribution and rising inequality. Second, even successes in the socioeconomic domain have hardly been due to the application of a normative framework of human rights, the birth of a formal regime of human rights law, or the mobilizational activism of any human rights movement. In fact, the lion's share of poverty reduction in the last few decades (indeed, given the population numbers involved, in world history by far) is due to a single factor: the policies of the Chinese state.[49] And although a wide range of factors account for the remainder of poverty reduction – food and water access, health improvement, and so on – it does not seem as if human rights protection or promotion as frameworks or projects rank high among them, if they figure on the list at all.

Now consider this deflationary perspective about the value of economic and social rights agendas (set off from the protection of those rights achieved through other frameworks or thanks to other means) by starting with domestic or national protection and then turning to more transnational and global protection. There is no doubt that, after the first phase of human rights history in the 1970s and 1980s, during which a global dialogue concerning economic and social rights was largely absent, such discourse has surged. But, sadly, this rhetorical and framing (or, more generously, standard-setting) work has caused no shifts in real-world outcomes independently. This is most graphically clear when it comes to the highly prestigious model of judicial enforcement of socioeconomic rights, especially when national judiciaries interpret constitutional norms in the spirit of international human rights law (notably by relying on its notion of a minimum core of protection).

48 See Thomas Piketty, *Capital in the Twenty-First Century*, trans., Arthur Goldhammer (Cambridge, MA: Harvard University Press, 2014).

49 According to one source, China brought more than 600 million people out of poverty across the era of neoliberalism (1980–2010), accounting for three-quarters of all poverty reduction worldwide. See 'Towards the End of Poverty', *The Economist*, last modified June 1, 2013, available at http://www.economist.com/news/leaders/21578665-nearly-1-billion-people-have-been-taken-out-extreme-poverty-20-years-world-should-aim

For many years, South Africa was credited as the laboratory where these developments were pioneered, especially after the landmark *Grootboom* case.[50] In particular, for several years, some leading American academics praised the 'democracy-forcing' manner in which South African courts both advanced socioeconomic rights and respected democratic legitimacy when it came to policy choices.[51] On this interpretation, courts could invalidate policies that failed to respect a designated minimum core of socioeconomic rights protection while refusing to craft enforcement remedies of their own, thereby prompting democratic branches of government to do so.[52] But especially on this minimalist and noninterventionist model, the final results have been disappointing: it turns out that the South African judiciary, instead of encouraging legislative or political action, forced the democratic branches into a non-response. Unfortunately, it is plausible to conclude that judicial enforcement has failed to make a great deal of difference, both in South Africa and beyond.[53] In particular, as David Landau has shown, enforcement of economic rights by courts tends to favor the well-off (such as pensioners defending entitlements against state rollback under budgetary pressure) rather than the weakest and most vulnerable.[54] Of course, the failure of judicial enforcement of socioeconomic rights does not mean that other attempts to protect socioeconomic rights have necessarily failed. But, so far, there is no powerful evidence confirming the value that a human rights framework brings to the reformulation of citizenship in a welfarist direction thanks to other forces (for example, partisan mobilization, which Simmons has credited for improvement when it comes to political and civil rights).[55]

Meanwhile, in international law, there is currently a burgeoning debate about how international human rights norms do or might tame or counteract globalization, especially in its recent neoliberal mode. This debate has exploded in two concurrent arenas: international trade law and policy on the one hand, and corporate social responsibility on the other. But the most generous thing to say is that it is too early for much more than the declaration of normative applicability of human rights principles in either domain.

50 See *Republic of South Africa v. Grootboom* 2001 (1) SA 46 (CC) (S. Afr.) (vindicating social and economic rights of applicants and forcing government policy to implement them).

51 See Cass R. Sunstein, *Designing Democracy: What Constitutions Do* (New York: Oxford University Press, 2001), 221–38; Mark Tushnet, *Weak Courts, Strong Rights: Judicial Review and Social Welfare Rights in Comparative Constitutional Law* (Princeton, NJ: Princeton University Press, 2009), chaps 6–8.

52 See Sunstein, *Designing Democracy.* It is a story that likely seemed especially appealing to Americans because of their own country's failure to constitutionalize social rights at the zenith of liberal judicial power and persistent worries since of the political power of the charge that judges might 'legislate from the bench'.

53 See Paul O'Connell, 'The Death of Socio-Economic Rights', *Modern Law Review* 74 (2011): 532–554.

54 See David Landau, 'The Reality of Social Rights Enforcement', *Harvard International Law Journal* 53 (2011): 189–247.

55 See Simmons, *Mobilizing for Human Rights.*

Petersmann and many others have argued that, by and large, the relationship between globalization and human rights is essentially one of mutual reinforcement or even common identity, especially when rights of property and free enterprise are made the key to the enjoyment of other human goods since property rights and free enterprise allow the funding for these other goods to materialize.[56] The more that free trade is allowed to maximize wealth for all, the better the outcomes will be across all dimensions of concern that human rights aim to cover. The response of mainstream human rights scholars to this claim is to insist on the separability and priority of the norms of which they are the stewards, guarding them against being falsely represented as simple side effects or fringe benefits of some other project, like economic growth.[57] Although optimists in the mainstream continue to hold out hope for 'linkage' in the trade arena and the rise of rights principles within corporate social responsibility, it is hard to conclude that the grounds for hope are justified on the basis of the record so far.[58]

In perhaps the most developed version of this mainstream account, David Kinley has argued that if globalization is tweaked in the name of external international human rights standards that it sometimes regrettably fails to respect, it can indeed provide the benefits that its more naïve enthusiasts celebrate as automatic.[59] His position is that, if the equally unsalutary extremes of uncritical partisanship and skeptical demonization of globalizing markets are avoided, the large amount of overlap between market forces and human rights can be discovered and 'crossovers and complementarities' between the two maximized.[60] For Kinley and others writing in this vein, neoliberal market fundamentalists are bad apples who inappropriately extend their otherwise healthy respect for the ability of free trade and multinational corporations to raise humanity out of indigence, and transform this respect into the mistaken beliefs that there are no defects to globalizing capital and that all human goods are advanced by it. Conversely, critics of 'neoliberalism' refuse to see that globalization has progressive features and believe that it is purely evil.[61] With a prophylaxis against the extremes, the task of ethical globalization is where hope for the future lies.

Yet just as in the case of social rights prospectively enforced by judicial authority, it is unsurprising that in both international trade law and corporate social

56 See Petersmann, 'Time for a United Nations'.
57 See Alston, 'Resisting the Merger'.
58 Petersmann has made much clearer in response to the polemics of a decade ago that he does not regard 'linkage' of human rights and trade liberalization to be solely on the latter's terms, thus making his proximity to mainstream optimists about the possibility of finding a zone of overlap between capitalism and human rights (and vice versa) clearer than before. See Ernst-Ulrich Petersmann, 'The Promise of Linking Trade and Human Rights', in *Linking Global Trade and Human Rights: New Policy Space in Hard Economic Times*, eds, Daniel Drache and Lesley A. Jacobs (New York: Cambridge University Press, 2014).
59 See Kinley, *Civilising Globalisation*.
60 ibid., 32.
61 Howard-Hassman, *Can Globalization Promote Human Rights?*

responsibility, human rights have proved distressingly ineffective, and this seems unlikely to change.[62] To be sure, human rights have made discursive inroads, albeit surprisingly recently, in the trade debate. As late as 2006, when World Trade Organization (WTO) Director-General Pascal Lamy offered a call in Santiago to move beyond the Washington Consensus, human rights did not figure into the discussion.[63] But, then again, the raft of criticism of the Washington Consensus before that date rarely appealed to human rights.[64] (It more frequently insisted that trade arrangements pay developmental benefits for the worst off rather than that they respect human rights.) With surprising speed, however, the intersection of international trade and human rights has taken on something of the character of an obligatory topic in WTO circles, and it seems plausible (though, as noted above, no one has undertaken to prove it empirically) that, in the areas of labor regulation and pharmaceutical patents, human rights have had some salutary effects in framing claims and even in promoting better outcomes.

But it is another matter to hypothesize much of a general reorientation of trade law by international human rights norms, law, or politics. Even mainstream analysts acknowledge that human rights norms have made little rhetorical headway in trade debates, and although the WTO's dispute resolution mechanism has teeth, it is not a plausible agent for the general advancement of human rights outcomes.[65] Andrew Lang's brilliant essay on neoliberal trade law sympathetically considers what would work, compared to recent history, in which human rights have provided little beyond discursive sensitization.[66] Lang plausibly worries that it is only a reform of the collective purposes of the trade regime itself that would provide better normative guidance (and, one might add, more robust politicization both in theory and practice).[67] A focus on the effect of trade on human rights law from the outside, as it were, has the function:

> of occluding the question of collective purpose in the conduct of international economic governance. Where critical voices should be generating a debate

62 See *Economic Globalisation and Human Rights*, eds, Wolfgang Benedek, Koen de Feyter and Fabrizio Marrella, EIUC Studies on Human Rights and Democratization (Cambridge: Cambridge University Press, 2011) (providing survey of the human rights prospects in diverse areas of economic law).

63 See Pascal Lamy, Director-General, World Trade Organization, 'Humanising Globalisation' (speech, Santiago, Chile, January 30, 2006), http://www.wto.org/english/news_e/sppl_e/sppl16_e.htm

64 See ibid.

65 According to Kinley, 'I have lost count of the number of trade specialists (lawyers, economists, national and international bureaucrats, and academics) who roll their eyes whenever mention is made of human rights and trade.' Kinley, *Civilising Globalisation*, 91. On dispute resolution, see James Harrison, *The Human Rights Impact of the World Trade Organisation* (Oxford: Hart Publishing, 2006).

66 See Andrew Lang, *World Trade Law after Neoliberalism: Reimagining the Global Economic Order* (Oxford: Oxford University Press, 2011).

67 Ibid., 190–220.

> about the fundamental purposes of global trade governance, instead they have given rise to a discussion of the relative priority to be accorded to the trade project vis-à-vis other projects of international order. What should be a debate about re-opening space for discussing the collective purposes of global trade governance, instead has to a large extent become a debate about the appropriate allocation of authority between the global trade regime and other centres of regulatory and political authority [like human rights law] … [A]ttempts to integrate consideration of 'social' values and objectives into the trade regime are unlikely to bear much fruit unless they are accompanied by a much more fundamental challenge to prevailing understandings of the nature and purpose of the trade regime.[68]

Lang himself casts this possible move as a return to the 'embedded' liberalism of the immediate post-World War II years, and he thinks human rights are potentially part of the normative vocabulary that would provide this return or renewal.[69] Whether or not he is persuasive on either count, it seems hard to doubt his conclusion that the superficiality of the effects of human rights politics on trade outcomes so far demands some other approach.

Similar observations apply to corporate social responsibility, which has a history that is even shorter with regard to the incorporation of human rights norms, but which is subject to a parallel analysis as that of international trade law. Indeed, the rise of human rights in the governance of corporations (especially among multinational corporations) is not only more recent but has come about in explicitly nonlegal, 'moral' form. Famously, after the death of the UN Norms on the Responsibilities of Transnational Corporations and Other Business Enterprises with Regard to Human Rights, John Ruggie stepped in as special representative to offer 'pragmatic' and nonlegal Guiding Principles on Business and Human Rights, approved by the Human Rights Council in 2011.[70] Charitably, it is far too early for optimism about the meaningful chastening of corporations simply because of the existence of these principles, especially given the step away from legality (and sometimes rights themselves) that Ruggie controversially took in order to make consent toward them possible.

As a general matter, mainstream proponents of human rights mechanisms in the socioeconomic domain place faith in what one might call an 'infiltrative' model of

68 Ibid., 10–11. However, Lang, I believe, goes too far in saying that a human rights strategy is 'inadvertently complicit in the basic neoliberal move of occluding' collective purpose – unless it could be shown that human rights seriously obstruct it, as opposed to distract from or simply fail to reach it.

69 Ibid., 313–354.

70 John Gerard Ruggie, *Report of the Special Representative of the Secretary-General on the Issue of Human Rights and Transnational Corporations and Other Business Enterprises*, UN Doc. A/HRC/17/31 (Mar. 21, 2011). See also John Gerard Ruggie, *Just Business: Multinational Corporations and Human Rights* (New York: W.W. Norton, 2013).

politics, in which what is introduced as apparently harmless subterfuge will end up creating conditions for a powerful threat. But Ruggie's principles seem even less likely to change behavior than other generally empty Trojan horses that the human rights movement has built across its short history. Of course, this hardly implies that the new principles are worthless – let alone so accommodating as to provide collusive shelter to global corporate power. Time alone will tell if they transcend their current uselessness, but it is not a good bet.

In an era when human rights chiefly have a rhetorical value in international trade and corporate responsibility alike, the main effect they do risk is a compensatory one, even as the chief practical challengers of neoliberalism, from the Seattle protests against the WTO of 1999 to Occupy Wall Street fifteen years later, generally skirt the normative claims, legal regimes, and mobilizational strategies of human rights in favor of other rubrics and styles. As Lang puts it:

> it is important not to overstate the extent to which human rights have been adopted more broadly as the language of the global justice movement. For every NGO that adopts a rights perspective or uses rights language, there are many more which do not, and still more who do so only partially or tangentially.[71]

Alas, this does not mean that anyone is, as of yet, in possession of a plausible framework of opposition to market fundamentalism, either intellectually or practically. But this hardly makes human rights necessary or inevitable as a means of reorienting economic affairs, especially given their failures to change the world so far.

V Conclusion: forms of criticism of human rights

Whatever the obscure prehistories of international human rights and global neoliberalism were up until the 1970s, when both began to ascend in prominence, each of these phenomena enjoyed only minor successes until the era surrounding the end of the Cold War, which provided each an extraordinary space of opportunity. The World Conference on Human Rights, which took place in Vienna in 1993, provided a moment of imaginative relaunching of human rights corresponding to the founding of the WTO in 1995. The trouble is that so far – and in contrast to their signal role in targeting and stigmatizing totalitarian and authoritarian states – human rights have remained chiefly rhetorical in their inroads into the socioeconomic domain, whereas neoliberalism has transformed the globe profoundly. More challengingly, even when it comes to the ends of

71 Lang, *World Trade Law after Neoliberalism*, 100 (rigorously cataloguing the rise of human rights in trade debates after the catalytic period of 1997–2000, particularly around the TRIPS agreement). Cf. Tomer Broude, 'From Seattle to Occupy: The Shifting Focus of Global Protest', in Drache and Jacobs, *Linking Global Trade and Human Rights*.

human rights protection, neoliberalism has sometimes done a better job than actual human rights movements: even as neoliberalism has had disastrous effects on wealth distribution both within states and across the globe, it has provided more poverty reduction, especially in its Chinese form, than any other agent. (This is not to say that neoliberalism unerringly works for the benefit of all humanity, as some of its proponents claim.)

In part for this reason, marginal skeptics about the role of human rights in the global economy reply to mainstream optimists that the tweaks they entertain to the international economic order are not enough. According to skeptics, the mainstream is too uncritical of globalization itself to be trusted with the task of separating the wheat from the chaff. The mainstream puts a high premium on successfully avoiding naïve celebration of market fundamentalism, but puts an only slightly modified version of that same set of commitments in its place. For Paul O'Connell, there is no way to save globalization from neoliberalism without the drastic transformation of politics and economics that he calls 'subaltern globalization'.[72] Susan Marks, for her part, focuses on the way in which human rights law, even when it purports to seek root causes of human rights violations, is not currently organized to permit the sort of structural critique eventually needed to target neoliberalism – or perhaps capitalism in any of its possible variants.[73] A new approach to politics and law would require a systemic evaluation of the causes of and alternatives to 'planned misery'.[74] In their current forms at least, international human rights generally provide a distraction from both the necessary diagnosis and the necessary remedy.[75]

Although it is hard to gainsay the sobering conclusions of such critics, I have been concerned in this chapter with a cautionary point. For it is equally hard to conclude that blaming human rights regimes and movements of 'complicity' with neoliberalism is itself productive. As I have indicated, I do not think human rights do or should provide the final normative standards against which economic arrangements should be judged wanting: they are too minimalistic to do so, especially in the socioeconomic domain, where an egalitarian theory of social justice provides a more defensible (and much higher) bar to meet.[76] But the

72 Paul O'Connell, 'On Reconciling Irreconcilables: Neo-liberal Globalisation and Human Rights', *Human Rights Law Review* 7 (2007): 483–509, 487, 493–495. See also Rhoda E. Howard-Hassmann, 'Reply to Paul O'Connell's Article on Neo-liberal Globalisation and Human Rights', *Human Rights Law Review* 9 (2009): 127–133; Paul O'Connell, 'Not Seeing the Forest for the Trees: A Reply to Rhoda Howard-Hassmann', *Human Rights Law Review* 9 (2009): 135–141.

73 See Marks, 'Human Rights and Root Causes'.

74 See ibid.

75 See Marks, 'Four Human Rights Myths'.

76 For this reason, it seems mistaken to me for O'Connell to treat human rights norms as the main normative standards against which to judge neoliberal globalization wanting, and to motivate the call for a subaltern globalization. After all, there is a wide range of ends international human rights are simply not trying to achieve, equality perhaps first among them.

minimalist standards of judgment for gross failure that human rights norms offer hardly themselves pose an obstruction (let alone the main one) to maximalist alternatives. The ethical standards of human rights are not necessarily 'part of the problem' in the quest to develop either a higher standard for judgment or the political basis for a movement to meet it. The same, *mutatis mutandis*, is true of human rights regimes and movements. But this defense of human rights in an age of galloping inequality is obviously faint praise.[77]

It also follows that criticizing either the norms or the movements for distraction and insufficiency is important but minimal in itself. In an era in which human rights norms and movements are frequently overloaded with expectation, the best conclusion is that a Band-Aid is not an adequate response to a charnelhouse (even if Band-Aids have their uses). Analytically and politically, the mere act of criticizing human rights does little to provide useful alternatives to human rights frameworks, regimes, and movements that might succeed in areas where human rights have failed – in part because human rights are (so far) not designed to succeed in those areas. To bring the limited aims and often glancing successes of human rights movements into focus is simply to demand another politics to supplement goals that are inadequate in the first place and strategies that rarely work, especially in the socioeconomic domain. A threatening enemy, rather than a powerless companion, is what market fundamentalism demands.

77 Cf. David Kennedy, 'The International Human Rights Movement: Part of the Problem?', *Harvard Human Rights Journal* 15 (2002): 101–125. When Kennedy revisited his classic essay ten years later, his verdict was different – and in my opinion more correct: 'Perhaps the [human rights] movement bit off more than it could chew'. David Kennedy, 'The International Human Rights Movement: Still Part of the Problem?', in *Examining Critical Perspectives on Human Rights*, eds, Rob Dickinson et al. (Cambridge: Cambridge University Press, 2012), 21.

Chapter 8

An unlikely resonance? Subjects of human rights and subjects of human capital reconsidered

Zachary Manfredi

I Toward a history of hybrid governmentalities

Critical historiography over the past decade has called into question the continuity between late twentieth-century human rights advocacy and earlier eighteenth-century conceptions of human rights *qua* 'the rights of man'.[1] One way in which critics have sought to distinguish contemporary human rights from their historical forebears is by calling attention to the 'minimalist' nature of the international human rights project that emerged in the 1970s.[2] Contemporary historians note that in the 1970s international human rights advocates focused on stopping state abuses for the 'most grievous' offenses of torture, disappearance and violent responses to political dissent.[3] On this account, human rights advocates proffered a moral reproach of authoritarian states, but largely abandoned – or at least proved inefficacious at – challenging other social ills such as deep, structural social and economic inequality. This account of 'human rights minimalism' undoubtedly has support from the historical record.[4]

1 This view is perhaps now most popularly associated with Samuel Moyn's *The Last Utopia: Human Rights in History* (Cambridge: Harvard University Press, 2010).

2 These critics, for example, take note of Michael Ignatieff's oft cited work *Human Rights as Politics and Idolatry*, in which he observes that '[H]umans rights activism likes to portray itself as an anti-politics, in defense of universal moral claims designed to delegitimize "political" (i.e., ideological or sectarian) justifications for the abuse of human beings.' Michael Ignatieff, *Human Rights as Politics and Idolatry* (Princeton: Princeton University Press, 2001), 9.

3 For a debate between Moyn and Seyla Benhabib on this point, see Seyla Benhabib, 'Moving beyond False Binarisms: On Samuel Moyn's The Last Utopia', *Qui Parle*, 22 (2013): 81–93; and Sam Moyn, 'The Continuing Perplexities of Human Rights', *Qui Parle* 22 (2013): 95–115.

4 Moyn documents the narrow focus of early human rights movements in the late 1970s and early 1980s. Although I do not address it here, the view of human rights as a 'minimalist' political doctrine likely has support in the work of early analytic political philosophy. In his famous application of his theory of justice to the international scene, *The Law of Peoples* (Cambridge: Harvard University Press, 1999) John Rawls argued that, while the protection of human rights remains necessary for any 'decent society', such rights should not be confused with the more robust set of legal rights that a truly liberal constitutional state must also secure.

Indeed, it has opened up new vistas of critique[5] and avenues for historical research on human rights in the late twentieth century.[6] One significant, yet unresolved, debate within this historical literature concerns the relationship between the outburst of human rights discourse in the late twentieth century and the contemporaneous rise of 'neoliberalism' as a political and economic project. Even among those who acknowledge that the 1970s mark something of a watershed moment in the history of human rights, important disagreements persist about the political entailments of human rights' preeminence.

Consider, for example, Samuel Moyn's recent critique (reprinted in Chapter 7 of the present volume) of Naomi Klein and other leftist critics who, he suggests, too readily equate international human rights with neoliberal economic rationality.[7] As an historical matter, Klein and others observe that neoliberal economic policies and the 'minimalist' Western conception of international human rights advocacy both flourished in close geographic and temporal proximity.[8] In her famous work on the global North's 'export' of 'free market' principles, *The Shock Doctrine*, Klein highlighted the contemporaneous Nobel Prize victories of Milton Friedman and Amnesty International as an index of the ostensible compatibility of neoliberalism and human rights.[9] On her account, Chicago School interventionism into the Southern Cone coincided with new forms of human rights activism in the region; she describes how (that particular) human rights movement's narrow focus 'purely on the crimes [of the dictators and military juntas] ... helped the Chicago School ideology to escape from its first bloody laboratory virtually unscathed'.[10] In Klein's story, human rights advocates obscured the deep harms associated with the structural transformations of South American states' social and economic orders. In limiting their analysis to select grave instances of torture, disappearance and the suppression of associational rights, they also distracted from the role of Western states in overthrowing governments, such as the CIA-backed coup against Salvador Allende in Chile.

5 For a discussion of the political valences of different approaches to human rights historiography, see Ben Golder, *Foucault and the Politics of Rights* (Stanford: Stanford University Press, 2015), 4–5.

6 The twentieth-century turn in human rights historiography has not been without its critics as well. For an overview of some of these critiques from the perspective of some legal scholars, see Caroline Anderson, 'Human Rights: A Reckoning', *Harvard International Law Journal* 53 (2012): 549–562; Christopher McCrudden, 'Human Rights Histories', *Oxford Journal of Legal Studies* 35 (2015): 179–212; Justin Zaremby, 'On the Uses and Disadvantages of History for Human Rights Law: Reading Samuel Moyn's The Last Utopia: Human Rights in History', *Yale Human Rights Development Journal* 15 (2014): article 5.

7 Samuel Moyn, 'Powerless Companion: Human Rights in the Age of Neoliberalism', *Law & Contemporary Problems* 77 (2014): 147–169.

8 Namoi Klein, *The Shock Doctrine: The Rise of Disaster Capitalism* (New York: Picador, 2007), 145–155.

9 Klein, *The Shock Doctrine*, 145–150.

10 Klein, *The Shock Doctrine*, 119 (this analysis focuses on Uruguay, Chile, Argentina).

Moyn, however, cautions against a full acceptance of Klein's narrative. Instead, he describes the relationship that human rights bears to neoliberal political projects as akin to that of a 'powerless companion'.[11] On his view, human rights may not intrinsically collaborate with or enforce neoliberal political projects and their attendant exacerbation of social and economic inequality, but they have done little, if anything, to deter the recent historical ascendancy of those projects. Moyn thus inaugurates a debate about the history of human rights in the twentieth century with those he labels as 'Marxists'[12] – Moyn critiques the work of the international legal theorist, Susan Marks, and that of political theorist Wendy Brown as too readily condemning international human rights for their complicity with neoliberal political rationality.[13] On his account, early human rights

11 Moyn, 'Powerless Companion', 151 ('human rights have not made enough of a difference in the short timeframe and global space they share with their neoliberal *frère ennemi*. They have been condemned to watch but have been powerless to deter. Added to the fact that human rights at least as canonically established have nothing to say about the principal value of equality that neoliberalism threatens, it seems hard to conclude that they are a useful resource in response').

12 Moyn's simple description of Wendy Brown as 'a Marxist' seems curious and surprising. Brown's own thinking engages deeply with post-Marxist and feminist critiques of Marxist orthodoxy, as well as Foucault, Derrida and Baudrillard's challenges to structuralist re-formulations of Marxism and teleological narratives of revolution. For an intellectual historian deeply concerned with the political theory of human rights, Moyn's account falls short of genuine theoretical engagement with the work of one of human rights' significant contemporary left critics. For Brown's significant earlier work on theories of rights, that engages with Foucault's notion of disciplinary power as a supplement to older Marxian critiques of rights, see Wendy Brown, 'Rights and Losses', in *States of Injury: Power and Freedom in Late Modernity*, ed., Wendy Brown (Princeton: Princeton University Press, 1995), 96–134. For some of her early work on rethinking the concept of power in Marx's writing see 'Power without Logic, without Marx', in Wendy Brown, *Politics Out of History* (Princeton: Princeton University Press, 2001), 62–90. In Brown's critique of Michael Ignatieff and the post-Cold War notion of international human rights in particular – which Moyn does cite – her account actually shares much greater affinity with his own discussion of rights in 'A Powerless Companion' – there, Brown laments that human rights as currently framed respond to a narrow set of concerns, but do not contest larger structures of power in the current global order: 'If the global problem today is defined as terrible human suffering consequent to limited individual rights against abusive state powers, then human rights may be the best tactic against this problem. But if it is diagnosed as the relatively unchecked globalization of capital, postcolonial political deformations, and superpower imperialism combining to disenfranchise peoples in many parts of the first, second, and third worlds from the prospects of self-governance to a degree historically unparalleled in modernity, other kinds of political projects, including other international justice projects, may offer a more appropriate and far-reaching remedy for injustice defined as suffering *and* as systematic disenfranchisement from collaborative self-governance.' Wendy Brown, '"The Most We Can Hope For …": Human Rights and the Politics of Fatalism', *South Atlantic Quarterly* 103 (2004): 451–463, 461–462.

13 Susan Marks' own work comparing Brown and Moyn on their critiques of human rights is illuminative in thinking thorough the similarities and difference of their positions. See Susan Marks, 'Four Human Rights Myths', in *Human Rights: Old*

advocates focused on a narrow set of concerns, and often neglected – at least proved less efficacious in their advocacy regarding – 'socio-economic' issues.[14]

This ostensible disagreement opens up an important site for future debate among leftist scholars about how best to characterize the relationship between human rights and neoliberalism. However, as currently formulated, this exchange appears to contemplate a circumscribed set of options for thinking about the relationship between human rights and neoliberalism: first, human rights either collaborate with neoliberalism to produce inegalitarian orders (or simply are themselves tools for advancing neoliberal agendas *qua* claims to property rights); second, human rights are neither necessarily neoliberal nor anti-neoliberal, but 'powerless companions' to neoliberalism's rise that simply do not address the kinds of harms (exacerbating structural inequality) that neoliberal policies ostensibly produce; or third, human rights, in one form or another, may still be a site of resistance to and means of effectively challenging neoliberal rationality and policy.[15] While important and interesting positions in their own right, each of these accounts treats some of their constituent objects of analysis as relatively fixed and familiar. Both Moyn's account, and the view he attributes to Marxist critics, assume we know what 'human rights' and 'neoliberalism' mean in order to contemplate their relationship and judge their normative compatibility.

In this chapter, however, I offer a provocation that might lead to different accounts of the relationship between neoliberalism and human rights. On my account, neoliberalism and human rights need not be treated as independent notions whose compatibility can be judged by comparing their normative principles and historical aspirations. Instead, I contemplate the possibility that, in different historical configurations, both terms may prove co-constitutive. Neoliberal political rationality may, in certain contexts, amalgamate with human rights in

Problems, New Possibilities, eds David Kinley et al. (Northampton: Elgar Publishing, 2013), 217–235. For Marks' own account of the limitations of certain human rights discourse, and an alternative proposal orienting human rights advocacy to challenge the 'planned misery' of capitalist exploitation, see Susan Marks, 'Human Rights and Root Causes', *The Modern Law Review* 74 (2011): 57–78.

14 Moyn, 'Powerless Companion', 151–152, 160–166.

15 For an articulation of this, last, position, see David Harvey, *A Brief History of Neoliberalism* (Oxford: Oxford University Press, 2005), 175–177 ('The temptation in the light of this critique is to eschew all appeal to universals as fatally flawed and to abandon all mention of rights as an untenable imposition of abstract, market-based ethics as a mask for the restoration of class power. While both propositions deserve to be seriously considered, I think it unfortunate to abandon the field of rights to neoliberal hegemony. There is a battle to be fought, not only over which universals and what rights should be invoked in particular situations but also over how universal principles and conceptions of rights should be constructed. The critical connection forged between neoliberalism as a particular set of political-economic practices and the increasing appeal to universal rights of a certain sort as an ethical foundation for moral and political legitimacy should alert us … "Between two rights", Marx famously commented, "force decides." If class restoration entails the imposition of a distinctive set of rights, then resistance to that imposition entails struggle for entirely different rights.').

ways that transform both concepts. In offering this alternative approach to narrating the history of human rights, I do not intend to detract from the work of Moyn, Klein or Marks in developing critical accounts of human rights and neoliberalism. Rather, this chapter hopes to supplement the groundwork laid by earlier histories in order to gesture towards novel genealogies of human rights that might be developed in the future. Whether we understand human rights as a 'minimalist utopia' or a feature of a neoliberal political project, this may only scratch the surface of how different practices of human rights function in the world. Returning to the question of the recent history of human rights, we might endeavor to chart the complex tensions, elisions and divergences that attend various discourses of rights as they move across spatial and geographic boundaries.[16] What kinds of subjects do different notions of human rights encode or assume? What mechanisms of power, logics of governmental reason, or normative visions do different accounts of rights carry with them? How are different notions of human rights in turn, contested, transformed and reoriented as they encounter other practices of social control and new ideologies? Additionally, what novel, complex, and hybrid governmentalities might be found when narratives of international human rights tell stories beyond the rhetorics of 1970s Western advocates?

As a gesture towards one possible site of study, I consider how some of the late 1980s and early 1990s discourses about 'human development' borrow elements from both human capital theory and older traditions of human rights. Focusing on human capital theory, as opposed to 'neoliberalism' writ large, also helps to concretize and refine my analysis. Neoliberalism remains a term largely defined by those critical of it as a social, political and economic project – few theorists labeled as 'neoliberals' avowedly endorse or promote their work under the sign of neoliberalism. Consequently, a focus on human capital avoids the risk of applying an ideological label to theorists who themselves eschew such a description of their work – for example, leading Chicago School exponents of human capital theory, Gary Becker and Theodore Shutlz rarely self-describe as 'neoliberals', yet remain deeply invested in the concept of human capital as an analytical tool. It bears remembering that the various concepts and practices associated with neoliberalism may have resonances with thinkers and movements far beyond the early programs of Reaganism and Thatcherism. Work on human capital offers concepts and rationalities that may also travel to sites other than those traditionally identified with neoliberal intervention. Additionally, focusing attention on 'human capital'

16 Moyn gestures towards the importance of this approach in a piece on the historiographic turn in human rights scholarship within the discipline of history. Samuel Moyn, 'Substance, Scale, and Salience: the Recent Historiography of Human Rights', *Annual Review of Law and Social Science* 8 (2012): 123–140. My approach here is also a suggestion that greater attention should be shown to the contribution of disciplines such as political theory, philosophy, critical theory, law, and area studies, as they may more fruitfully expand the depth of analysis and levels of engagement on which we track the various practices of human rights.

theory avoids some of the immediate normative baggage associated with a left critique of neoliberalism – analyzing the legacy and influence of human capital theory requires more than the generation of moral opprobrium, but instead necessitates renewed attention to how the adoption of different 'explanatory' frameworks may itself influence social policy.

In this chapter I focus attention on how the language of human rights entered into the discourse of international economic development in the latter decades of the twentieth and the early years of the twenty-first centuries. Just as human rights have risen to prominence in the late twentieth century, so did the institutions and rhetorics of 'development' in turn proliferate; few other discourses that emerged in the post-war international order have seen as much expansion, investment, institutional development, and dynamic change as the landscape of 'development'. Not unexpectedly, in the past decades the practices and discourses of international economic development have intersected with those of human rights in novel, complicated, and surprising ways. This chapter thus considers how respecting human rights may now function as an indicia of development, or a metric for assessing the viability of capital investment in a population. Michel Foucault's early insights into the 'heterogeneous accounts of freedom' offered by liberal governmentality and natural rights theory guides my analysis. In his 1979 lectures at the Collège de France, Foucault offers details about how theories of natural and subjective right might conflict with, but also become complexly intertwined with, the logics of liberal (and later neoliberal) governmentality. Reading examples of the incorporation of human rights frameworks into the logic of development with Foucault in mind helps us trace a fascinating intersection between theories of governmentality and human rights – and furthermore allows us to consider the different notions of 'the human' and kinds of subjects contemplated (and generated) by such hybrid approaches. My chapter concludes with a suggestion that some techniques of modern international economic governance yoke both theories of human 'capital' (or human 'capabilities') to notions of human rights in complex, ambivalent and potentially promising ways. We may have only begun to understand the logics that are at play in the many contemporary forms of governmentality that speak in the language of human rights.

II Liberal governmentality vs natural rights? Revisiting Foucault on rights and liberal governmentality

In his 1979 lecture course at the Collège de France, published in English as *The Birth of Biopolitics*, Foucault offers an intriguing theoretical observation about the contemporary human rights advocacy[17] of his time:

17 Foucault's own views on human rights advocacy prove complex and have recently been the subject of significant scholarly commentary. While indebted to that body of work, my analysis here does not engage in debates about Foucault's assessment of the viability of human rights as a vehicle for resistance to modern forms of disciplinary

> With regard to the problem of what are currently called human rights, we would only need to look at where, in what countries, how, and in what form these rights are claimed to see that at times the question is actually the juridical question of rights, and at others it is a question of the assertion or claim of the independence of the governed vis-à-vis governmentality.[18]

In the above quotation, Foucault suggests that claims for the vindication of 'human rights' may function in radically different ways depending upon the context in which they are invoked. Foucault's distinction between the 'juridical question of rights' and the 'independence of the governed' emerges from his assessment of the history of European governmentality. In this lecture, he describes a 'shift in the center of gravity of public law' that occurred at the end of the eighteenth and the beginning of the nineteenth century. In earlier historical epoch, Foucault argues, questions of public law concerned the conditions for the foundation of sovereignty and legitimate exercise of the sovereign's rights. The new problematic Foucault traces concerns the 'exercise of power by public authorities' through the setting of a juridical limit; earlier doctrines of public law asked questions about how far sovereign authority could be maintained while still generally presupposing that sovereign power entails omnipotence and absolute authority. The new scheme, rather than beginning with the assumption of sovereign power and the concern about its potential limits, asserted that the origins of governmental regulation first needed to be thought from the perspective of their basic limitations and constraints. The 'natural or original rights' approach to the problem of governmental limitation operated by first defining what rights 'belong to every individual' that they would then, under certain conditions, willingly concede or set limits upon in order constitute the sovereign.[19] Foucault associates this way of addressing the problem of public law with Rousseau, calling it both 'the axiomatic, juridico-deductive approach' and the 'revolutionary approach'.[20]

power and governmentality. Instead, I engage Foucault's thinking primarily for its methodological insights into how we might complicate the conceptualization of contemporary formulations of international human rights. See, e.g. Golder, *Foucault and the Politics of Rights*, 1–15; and *Rethinking Foucault on Law, Power and Rights*, ed., Ben Golder (Oxford: Routledge, 2013).

18 Michel Foucault, *The Birth of Biopolitics: Lectures at the College de France 1978–1979*, trans., Graham Burchell (New York: Picador, 2008), 42.

19 Foucault, *Birth of Biopolitics*, 39.

20 While the connection to the Rousseau of *The Social Contract* is obviously clear in this reading, as well as the direct association with the Declaration of the Rights of Man and Citizen, it seems that one could trace a longer legacy of social contract thought in regard to this problematic as well. Foucault does not mention Hobbes in this regard and generally tends to associate his thought with the earlier problematic of 'sovereign juridical power.' However, one would need to acknowledge the origins of a model of 'natural right' as the basis for social contract theory in Hobbes's own thought. His distinction between '*jus*' and '*lex*' *naturalis* (natural right v. natural law) has often been seen as an essential historical touchstone for the rise of certain notions of human rights. Hobbes's model of sovereignty by conquest as well as his fundamental concern for how

On this view, Foucault summarizes that one 'starts with the rights of man in order to arrive at the limitation of governmentality by way of the constitution of the sovereign.'[21] He further attributes this tactic to the 'revolutionaries' of the period, and describes it as 'retroactive' or 'retroactionary' in so far as it opposes the notion of rights and public law to the discourse of *raison d'Etat* as had been done in the seventeenth and eighteenth centuries.[22]

Foucault juxtaposes the 'radical' English tradition associated with 'utilitarian' thought with the revolutionary approach. In the 'radical' theory, one begins not from the question of law, but rather from that of governmental practice itself and its historically and materially constituted limits. The radical approach thus asks what practices of government – given extant circumstances and resources – will produce beneficial effects regardless of the question of fundamental 'rights' or 'legal restrictions' on actions. Limits on government derive from the efficacy of potential practices and are determined by the ability to manipulate relevant variables (natural resources, trade, labor forces, prices, etc.) toward the production of greater utility.[23] This modality of governmentality, here first associated with nineteenth-century utilitarianism, forms the basis of what Foucault will elaborate as 'liberal governmentality' – an art of governing the 'conduct of conduct', which focuses on how to achieve desired market effects by lessening direct control over individual choices, while also manipulating variables that maximize a population's overall production of value.

On its face, this reading appears to affirm the view that Foucault considers the rights of man to remain inscribed within a model of sovereign juridical power. The subject of right may be cast as the basic unit for determining the limits of governmental power, but that subject nevertheless remains one of rational consciousness that acts through the imposition of its will on the world. As Foucault states the problem, the revolutionary approach functions as 'a system of will-law': 'The problem of will is, of course, at the heart of all the problems of right, which again confirms that this is a fundamentally juridical problematic. The law is therefore conceived as the expression of a collective will indicating the part they wish to hold on to.'[24] Alternatively, the 'radical utilitarian' approach begins not with the presumption of a fundamental set of rights belonging to the subject, but with the notion of 'the independence of the governed,' i.e. the basic

to legitimate and stabilize sovereign power, however, likely still distinguishes him from the 'revolutionary approach' to the problem of public law as Foucault discusses it. Hobbes's motivating concern remains how to establish sovereign authority (in order to provide security and protect against the threat of violent death), not how to limit governmental power by respecting natural rights. For Foucault's own direct and more extended engagement with Hobbes, see *Society Must be Defended: Lectures at the College de France 1975–76*, trans., David Macey (New York: Picador, 2003), Lecture 5, February 4, 1977.

21 Foucault, *Birth of Biopolitics*, 39.
22 Foucault, *Birth of Biopolitics*, 30.
23 Foucault, *Birth of Biopolitics*, 39–41.
24 Foucault, *Birth of Biopolitics*, 41.

presumption that the freedom of anyone consists in the degree to which individuals remain independent of direct governmental regulation. While he acknowledges that these two rationalities offer 'two absolutely heterogeneous conceptions of freedom', he observes that they were often intertwined in fraught and complicated ways.[25] In an additional section of notes that Foucault skipped over in his lecture, he adds that one also finds many connections and co-mingling between these two approaches historically; indeed, he suggests that in the American context, the problematic of 'revolutionary thought' may be 'precisely … [how] to think at the same time the utility of independence and the axiomatic of rights.'[26]

Extending this logic to his present, Foucault observes that, although human rights may sometimes concern the older 'revolutionary' problematic, they are now also invoked to address concerns that follow the 'radical utilitarian' approach to regulating government. I suggest, however, that Foucault's writing may assist us in analyzing novel amalgamations of human rights and liberal governmentality as well.

In this regard Foucault provides two essential insights. First, in contradistinction to the historical analysis of 'human rights minimalism', Foucault helps us to imagine alternative ways of marking the difference between earlier historical conceptions of human rights and their contemporary manifestations. Different conceptions of rights may assume different notions of what it means to be human, or elaborate different theories of governance as the means for best protecting and promulgating rights. Human rights to private property and freedom of contract, for example, might imagine very different kinds of state intervention and action for their protection, than might human rights to water, food, shelter and housing. Similarly, different formulations of human rights may also encode *different accounts of subjectivity* into their substantive guarantees of particular rights – one theory of rights might imagine human subjects as entrepreneurial creatures who thrive in the absence of state regulation of their conduct, while another might conceive of humans as vulnerable creatures whose very survival hinges upon states ensuring that their basic needs are met.

Second, Foucault helps escape the binary choice of thinking of human rights as a political project that either opposes or endorses neoliberal political rationality. Instead, we might ask, with Foucault, what it means to formulate theories of human rights in relation to *different* political rationalities (liberal, utilitarian, neoliberal, Marxist, post-Marxist, etc.). How do conceptions of human rights change – both in terms of the context of particular rights and the governing logics about how rights are to be actualized – when formulated through different political rationalities? How, in turn, does the incorporation of a conception of

25 Foucault, *Birth of Biopolitics*, 41–42

26 Nevertheless, Foucault does emphasize in the concluding remarks of the lecture that the radical approach to public law historically appears to win out over its revolutionary alternative: 'Overwhelmingly, and not without some reversals, regulation of the public authorities in terms of utility prevails over the axiomatic of sovereignty in terms of original rights.' Foucault, *Birth of Biopolitics*, 42.

'human rights' into different political rationalities transform those rationalities? What diverse, hybrid and heterogeneous logics and practices of governmentality emerge at the interstices of human rights and neoliberalism?

While Foucault's own formulation may lead us to characterize contemporary human rights discourse as either 'revolutionary' or 'radical' in scope, I suggest that his analysis in fact offers a more interesting and productive set of insights into the necessarily hybrid nature of forms of governmentality and of human rights. As Foucault himself already noted in 1979:

> With regard to the problem of what are currently called human rights, we would only need to look at where, in what countries, how, and in what form there rights are claimed to see that at times the question is actually the juridical question of rights, and at others it is a question of ... [the] assertion or claim of the independence of the governed vis-à-vis governmentality.[27]

In the next section of this chapter I use Foucault's insights to think about the complicated relations between human capital, human development and human rights. In the development context, the rights of the governed to freedom, autonomy and self-determination may now be inextricably linked to states' investment in securing and upholding 'natural rights'. 'Achieving' human rights requires governmentality to invest power in individuals' physical and social well-being – a 'material making of humanity', as described by Pheng Cheah[28] – so that they might achieve 'self-determination'. Under such conditions the traditional divisions between negative and positive liberty may become inverted. In this vein, new techniques of governance reimagine human rights protection as part of their labor; tracing the development of the complicated and intertwined logics of 'radical' and 'revolutionary' in the approaches to human rights may thus benefit from defamiliarization. We may benefit from not assuming the meaning of 'human rights' as we attempt to trace their complicated history. Familiar notions of human rights as either a minimalist project focused on narrow moral claims, or as an ideological construction of capitalist property rights may obscure the ways in which actual practices of rights make subjects and reorient social forces today. In the spirit of provoking future exercises in defamiliarization, I now turn to reconsideration of the intersections of human rights and human capital theories in the context of the discourse of international economic development.

III Genres of the human? Capital, rights, capabilities

> [A] comment on poor countries, for which there are virtually no solid estimates. I have been impressed by repeatedly expressed judgments, especially by those who have a responsibility in making capital available to poor countries,

27 Foucault, *The Birth of Biopoliitics*, 42.

28 Pheng Cheah, 'Human Rights and the Material Making of Humanity: A Response to Samuel Moyn's The Last Utopia', *Qui Parle* 22 (2013): 55–61.

> about the low rate at which these countries can absorb additional capital. New capital from outside can be put to good use, it is said, only when it is added 'slowly and gradually'. But this experience is at variance with the widely held impression that countries are poor fundamentally because they are starved for capital and that additional capital is truly the key to their more rapid economic growth. The reconciliation is again, I believe, to be found in emphasis on particular forms of capital. The new capital available to these countries from outside as a rule goes into the formation of structures, equipment and sometimes also into inventories. *But it is generally not available for additional investment in man. Consequently, human capabilities do not stay abreast of physical capital, and they do become limiting factors in economic growth. It should come as no surprise, therefore, that the absorption rate of capital to augment only particular nonhuman resources is necessarily low. The … optimum rate of investment which treats knowledge and skill as a critical investment variable in determining the rate of economic growth is both relevant and important.*[29]
>
> The significant transformation that has occurred in recent years in giving greater recognition to the role of 'human capital' is helpful for understanding the relevance of the capability perspective. If a person can become more productive in making commodities through better education, better health and so on, it is not unnatural to expect that she can, through these means, also directly achieve more – and have the freedom to achieve more in leading her life.[30]

A definitive conceptual history of 'human capital' remains to be written. Although the term has antecedents dating back to the nineteenth century, and its exponents often claim a heritage dating to the work of Adam Smith, in its modern formulation human capital theory began to flourish in the late 1950s and early 1960s. An early essay in 1958 in the *Journal of Political Economy* by noted labor economist Jacob Mincer proposed measuring investment in training, skills, and educational development as a means of accounting for Pigou observations about the disparity between income inequality and the natural distribution of talents in a given population.[31] Theodor Schultz published his influential pieces, 'Investment in Human Capital' and 'Reflections on Investment in Man', in 1961 and 1962 respectively, and in 1964 Gary Becker published his monograph, *Human Capital*, that became a landmark text in the field.[32] In these early analyses human capital served as a measure of the value of investing in 'skills and knowledge' on future income outputs. In 1961 Schutlz, for example, observed, despite being largely overlooked by previous generations of economists, that human capital is 'a substantial part of deliberate investment', and that it

29 Theodore W. Schultz, 'Investment in Human Capital', *The American Economic Review* 51 (1961): 1–17, 10 (emphasis added).

30 Amartya Sen, *Development as Freedom* (Oxford: Oxford Paperbacks, 2001).

31 Jacob Mincer, 'Investment in Human Capital and Personal Income Distribution', *The Journal of Political Economy* (1958): 281–302.

32 Gary S. Becker, *Human Capital: A Theoretical and Empirical Analysis, with Special Reference to Education* (Chicago: University of Chicago Press, 2009).

'has grown in Western societies at a much faster rate than conventional (nonhuman) capital.'[33] Schultz's and other cognate accounts focused on creating metrics of 'human capital' as a means of explaining how the national outputs of Western states had outpaced increases in traditional measures of capital investment (i.e. 'land, man-hours, and physical reproducible capital').[34]

Proponents of human capital theory saw their analysis as a source of guidance and insight for states hoping to maximize their returns on investment in their populations – by creating more refined indicia to analyze how investment in skills and training led to overall increases in outputs, states could better maximize their return on capital investment. For individuals, this analysis also functioned as a science of risk management: understanding human capital development could help one predict when investment in educational skills and training might allow for higher income at a later time and counsel in favor of temporarily accepting a comparatively lower income.[35] Historically, human capital analysis has become ubiquitous, and scholars have traced its influence on public policy across many issue areas (regulation of crime, reproductive health and fertility rates, educational investment and vocational training programs to name but a few areas where this research has proven highly influential).[36]

Critical theorists have analyzed the development of human capital theory, and also documented how its dissemination to a broader public expanded its application to other aspects of social life. Michel Feher, for example, observes two key shifts in human capital theory that accompanied its historical dissemination beyond the field of economics. First, 'the definition of human capital was broadened [beyond measures of direct educational investment] so that its evaluation would include a multiplicity of factors', including innate genetic background and talents, parental investments in children's development, and social, physical and psychological factors associated with personal habits and networks.[37] Second, following this expansion of possible inputs, human capital became construed not just as a measure of future income, but as a metric for assessing 'capital growth or appreciation'.[38] Under Feher's analysis, these two shifts require individuals seeking to maximize their human capital to engage in a constant re-evaluation of self and instrumentalization of nearly every aspect of their lives in order to avoid 'depreciation'. Wendy Brown, in her forceful critique of the broad application of human capital rationalities to political life, observes that:

33 Theodore W. Schultz, 'Reflections on Investment in Man', *The Journal of Political Economy* (1962): 1–8.
34 Schultz, 'Investment in Human Capital', 1–3.
35 Schultz, 'Investment in Human Capital', 1–3.
36 See, e.g. Bernard E. Harcourt, *Against Prediction: Profiling, Policing, and Punishing in an Actuarial Age* (Chicago: University of Chicago Press, 2008); and Bernard E. Harcourt, *The Illusion of Free Markets* (Cambridge: Harvard University Press, 2011).
37 Michel Feher, 'Self-Appreciation; Or, the Aspirations of Human Capital', *Public Culture* 21 (2009): 21–41.
38 Ibid., 26.

> for the figure of human capital … no longer is there an open question of what one wants from life or how one might wish to craft the self. Human capitals, like all other capitals, are constrained by markets in both inputs and outputs to comport themselves in ways that will outperform the competition and align themselves with good assessments about where those markets may be going.[39]

Without weighing into their normative assessment of how the theories of human capital impact upon democracy or other political values, the work of both Feher and Brown still offers essential insights for understanding human capital theory. They both document the expansion of the logic of human capital as it traveled beyond the work of the early Chicago School economists, and note how the shift from a focus on 'income' to 'appreciation' follows from it.

Critical for my purposes here, however, is the way in which the logic of human capital emerges in the context of international development programs. As Antony Anghie notes, in addition to human rights, 'development' emerged as another important utopia for internationalists in the late twentieth century: 'the vast majority of governments and people in the 1970s were preoccupied in their struggle for a very different utopia, the utopia of 'development'.[40] In the dominant recounting of the history of international development, the initial frameworks and logics of development did not make significant use of the language of 'human rights'; the late 1980s and early 1990s, however, produced significant transformations in the frameworks applied by international governmental organizations.[41] The close of the Cold War also provided new opportunities for Western economic investment in post-colonial states. Significantly, however, the 1980s structural adjustment policies of the International Monetary Fund and the development regime of the World Bank contributed to renewed critiques of international development programs. From 1981 to 1986, World Bank president Alden W. Clausen and chief economist Anne Krueger increased structural adjustment lending and imposed loan conditionalities on 'developing' countries that many argued exacerbated economic crises.[42] Developing states increasingly felt the consequences of structural adjustment conditionalities, and significant debate emerged about the impact of these policies. This critical position, coupled with the perceived success of the OPEC oil embargo in previous years, gave renewed

39 Wendy Brown, *Undoing the Demos: Neoliberalism's Stealth Revolution* (New York: Zone, 2015), 125.

40 Antony Anghie, 'Whose Utopia?: Human Rights, Development, and the Third World', *Qui Parle* 22 (2013): 63–80.

41 For an interesting discussion of this history, see Jocelyn Viterna and Cassandra Robertson, 'New Directions for the Sociology of Development', *Annual Review of Sociology* 41 (2015): 243–269.

42 Adrian Robert Bazbauers, 'The Wolfensohn, Wolfowitz, and Zoellick Presidencies: Revitalising the Neoliberal Agenda of the World Bank', *Forum for Development Studies* 41 (2014): 91–114; Antje Vetterlein, 'Seeing Like the World Bank on Poverty', *New Political Economy* 17 (2012): 35–58.

vigor to many who believed that so-called Third World states required new access to resources in order to foster economic growth.

After considerable debate and controversy, the United Nations General Assembly adopted the Declaration on the Right to Development in 1986 – and the connection between human rights and development became both more explicit and more complex.[43] The African Charter of Human and Peoples' Rights laid some groundwork for this connection and had previously acknowledged a right to development; the General Assembly resolution, however, newly tied the idea of development to human rights as a matter of international law.[44] Article 1 of the Declaration states that 'The right to development is an inalienable human right by virtue of which every human person and all peoples are entitled to participate in, contribute to, and enjoy economic, social, cultural and political development, in which all human rights and fundamental freedoms can be fully realized.'[45] Much of the rhetorical and political force of the Declaration centered around developing states' rights to use and control over natural resources – but the Declaration also set the stage for a broader linking of human rights protection to achievement of economic development.[46] According to the Declaration, the 'realization' of human rights hinged on collective participation in economic and social development.[47] While largely only a rhetorical victory at the time of its passage, since 1998 an inter-governmental Working Group on the Right to Development has reported to the UN Human Rights Council and the General Assembly. Subsequently, the norms and standards inaugurated by the Declaration have been incorporated into a variety of international legal instruments and intergovernmental programs.[48]

43 Declaration on the Right to Development, A/RES/41/128, UN General Assembly, Dec. 4, 1986.
44 The declaration was neither a treaty, nor yet recognized as customary international law, so is without binding force as a matter of international law.
45 Declaration on the Right to Development, Article 1.1.
46 For an historical and critical account of the colonial legacy of international law and its relationship to the rise of the development paradigm, see Sundhya Pahuja, *Decolonising International Law: Development, Economic Growth and the Politics of Universality* (Cambridge: Cambridge University Press, 2011). Pahuja discusses both how the logic of development intersected with the aspirations of post-colonial nationalism in fraught ways, and the ways in which international law – and its long history as a tool of colonial governance – exacerbated problems with those who sought to escape the inequalities rooted in the long history of European colonization.
47 For a contemporary discussion of the early notion of development as a human rights, see R.L. Barsh, 'The Right to Development as a Human Right: Results of the Global Consultation', *Human Rights Quarterly*, 13 (1991): 322–338.
48 Declaration on the Right to Development was re-affirmed in several instruments including the 1992 Rio Declaration on Environment and Development, the 1993 Vienna Declaration and Programme of Action, the Millennium Declaration, the 2002 Monterrey Consensus, the 2005 World Summit Outcome Document and the 2007 Declaration on the Rights of Indigenous Peoples.

In line with the new international focus on development rights, in 1990 the United Nations Development Program (UNDP) also published its first *Human Development Report*. The first chapter of the report opens with the observation that 'people are the real wealth of nations. The basic objective of development is to create an enabling environment for people to enjoy long, healthy, and creative lives.'[49] The report offered a methodological innovation with its Human Development Index (HDI) as a new metric for tracking human development. The HDI included three primary dimensions: life expectancy, knowledge and education (combining adult literacy rates, and educational gross enrollment ratios), and standard of living (modeled as the natural logarithm of GDP and purchasing power parity[50]). The report placed countries on a final index that included a combined assessment of these three variables.[51] The inclusion of the measure of standard of living in terms of purchasing power parity proved particularly innovative, and helped measure income in relation to 'the fulfillment of human needs'.[52] In combining these concepts the report famously linked development to 'human freedom' – describing freedom in terms of 'people's capacities, or in other words, people's strengths to manage their affairs.'[53]

Economists Mahbub ul Haq and Amartya Sen first conceived of the HDI and designed and implemented the first report. The report famously reflects the theoretical innovations of Sen's 'capabilities approach', in which Sen, who had earlier gained fame for his powerful critique of welfare economics, described development as a process designed to enhance individuals' capabilities to achieve their life goals. Sen developed the approach with philosopher Martha Nussbaum, and it has been the subject of much reflection and debate among academics and international development practitioners ever since. While a full assessment of these debates exceeds the scope of the present analysis, reflecting on Sen's highly influential theory helps illuminate the ambivalent legacy of human capital theory in development economics. In later writing, both Sen and Nussbaum also reflect on how their approach intersected with, and departed from that of human rights – before turning to these later reflections (which risks a certain revisionism), it is worth pausing to consider how the logic of rights first intersected with the novel approaches to development and human capital and their various methodologies and strategies for securing greater human freedom.

49 UNDP, *Human Development Report*, 9, 1990 (HDR, 1990).

50 For an early assessment of the HDI, see Harald Trabold-Nübler, 'The Human Development Index – a New Development Indicator?', *Intereconomics* 26 (1991): 236–243; Allen C. Kelley, 'The Human Development Index: Handle with Care', *Population and Development Review* (1991): 315–324; Ambuj D Sagar, and Adil Naja, 'The Human Development Index: a Critical Review', *Ecological Economics* 25 (1998): 249–264.

51 The formulate was substantially changed in 2010. For a discussion of the difference, see Paolo Palazzi and Alessia Lauri, 'The Human Development Index: Suggested Corrections', *PSL Quarterly Review* 51 (1998): 193–221.

52 HDR, 13, 1990.

53 HDR, 15, 1990. (See Box 1.5.)

On its face, the early HDI report both shares essential premises with early theorists of human capital, but also explicitly breaks with such theories (regarding the issue of income and choice). Consider for instance, the following two passages:

> [T]here is nothing in the concept of human wealth contrary to his idea that it exists only for the advantage of people. By investing in themselves, people can enlarge the range of choice available to them. It is one way free men can enhance their welfare.[54]

and

> Human development is a process of enlarging people's choices... income is clearly only one option that people would like to have, albeit an important one. But it is not the sum total of their lives. Development must, therefore, be more than just the expansion of income and wealth. Its focus must be people.[55]

The first is from Schultz's early and highly influential 1961 piece, 'Investment in Human Capital', the second comes from the definition of 'human development' offered in the first 1990 *Human Development Report.* These passages motivate reflection on the relationship between human capital theory and the Sen-inspired philosophy of human development. First, human capital in Schultz's early formulation already contemplated human capital as a means of enhancing human freedom – and understood freedom as a means of developing human welfare that exceeds basic measures of income. The human development formulation takes many of the essential insights of human capital theory for granted: it assumes investment in education and skills training are essential for attainment of higher incomes and greater achievement of human welfare. Indeed, one seeking to integrate the two theories might describe investment in human capital as a means of increasing human capabilities. As a matter of state and policy planning both theories recommend a focus on demographic variables as a means of achieving success: promotion of life expectancy, public health, and investment in increased primary and secondary education. (It should come as no surprise that these variables also map onto Foucault's account of the development of liberal governmentality and biopolitics.)[56]

Significantly, however, both the text of the *Human Development Reports* and Sen's own writings endeavor to distinguish their approach from that of human capital theorists. In the 1990 report, development is distinguished from a focus on

54 Schultz, 'Investment in Human Capital'.

55 HDR, 10, 1990. (Box 1.1, 'Human Development Defined'.)

56 For a discussion that relies on Foucault in the context of global public health, see Andrew Lakoff, 'Real-Time Biopolitics: the Actuary and the Sentinel in Global Public Health', *Economy and Society* 44 (2015): 40–59.

'income' and treating humans as 'singularly economic creatures' by reference to the independent value of human rights:

> The purpose of development is to offer people more options. One of their options is access to income – not as an end in itself but as a means to acquiring human wellbeing. But there are other options as well, including long life, knowledge, political freedom, personal security, community participation and guaranteed human rights. People cannot be reduced to a single dimension as economic creatures.[57]

In this formulation, income and economic success serve as one possible – although ultimately essential – value that persons may choose to pursue. Some degree of economic security may be a necessary pre-requisite to achieve human freedom where real 'choice' is possible, but other dimensions of human life offer values that are not merely subsumable within the economic sphere. For the authors of the early reports, 'guaranteed human rights' formed at least one kind of 'outside' to economic valuation – from their approach economic success might be seen as valuable only insofar as it could contribute to the security and protection of fundamental rights and capabilities.

Sen's later philosophical work provides a deeper theoretical framework to address the connections, conflicts, and contradictions at stake in the relationship among accounts of human capital, human rights, and human capabilities. He treats the problematic most explicitly in the conclusion to his groundbreaking monograph, *Development as Freedom*.[58] In this text, Sen acknowledges the essential affinity between the two theories of human capital and human capabilities: both draw on Adam Smith's 'integrated approach to economic and social development', both emphasize the interconnection of individuals, humans and populations ('in particular the actual abilities they achieve and acquire'),[59] and both focus on education and skill formation as a means via which human freedom is best achieved.[60]

Sen describes human capital theory as concentrating 'the agency of human being in augmenting production possibilities', whereas the human capabilities approach emphasizes a 'more substantive' account of freedom as 'the ability … of people to lead the lives they have reason to value and to enhance the real choices they have.'[61] In developing this contrast, Sen relies on a distinction between 'direct' and 'indirect' reasons for which a person values something. Direct valuation includes that which immediately 'enriches' a person's life, including health and nourishment, whereas indirect valuation concerns the further production or

57 HDR, 'Forward', iii, 1990.
58 Sen, *Development as Freedom*, 292–293.
59 Sen, *Development as Freedom*, 293.
60 Sen, *Development as Freedom*, 293–294.
61 Sen, *Development as Freedom*, 294.

command of a 'price in the market'.[62] In this vein, Sen describes the difference between a human capabilities and a human capital approach in terms of 'means and ends'. Human capital theory fails to tell us 'why economic growth is sought in the first place', whereas a human capabilities approach focuses on 'the expansion of human freedom to live the kind of lives that people have reason to value.'[63] In conclusion, Sen acknowledges a more explicit debt to human capital theory, arguing that 'we must go beyond the notion of human capital, after acknowledging its relevance and reach. *The broadening that is needed is additional and inclusive, rather than, in any sense an alternative to the "human capital" perspective.*'[64] In Sen's evaluation, human capital theory understands the mechanisms via which individuals may increase their freedom, but it too readily instrumentalizes that freedom in service to the value of capital accumulation.

Returning to Foucault's analysis, we might query whether human development theory itself tries to reconcile 'heterogeneous accounts of freedom'. For Sen, human freedom consists in one's capacity to live a life that achieves those things an individual chooses to value; that freedom cannot simply be a measure of the degree to which an individual remains 'ungoverned', as in the conception of liberal governmentality that Foucault traces. In order to develop individuals' 'capabilities' the state must often invest in populations and expend substantial resources. Yet, freedom requires that individuals develop capabilities to choose how they invest their time and resources, and to ultimately choose the very things they 'value'. Subjects of human development must be governed just enough to be able to govern themselves. Even though the capabilities theory strives to accept the plurality of human experience, and the myriad possibilities that individuals will value different kinds of lives when capable of doing so, Foucault's account of governmentality might caution against an uncomplicated acceptance of this account of freedom. In what ways must the powers and resources of the state already be mobilized and in place in order to secure a population's development? How autonomous are choices to develop skills and talents when they must be promoted from an early age – how does the imperative to 'increase capability' to achieve goals influence the development of the subject, especially when 'capability' often correlates with capital accumulation?

In the context of human development discourse, the logic of human rights also intertwines with older notions of governmentality and complicates the question of human freedom. Human rights serve as 'values' that individuals should be 'allowed to choose' – and even values that they should be permitted to prize above increased capital accumulation. Yet when development itself is framed as a 'human right', such rights also form the basis for the normative demand of governance and the investment of 'capital' into humans in the first place. We might thus ask after the normative and ontological priority of the human right to

62 Sen, *Development as Freedom*, 296.
63 Sen, *Development as Freedom*, 295.
64 Sen, *Development as Freedom*, 296 (emphasis added).

development in a theory of human freedom. For example, does the right to development also encompass a 'right *not* to develop'? At a level of individual choice, the answer might appear clear – Sen would counsel that any decision to develop one set of capabilities likely comes at the expense of another possible choice. Yet, when capacity and capital are not so easily distinguishable, the question becomes more difficult; when does a subject know to stop accumulating human capital and start expending it on that which they value? More troublingly still, in a world where human capital preservation proves ubiquitous, the very basis for what a subject 'values' may already be highly influenced by the logics of capital maximization. In what ways does the subject of human capital preserve the inner core of freedom as the ability to 'choose what it values', in a world where it is consistently told to value capital accumulation? Foucault asks us to consider how governmentality produces not only productive subjects, but also how it *shapes the desires of those subjects* and the kinds of values they may hold.

IV Concluding reflections

In conclusion, I offer reflections on two different possibilities that might emerge in different contexts where the discourse of human development, human capital, and human rights intersect. First, as a matter of social movement politics, it is helpful to return to Feher's work. Feher helps us consider how Sen's effort to distinguish his approach from human capital theory might compare to other left political projects hoping to challenge neoliberal political orders. Feher suggests that the Left has failed to avail itself of a strategy of challenging 'the hegemony of neoliberalism'. He argues that the political Left typically calls for either the introduction of policies that would 'lessen the social effects of neoliberal policies', or 'a frontal assault on neoliberalism, advocating an unapologetic program of wealth redistribution' and greater public services.[65] Feher proposes a 'third way' approach in which the Left could defy neoliberalism from 'within by embracing the very conditions that its discourses and practices delineate.'[66] In particular, Feher calls for a willing 'inhabiting' of a certain mode of neoliberal subjection in order to redirect neoliberal policies.[67] Could the human development paradigm already provide a means of redirecting the subjective condition of existing as 'human capital' from within that paradigm? Within the discourses and texts of development theory, there already exists a wealth of resources focused on questions of autonomy, self-determination, and the rejection of purely instrumental economic valuation. Could human development theory provide space for a Left politics that rejects the larger macro-economic policies of international financial institutions? A politics that perhaps calls for the 'right to reject' certain forms of capital investment that produce and sustain extreme structural inequality? Could human

65 Feher, 'Self-Appreciation', 21–41.
66 Feher, 'Self-Appreciation', 21.
67 Feher, 'Self-Appreciation', 22–23.

rights – as a strange and hybrid site of investment of governmental technology – become a fulcrum from which to push development discourse from within?

Sen himself remarked in a 1994 piece on famine that:

> Political rights are important not only for the fulfillment of needs, they are crucial for the formulation of needs ... we now frequently hear the working classes called 'the population', just as animals upon a farm [are called] 'the stock'. The importance of political rights for understanding economic needs turns ultimately on seeing human beings as people with rights to exercise, not as parts of a 'stock' or a 'population' that passively exists and must be looked after.[68]

Sen's text explicitly calls for resistance to the pastoral power of liberal governmentality of which Foucault sought to provide a genealogy. Yet, significantly, Sen does not oppose the political right to self-government to the investment of capital in individuals – rather, he calls for preserving a notion of human rights as a way of securing *political autonomy* and avoiding the ultimate instrumentalization of politics in the service of capital accumulation. It would require much greater empirical and historical investigation to document when the discourse of development used human rights as a vehicle for resisting neoliberal logics of capital maximization and in what ways it did so. Nevertheless, Sen's theory of human development may have more to offer Leftists hoping to resist, what Feher calls, the 'neoliberal political condition' than was previously contemplated.

Second, in a parallel but different vein, human rights themselves might function as a novel technique of governance – the political implications of an account of human rights as techniques of government might sit in tension with their potential to serve as a tool of resistance to neoliberal political orders. For indeed, when human rights are viewed in this way, the distinction between human capital theory and the human capabilities approach may be more difficult to preserve in practice. Consider, for example, a 2010 Working Paper the World Bank Human Development Network Education Group produced, evaluating the success of the 'Schultz Hypothesis' over the past few decades. The report's title alone proves illuminating in highlighting the connections between human capital and human rights in the development context: 'Economic Freedom, Human Rights and the Returns on Human Capital: An Evaluation of the Schultz Hypothesis'.[69] The report sought to assess Schultz's notion that capital returns on skill development are highest when states have economic policies that best allow individuals to respond to market shocks. It notably concluded that empirical data supported the Schultz hypothesis in the development context: 'economic freedom benefits those workers who have

68 Amartya Sen, 'Freedoms and Needs', *The New Republic* (1994): 31–37.

69 Elizabeth M. King, Claudio E. Montenegro and Peter F. Oraze, 'Economic Freedom, Human Rights, and the Returns to Human Capital: An Evaluation of the Schultz Hypothesis', *Economic Development and Cultural Change* 61 (2012): 39–72.

attained the highest level of schooling as well as those who have accumulated the most work experience.'[70] The report used a 'human rights data set' – including the 'Empowerment Rights Index' – to measure whether states' record of securing human rights correlated with individuals' capacity to achieve the highest returns on their individual human capital. In this way, the report conceives of the relationship between human rights and human capital valuation differently than does Sen's theory of development: individuals' returns on education and training 'may depend on the protection of individual political rights.'[71] This formulation resonates with Talal Asad's description of contemporary world human rights discourse 'as a mode of converting and regulating people, making them at once freer and more governable in this world.'[72] In this sense, human rights put 'freedom' to work as a kind of regulative principle of subjectivity:

> The employment of cost-benefit analysis derived from neoliberal economics has the advantage of defining 'freedom' quantitatively ... for the consuming subject in terms of behavior. It also provides a pragmatic principle for deciding when and to what extent the government of the population requires restriction or abrogation of particular individual freedoms. The historical convergence between human rights and neo-liberalism may not be purely accidental.[73]

As discussed above, one may see many historical and conceptual reasons for following Asad in diagnosing an affinity between the rise of the language of human rights and practices of neoliberal governance. Human rights discourse converges with certain accounts of 'self-ownership' and 'entrepreneurship': individuals are given rights in order that they might be free to pursue the augmentation of their own interests. The freedom of interest becomes the freedom of self-investment as human capital. Technologies of human rights thus set limits on how state actors

70 King, et al., 'An Evaluation of the Schultz Hypothesis'.

71 King, et al., 'An Evaluation of the Schultz Hypothesis': 'The Human Rights Dataset by Cingranelli and Richards (2005) provides measures of personal freedoms for 198 countries from 1981–2004. We use the Empowerment Rights Index which is constructed from measures of the extent to which individuals in the country had freedom of movement within or out of the country; freedom of speech without government censorship; freedom to participate in politics; freedom of religion; and worker rights protections. This index is positively correlated with the Economic Freedom Index, but at 0.44, the correlation suggests that the two indexes are not identical. Again we will examine how the subcomponents of the index perform relative to the aggregate index, although a single factor loading explains virtually all of the common variation among the subcomponents to human capital as are individual economic freedoms, and yet these freedoms could contribute to a climate of creativity and innovation. Florida (2007) emphasizes that acceptance of individual differences fosters innovation and a climate of entrepreneurship.'

72 Talal Asad, 'Redeeming the Human Through Human Rights', in *Formations of the Secular*, ed., Talal Asad (Stanford: Stanford University Press, 2003), 157.

73 Asad, 'Redeeming the Human', 157.

may intervene in the social field, while also providing countless indicia for determining the ways in which human capital may be measured: accounts of access to education as the acquisition of marketable skills, health as a barometer for one's ability to work, and political freedom as the ability to access and participate in the market economy. Through such measures of human rights performance knowledge-workers (in the form of international NGOs, UN human rights bodies, and governmental human rights agencies) use human rights as tools both for mapping the social field, but also as justifications for its transformation. In this formulation, human rights protections function as a new kind of knowledge and technology of governance: human rights protections are useful insofar as they may measure when human capital returns are likely to be maximized. This knowledge undoubtedly becomes a new tool in the contemporary context of different forms of governmentality – human rights protection becomes instrumentalized insofar as it may become a means and metric for increasing the production of capital. In the complex field of human development, it remains to be seen just when, how and under what conditions, rights and capital may interact to shape the future of humanity.

In the conclusion of her essay on Post-Cold War liberals' resignation to a limited account of international human rights, Wendy Brown reminds us that:

> It is an old ruse of liberal reformers, in pursuing agendas that have significant effects in excess of the explicit reform, to insist that all they are doing is a bit of good or holding back the dark. On this view, rights simply set people free to make the world as they see fit – they do not have normative- or subject-producing dimensions; they do not carry cultural assumptions or aims; they do not prescribe or proscribe anything; they do not configure the political in a particular way or compete with other political possibilities or discourses. They simply expand autonomy and choice. I have suggested otherwise and … argued that we must take account of that which rights discourse does not avow about itself. It is a politics and it organizes political space …[74]

In this short chapter, I offer early thoughts on where we might look to expand the history of how different human rights discourses both make subjects and organize political space. The rhetoric of human development showcases how human rights may come to possess unanticipated meanings – at once evaluated as *a measure of how human capital should be invested*, human rights are also invoked by development economists as a *limiting principle against the excessive instrumentalization of human freedom by capital.*

Of course, my brief effort in this chapter to de-familiarize some standard accounts of human rights and development economics has only scratched the surface of a more complicated relationship between human capital and human rights. Still, I think it is enough to help show that neither lamenting the powerlessness of human rights to combat neoliberal expansionism, nor condemning

74 Brown, 'Human Rights and the Politics of Fatalism', 461.

rights as collaborators in that expansion, will give us insight into the particularities of their contemporary practices. Moreover, observing the intersections and tensions between human rights and human capital should remind us that neither has ever been powerless – rather both rights and capital are exemplary sites through which power operates, distributes, and governs subjects in the contemporary world. Today, critical human rights scholarship requires renewed attention to the complex, dynamic and unanticipated ways in which human rights discourse invests and mobilizes contemporary forms of power as it travels to ever more scenes of political struggle.

Chapter 9

Articulating human rights discourse in local struggles in a neoliberal age

Zeynep Kıvılcım

Introduction

David Harvey stresses that the privatization of water constitutes a new wave of 'enclosing the commons' and a mechanism of 'accumulation by dispossession'.[1] The commodification of water represents 'a distinct dimension of the neoliberalization of nature'[2] and is understood as a crucial phase of the expansion of the market into new spaces of life.[3] As Erik Swyngedouw suggests,[4] over the last two decades water has become one of the central testing grounds for the implementation of global and national neoliberal policies. Moreover, multilateral organizations such as the World Bank and the International Monetary Fund or the European Union (EU) have been centrally involved in regulating and organizing the privatization and dispossession of water.

The Turkish government is currently planning to 'exploit the total hydropower potential of the country' through the construction of about two thousand river-type hydroelectric power plants (HPPs) by the end of 2023.[5] The official statistics reveal that the vast majority of HPPs are and will be constructed and operated by private companies licensed for the exclusive use of the water derived from those rivers.[6] The opposition to HPPs is spread throughout Turkey due to the construction of these plants in almost every region of the country.

1 David Harvey, 'The "New" Imperialism: Accumulation by Dispossesion', *Socialist Register* 40 (2004): 63–87, 75.
2 Karen Bakker, 'Neoliberalizing nature? Market environmentalism in water supply in England and Wales', *Annals of the Association of American Geographers* 95, no. 3 (2005): 542–565, 544.
3 Adrienne Roberts, 'Privatizing Social Reproduction: The Primitive Accumulation of Water in an Era of Neoliberalism', *Antipode* 40, no. 4 (2008): 535–560, 540.
4 Erik Swyngedouw, 'Dispossing H_2O: The Contested Terrain of Water Privatization', *Capitalism Nature Socialism* 16, no. 1 (2005): 81–98.
5 See the statement on the official website of Ministry of Energy and Natural Resources: Yenilenebilir Enerji Genel Müdürlüğü, Enerji ve Tabii Kaynaklar Bakanlığı, *Türkiye'nin Hidroelektrik Potansiyeli*, http://www.eie.gov.tr/yenilenebilir/h_turkiye_potansiyel.aspx, accessed December 5, 2015.
6 Only 10 per cent of the HPPs are planned, constructed and operated by the State. According to the numbers given by the General Directorate of State Hydraulic Works,

As the Marxist legal scholar Robert Knox reminds us, law is pervasive in the contemporary world and hence almost all political debate is conducted in juridical terms.[7] The political controversy over HPPs in Turkey is no exception. Law and legal terms are indeed the critical tools in the context of political struggles over water privatization in Turkey. Knox proposes the use of law with what he labels 'principled opportunism',[8] but the problem with this approach is that a legal intervention that is successful in 'tactical' terms, so as to achieve the conjunctural aims of a political movement, can nevertheless be very problematic in 'strategic' terms, and thus potentially undermine the movement's systemic objectives in the long term. The use of a legalist human rights discourse for organizing political struggles can be considered risky in precisely these terms, since its use could potentially lead to the capitulation of political action to liberal legalism.

The 'right to water' constitutes one of the pivotal but controversial concepts of the anti-HPP campaign in Turkey. This right is not protected as a self-standing human right in Turkey's national legislation. Moreover, the scope of the right to water is not fully defined in international legal documents and its recognition does not foreclose (neither in theory nor in practice) the private sector participation in water management and supply.

In this context, the aim of this chapter is to study the use of human rights discourse in a local struggle against the commodification of water and to investigate the operational importance and limits of the concept of the 'right to water' as a new human right 'under construction' for local mobilization and resistance against the construction of HPPs in Turkey. Deploying the human right to water as a conceptual base for organizing or legitimizing the anti-privatization campaigns is problematized by several commentators. Karen Bakker points out that human rights are individualistic, anthropocentric, state-centric and compatible with the private sector provision of water supply, and as such represent a limited strategy for those seeking to refute water privatization.[9] Indeed, she stresses that the right to water not only fails to foreclose the possibility of increasing private sector involvement in water supply, but in fact serves as an argument *for* the privatization

the State institution responsible for the HPPs, by December 31, 2014 the number of active HPPs is 503 (65 of them are operated by the State) and there are 984 river-type HPP projects in the country, some of which are currently in the process of construction or at the planning stage (only 86 of them are projects run by the State) (see 'Anadolu'nun İl İl Baraj ve HES Soykırım Haritası', http://www.kuzeyormanlari.org/2015/03/30/anadolunun-il-il-baraj-ve-hes-soykirim-haritasi/, accessed December 5, 2015).

7 Robert Knox, 'Strategy and Tactics', in *Finnish Yearbook of International Law*, Vol. 21, ed., Jan Klabbers (Oxford: Hart Publishing, 2010), 210.

8 That would mean that 'law should always be openly invoked instrumentally and openly subordinated to political considerations' (ibid., 222).

9 Karen Bakker, 'The "Commons" versus the "Commodity": Alter-globalization, Anti-privatization and the Human Right to Water in the Global South', *Antipode* 39, no. 3 (2007): 430–455.

of water management.[10] Bronwen Morgan warns that rights have an inevitable regulatory face, and strategies to implement them will center on the articulation of substantive regulatory standards.[11] She argues that it 'makes more sense to think of a right to water not in direct opposition to market provision but as constituting a minimum acceptable baseline of market activity, a baseline constructed by regulatory intervention'.[12]

In fact, there is a proliferating conception of the right to water, according to which the private sector intervention in water management and supply is not a breach of this right, but on the contrary constitutes a necessary condition of its effective implementation. There are strong international movements which argue that water would be optimally allocated and the right to water would be effectively implemented *only* by making water marketable and by expanding the trade in water.[13]

However, while the concept of the right to water is articulated and instrumentalized for legitimating the privatization of water supply and management systems, the scope of this right is still not fully defined in international law. Accordingly, discussions continue in the international intergovernmental apparatus, and in particular within different organs and commissions of the United Nations, on the different possible normative formulations of the right to water. Water is an 'uncooperative' and 'resistant' commodity to neoliberal reforms with its symbolic, spiritual and ecological functions and appears as an 'ultimate frontier of privatization'.[14]

The contention of this chapter is that human rights are constituted by and through struggle about ideas and values. Antonio Gramsci explains that 'hegemony' operates through the shifts and modifications in the 'common sense' and

10 Bakker reminds us that proponents of private sector water supply management assert that market forces are the best means of fulfilling the right to water. They argue that 'this increasingly scarce resource which must be priced at full economic and environmental cost if it is to be allocated to its highest-value uses, and managed profitably by private companies whose accountability to customers and shareholders is more direct and effective than attenuated political accountability exercised by citizens via political representatives' (ibid., 432 and 439).

11 Bronwen Morgan, 'The North–South Politics of Necessity: Regulating for Basic Rights between National and International Levels', *Journal of Consumer Policy* 29, no. 4 (2006): 465–487.

12 Ibid., 469.

13 In this vein, principle no. 4 of the Dublin Statement on Water and Sustainable Development adopted at the closing session of the International Conference on Water and the Environment in 1992 recognized that 'water has an economic value in all its competing uses and should be recognized as an economic good … Past failure to recognize the economic value of water has led to wasteful and environmentally damaging uses of the resource. Managing water as an economic good is an important way of achieving efficient and equitable use and of encouraging conservation and protection of water resources.'

14 Bronwen Morgan, 'Social Protest against Privatization of Water: Forging Cosmopolitan Citizenship', in *Sustainable Justice: Reconciling Economic, Social and Environmental Law*, eds, Marie-Claire Cordonier Seggier and Judge C.G. Weeramantry (Leiden: Martinus Nijhoff, 2005), 9.

that the common sense is open to multiple interpretations and is for this reason potentially supportive of different kinds of social and political projects.[15] For Gramsci, counter-hegemony names the process by which subordinate classes challenge the dominant hegemony by countering and deconstructing the common sense,[16] in part by deploying concepts and symbols constitutive of the prevailing hegemony itself. Hence, as part of an emergent 'common sense', human rights can constitute elements of a counter-hegemonic strategy of political action. I follow Chantal Mouffe, who stresses that human rights have a political character and that the debate about human rights is taking place in a terrain shaped by power relations where a hegemonic struggle takes place and makes room for a plurality of legitimate understandings.[17] Wendy Brown argues in the same vein that rights are 'protean and irresolute signifiers, varying not only across time and culture but across the other vectors of power'.[18] The political potency of rights thus lies in their character as 'empty signifiers', and their becoming 'a project for discursive struggle whose parameters are invented rather than secured in advance and whose outcome is never guaranteed'.[19]

In the first part of the chapter I will give a brief overview of Turkey's anti-HPP movement. The movement perceives the right to water as a 'legal' concept, hence its acceptance and its instrumentalization by the movement depends largely on the general approach of different associations and actors active in the anti-HPP movement towards law and legal concepts. For this reason, in the second part I will investigate the relationship of the anti-HPP movement to law and legal instruments.

The fact that the scope of the right to water remains as yet undefined and that this legal concept is in *statu nascendi* is important while discussing its function(s) for the anti-HPP struggle in Turkey. For that reason, in the third part of the chapter I will briefly explain the concurrent, often discordant, legal texts adopted or still under discussion within different intergovernmental organizations relating the definition of the scope of right to water as an individual or collective right or with an ecological perspective in order to overcome the anthropocentrism of human rights discourse. Finally, in the fourth part, I will discuss the tactical and strategical functions of the right to water in the anti-HPPs movement in Turkey. The aim of this part is to investigate the eventual repercussions of the hegemonic struggles in the international organizations relating to the normative content of the right to water on its local understandings in the domestic struggle in Turkey.

15 Antonio Gramsci, *Selections from the Prison Notebooks of Antonio Gramsci*, eds and trans., Quintin Hoare and Geoffrey Nowell Smith (New York: International Publishers, 1971), 323–334.

16 Gramsci indicates that 'It must be a criticism of "common sense" ... it is not a question of introducing from scratch a scientific form of thought into everyone individual life, but of renovating and making "critical" an already existing activity' (ibid., 387–388).

17 Chantal Mouffe, *On the Political* (Abingdon: Psychology Press, 2005), 126.

18 Wendy Brown, *States of Injury: Power and freedom in late modernity* (Princeton, NJ: Princeton University Press, 1995), 97 and 116.

19 Ibid., 134.

My methodology rests both on documentary analysis and semi-structured interviews. The interviews were conducted during spring 2013 with five leading figures of the anti-HPP movement in Turkey. The interviewees were selected from different associations, initiatives and platforms in the anti-HPP struggle so as to collect empirical data about the diverse approaches adopted in different components of the movement.

The anti-HPP movement in Turkey

Turkey does not generate enough primary energy resources and hydropower is regarded as one of the most stable and economical energy sources by the government. The country has a mountainous landscape which favors the formation of high gradient mountain streams suitable for the development of small hydropower plants. Since 2000 several legislative attempts have been made to encourage private companies to invest in river type small hydropower plants.[20]

In many cases, different HPPs are planned so as to be constructed immediately one after the other over the same river. Because of the consecutive construction of many plants, the water is diverted into the pipes, canals and tunnels all along the river's roads, starting nearly from their very sources to where they empty into the sea. Consequently, these HPPs prevent local people from accessing the rivers and from making use of the water for agricultural and other purposes.[21] Furthermore,

20 The publication of Electricity Market Law (Law No. 4628) of March 2001 led to the establishment of the Electricity Market Regulatory Authority and it permits private sector legal entities to obtain a license granted from this authority to build and operate power plants. In 2001, the Industrial Development Bank of Turkey (TSKB) started to provide loans for setting up hydropower plants for electricity generation. With the Renewable Energy Law (Law No. 5346) of May 2005, the government guaranteed to buy electricity from legal entities with a fixed price for a duration of ten years. In addition to this, an 85 per cent discount is applied for forest land acquisition to build small size hydropower plants. In July 2008, Law No. 5784 allowed legal entities to be exempted from obtaining a license to generate electricity from renewable energy up to a capacity of 500 kW. According to this law, the government also guarantees to buy the excess electricity. The Environmental Impact Assessment (EIA) report was not required for HPPs up to an installed capacity of 50 MW until the issue of a regulation in July 2008. See further Serhat Kucukali and Kemal Baris, 'Assessment of Small Hydropower (SHP) Development in Turkey: Laws, Regulations and EU Policy Perspective', *Energy Policy* 37, no. 10 (2009): 3872–3879; Mehmet Capik, Ali Osman Yılmaz and İbrahim Cavusoglu, 'Hydropower for Sustainable Energy Development in Turkey: The Small Hydropower Case of the Eastern Black Sea Region', *Renewable and Sustainable Energy Reviews* 16, no. 8 (2012): 6160–6172, 6165.

21 The HPPs risk leading to the impoverishment of small-scale farmers; the yield will decrease first of all because of the irrigation problems, since the river water traditionally used for irrigation is diverted into pipes and canals and is not accessible for farmers. Additionally, the HPPs will cause important changes in the rainfall regime. See A. Aysu, 'Subsistence Agriculture and Water' (paper presented at the Alternative World Water Forum, March 14–17, 2012).

experts are warning that when the river is diverted into the pipes and tunnels for HPPs, the remaining water will be insufficient for natural ecosystems to function.[22]

The government is very committed to pushing forward the building of HPPs despite the social opposition and ecological risks. The Forestry and Water Affairs Minister declared that his government had eased the administrative burdens on building HPPs and boasted that his Ministry handles the transactions so fast that he is able to sign 300–350 permits in a day.[23] In December 2013, during his speech in the National Assembly defending the new budget, he argued that the HPPs are necessary and indispensable for the country.[24]

The anti-HPP struggle in Turkey started at the end of the 1990s. This growing movement actually comprises a multitude of valley associations, initiatives and unions established in a quite autonomous way in the affected provinces as well as in the larger cities of Turkey. Later on, these initiatives and associations came together under the umbrella of platforms or assemblies such as 'No to the Commercialization of Water Platform',[25] the 'Platform of Sisterhood-Brotherhood of Rivers',[26] the 'Council for the Protection of Munzur

22 Beyza Üstün (2009) 'Su'yu Korumak', *Doğa ve Toplum*, 1, https://ekolojiagi.wordpress.com/2011/02/11/%E2%80%9Csu%E2%80%9Dyu-korumak-beyza-ustun/, accessed December 5, 2015; Emine Girgin, 'Hidroelektrik Santrallerin Çevresel Etkileri', *Ölçü*, December 2010, 46–47, http://ikkistanbul.org/olcu/2010/webicin_icsayfalar.pdf, accessed December 5, 2015.

23 'Government to ease hydro plant construction for firms', *Hurriyet Daily News*, April 4, 2013, http://www.hurriyetdailynews.com/government-to-ease-hydro-plant-construction-for-firms.aspx?pageID=238&nID=44231&NewsCatID=348, accessed November 18, 2015.

24 'İki bakan arasında HES gerginliği', *Internet Haber*, December 14, 2013, http://www.internethaber.com/iki-bakan-arasinda-hes-gerginligi-618757h.htm, accessed November 18, 2015.

25 'No to the Commercialization of Water Platform' (Suyun Ticarileşmesine Hayır Platformu) started in April 2008. It struggles against the commercialization of water in Turkey, which is considered as posing a threat towards all peoples and living creatures. It urges providing domestic water free of charge and supplying cost-free water for irrigation, to those who engage in subsistence farming. The Platform considers 'the United Nations as part of the problem, not as part of the solution, due to the fact that it is the first international institution that defines water as a commercial good (commodity).' No to Commercialization of Water Platform, Istanbul Declaration against the 5th World Water Forum, March 15–22, 2009, Istanbul, http://labournet.de/internationales/tr/wasserplattform.pdf, accessed December 5, 2015. The Platform has an anti-capitalist perspective and stresses the need for ensuring the sustainability of all life and nature. Activist in No to the Commercialization of Water Platform, Beyza Üstün, interviews with author March 13, 2013, Istanbul, May 21, 2013, January 20, 2014.

26 'The Sisterhood/Brotherhood of Rivers Platform' (Derelerin Kardeşliği Platformu) was founded in 2007. The Platform consists of a network of different anti-HPP groups organized in different valleys of the Black Sea region and it is struggling against the privatization of the water and other natural resources. Derelerin Kardeşliği Platformu, *HES (Hidroelektrik Santralleri) Raporu*, March 17, 2010, http://derelerinkardesligi.org/web/pdf/derelerin-kardesligi-platformu-HES-raporu.pdf, accessed December 5, 2015; B. Kalın, electronic communication with author, May 12, 2013.

Valley'[27] and the 'Turkey Water Assembly'.[28] There are also individual lawyers and academics who are active in the movement.

The movement does not share a common ideological, social or cultural identity. Some components of the movement are established by the local people in the towns or villages where the HPPs are constructed, but some other components originate in the cities and remain active there.[29] The organizational practices as well as the political engagements differ in each locality, valley or association. Some local people active in the anti-HPP movement have been involved in political or social movements before, but for most of them this is the first time that they have organized against the state authorities, and the anti-HPP marches are the first demonstrations in which they have ever participated. The anti-capitalist emphasis is important for most of the activists in the anti-HPP movement, but not all people in the movement share a critical opinion about the capitalist system or about the government's policies in general. As a matter of fact, the population living in some localities affected by the HPPs is supportive of nationalistic and right-wing political discourses, whereas others have past or

27 Council for the Protection of Munzur Valley (Munzur Koruma Kurulu) was established in 1999 with the objective of bringing Munzur Valley to the public's attention and to prevent all kinds of activity which could cause ecological harm to Munzur Valley and its surroundings. Munzur Valley is situated in Eastern Anatolia, where the population is in major part Kurdish and Alevi (Anatolian Si'ism), H. Şen, interview with author, Istanbul, May 18, 2013.

28 The Turkey Water Assembly was established in January 2010 by declaring a *Water Manifesto*. According to that Manifesto, the Water Assembly adopts the non-commodification of water as a fundamental principle and commits itself to struggle against its privatization. The Assembly is severely criticized by other associations and platforms in the anti-HPP movement. These critics denounce the central arguments of the Turkish Water Assembly based on the EU Water Framework Directive. The Assembly approves and adopts the EU Directive key concept of 'integrated river basin management' (IRBM), whereas other associations in the movement strongly condemn the conceptual framework of the Directive that aims at the effective pricing of water (meaning its commodification). They also condemn the IRBM because it will open the river basins to the management by global water sector. See, e.g. the statement of the Supolitik Working Group and member of the 'No to the Commercialization of Water Platform' about the Turkish Water Assembly (Supolitik, *Büyük Anadolu Yürüyüşü ve Sermayenin Yeni Içerme Stratejileri*, http://www.supolitik.org/buyuk_anadolu_yuruyusu_ve_sermayenin_yeni_icerme_stratejileri.htm, accessed December 5, 2015), and the article written by Yusuf Gürcusu (from TÜRÇEP (Turkey Environmental Platform), member of the 'No to the Commercialization of Water Platform') in the daily newspaper *Evrensel* on February 26, 2011.

29 Turkey experiences a high level of internal migration, not only rural to urban migration but also massive and continuous displacement of Kurdish people. The migrants generally preserve their ties with their homeland, and the 'associations of fellow-countrymen' that they establish in cities are an important and active component of Turkey's civil society. The 'associations of fellow-countrymen' of different localities established in big cities are active in the struggle against the HPP construction in their home-valleys. The associations of fellow-countrymen of the Black Sea Region and of Munzur Valley are particularly important in this regard.

present ties with left-wing political movements as well as the Kurdish political movement.[30]

The movement's relationship with law and legal instruments

Social struggles can have an ambivalent relationship with law. As Rajagopal stresses, 'at one level, they tend to see law as a force for domination which must either be contested as part of a larger political struggle or largely ignored as irrelevant. Yet, they can hardly avoid the law as it also provides them space for resistance'.[31] Furthermore, the outcomes of social movements' engagements with the law are highly uncertain in terms of their impact either on law or on the movements themselves, since there are significant tensions between the internal logic of the law (its language, method and sources of legitimacy) and the logic of social movement struggles.[32] The emancipatory potential of law for social movements depends not only on the struggle over the translation of social conflict into legal categories, but also on the struggle over tactical and procedural matters. While using the law with a 'principled opportunism', there is a necessity to frame tactics in terms of strategy and not adopt 'those methods of intervening in the conjuncture which – whilst successful on their own terms – undermine the ultimate objective'.[33]

From their very beginnings almost all associations or platforms in the anti-HPP movement in Turkey made use of the available legal instruments as a tool of contestation. Some of the local anti-HPP associations were instigated by the lawsuits filed for the annulment of the HPP projects and the lawyers were the first community organizers. In many cases, several lawsuits were engaged for a single HPP project. This is because different court decisions were needed for the annulment of the Environmental Impact Assessment (EIA) report, for the agreement which gives to the private company the exclusive right to the use of the waters of the concerned river, and for the cancellation of the production license attributed by the Energy Market Regulatory Authority.

Since the end of 1990s more than 80 lawsuits have been filed before the administrative courts against dams and HPPs. Courts have given decisions for almost half of these cases. An overwhelming majority of the cases have resulted in the cancellation of HPP projects on the grounds that the submitted EIA reports were inadequate or misleading or the HPP projects were associated with protected areas.[34] Since the right to water is not protected as a self-standing right in Turkey's legislation, the

30 Özlem Saadet Işıl, 'Toplumsal Hareket Örneği: HES Karşıtı Mücadeleler', *Sosyolojik Tartışmalar* 3 (2012): 10–24.

31 Balakrishnan Rajagopal, 'Limits of Law in Counter-hegemonic Globalization: The Indian Supreme Court and the Narmada Valley Struggle', in *Law and Globalization from Below: Towards a Cosmopolitan Legality*, eds., Boaventura de Sousa Santos and César A. Rodríguez-Garavito (Cambridge: Cambridge University Press, 2005), 183.

32 Ibid., 184, 188.

33 Knox, 'Strategy and Tactics', 220.

34 Mahmut Hamsici, *Dereler ve İsyanlar* (Ankara: Note Bene, 2010), 193–196.

lawyers base their claims for the annulment of HPP projects on the right to life[35] as well as on the right to live in a healthy and balanced environment.[36] They do not directly refer to a 'right to water', but instead argue that the HPP projects breach the right to life because water is indispensable to sustain the life of all living elements of nature. They also maintain that the projects are equally in breach of the right to the environment, since they harm the natural hydrological cycles in the local ecosystems.

Although the individuals or associations in the anti-HPP movement are actively engaged in the use of lawsuits, the actors' points of view differ quite markedly concerning the function of legal instruments for organizing and orienting local struggles. They agree on the fact that law and legal discourse should be adopted as a tactic and not as a strategy. But they hold divergent opinions on when and how legal discourse should be used in order to win the conjuncture without destroying the ultimate objective. Some activists in the movement attribute a very important and vital role to the legal instruments. A lawyer active in the Black Sea anti-HPP movement, for example, stresses that, at the end of the 1990s, the lawsuits actually preceded and catalyzed the struggle in the social field and initiated the organization of the anti-HPP movement. The positive court rulings contributed to the local people's self-confidence and encouraged them to continue the resistance socially.[37] He thinks that the legal instruments continue to serve as means for demonstrating to the local people that the struggle against HPPs is necessary and that it is possible to prevent these projects.[38]

For some other lawyers and activists in the movement, the legal instruments have performed a more limited role and the legal language mainly compensates for the lack of a politicized ecological culture in Turkey. But even these commentators recognize law's tactical role. They stress that the legal instruments state the grounds for legitimacy of the local claims.[39] According to them, the law, in its official dimension in the lawsuits, exposes different sides of the struggles in a very concrete way. The legal adjectives of 'plaintiff', 'respondent' or 'intervener', make clear the positions and contribute to the organization of the struggle.[40]

Yet some activists suggest that the lawsuits have had some harmful impacts on the movement. Representatives of the platforms and lawyers active in the anti-HPP movement remind us that the positive court rulings do not foreclose the construction of the concerned HPPs, since the court decisions do not generally give the authorities the incentive for abandoning the related projects. They just slightly revise the part of the project which motivated the court decision and do not prevent its implementation in other respects.[41] The lawyers in the movements also admit that

35 Constitution of Turkey, art. 17.
36 Constitution of Turkey, art. 56.
37 Kalın.
38 Ibid.
39 M. Horuş, electronic communication with author, May 15, 17, 2013; H. Şen.
40 Horuş.
41 B. Üstün, interview with author, Istanbul, March 13, 2013, May 21, 2013, Jan 20, 2014; N. Fettahoğlu, fax communication with author, May 15, 2013.

they need to engage in several lawsuits for every single HPP project and that, given the huge number of the HPPs in construction or at the planning phase, there is no real possibility for using litigation as an effective tactic against the HPPs.[42]

Moreover, several activists in the movement stress that positive court decisions cause slackness in the movement, which proves very risky since in most cases the court decisions are not executed or the government enacts new legislation to avoid the effect of the court decisions.[43] The 2010 constitutional amendment[44] and the draft Law on Nature and Biodiversity Conservation presented to the Turkish National Assembly[45] further complicate the legal struggle against HPPs. The constitutional amendment provides for the restriction of the competence of the administrative courts and the draft Law on Nature and Biodiversity Conservation may lead to the protection status of all nature preserves being revoked. It will consequently have a very negative impact on the lawsuits concerning the HPPs constructed in the protected areas.

The anti-capitalist emphasis is important for most of the activists in the anti-HPP movement. Some think that the legal language should be used in courts, but not for organizing the wider resistance and struggle. According to them, the distinction is important and the arguments that the movement puts forward in the courts are just instrumental for stopping the projects. The argumentation before the judge could and should follow a different logic than the fundamental political principles that the movement asserts in the field.[46] The legal arguments are in many cases the fruits of tactical and opportunistic moves in the courtrooms and they can be harmful if they are converted into broader, political arguments.[47]

It seems that the instrumentalization of legal concepts remains an important controversy in the movement. However, a consensus is emerging on the fact that the transplantation of the legal arguments in the struggle's language and organizing the movement in the field with respect to this terminology need to be accomplished with some care. An arduous discussion still continues on how to find ways to ensure the cancellation of the HPP projects in the courts by making defensive use of already existing legal concepts in the legislation while, at the same time, the movement discusses the need to construct new and fertile concepts that will serve as 'weapons' in the hands of the activists who organize the resistance at the local level.[48] In this context, the articulation of the concept of right to water provokes controversy among different groups and activists in the movement.

42 Hamsici, *Dereler ve İsyanlar*, 195.
43 Fettahoğlu; Üstün; Şen.
44 An amendment of art. 125 of the Constitution which took place in 2010 restricted the competence of the administrative courts.
45 The draft law provides different system and new procedures for the attribution of the status of natural preservation areas.
46 Üstün.
47 Istanbul Bar Association, *HES Hidroelektrik Santralleri: Ekosisteme Etkileri Ve Dava Tipleri: Panel Notları*, İstanbul Barosu Yayınları Genel Yayın Sıra no. 194 (Istanbul: İstanbul Barosu Yayınları, 2011), 157.
48 Ibid., 154–160.

The right to water as a universal right in *statu nascendi*

In this part of the chapter I will describe the discussions over the last two decades within the intergovernmental organizations regarding the legal definition of the right to water. Against this background of the legal-semantic struggles over the construction of a new universal right, I will try to assess in Gramscian terms the 'counter-hegemonic' potential of the right to water for the local anti-privatization movement in Turkey.

Gramsci explains that counter-hegemony deploys concepts and symbols constitutive of the prevailing hegemony.[49] Ernesto Laclau and Chantal Mouffe, who further elaborate the concept of 'hegemony', stress that:

> the meaning of liberal discourse on individual rights is not definitively fixed; and just as this unfixity permits their articulation with elements of conservative discourse, it also permits different forms of articulation and redefinition which accentuate the democratic moment ... The elements making up the liberal discourse never appear as crystallized, and may be the field of hegemonic struggle.[50]

The definition and the legal recognition of universal human rights have historically been materialized as a result of social and political struggles. Different generations of human rights are socially constructed, distorted and reconstructed throughout history in the struggle for producing and modifying popular consent. Human rights take shape and are constituted by and through struggles about ideas and values. Hence, as a part of an emergent 'common sense', they constitute elements of a counter-hegemonic strategy of social transformation.[51]

Defending water as a human right produces and modifies the 'common sense' surrounding water provision. A substantial number of laws and statutes from different countries recognize the individual right to water.[52] The majority of these laws have been adopted during the past few years and they prioritize water for essential human needs over any other use.[53]

49 The counter-hegemonic project involves 'the concrete birth of a need to construct a new intellectual and moral order, and hence the need to develop more universal concepts and more refined and decisive ideological weapons'. Gramsci, *Selections*, 388.

50 Ernesto Laclau and Chantal Mouffe, *Hegemony and Socialist Strategy: Towards a Radical Democratic Politics*, 2nd edn (London: Verso, 2001), 176.

51 Alan Hunt, 'Rights and Social Movements: Counter-hegemonic Strategies', *Journal of Law and Society* 17, no. 3 (1990): 309–328, 325.

52 See, e.g. Constitution of the Democratic Republic of Congo, art. 48; Constitution of Ecuador, arts. 23. 42; Constitution of Nicaragua, art. 105; Constitution of South Africa of 1996, art. 27; Constitution of Uganda, preamble; Constitution of Uruguay; Palestinian Water Authority, Water Law (Law No. 3/2002), art. 3; Paraguay Law on Water Resources (Law No. 3239/2007), art. 3; WASH United, Freshwater Action Network and WaterLex, *The Human Right to Safe Drinking Water and Sanitation in Law and Policy – A Sourcebook* (2012).

53 See, e.g. Decree No. 2005-191, April 4, 2005 regarding priority uses and authority of government to control and allocate water in case of water shortage (Burkina Faso), art.

Water has not been explicitly recognized as a self-standing human right in legal international documents, but the right to access safe drinking water and sanitation has increasingly been recognized in core human rights treaties, mainly as part of the right to an adequate standard of living and the right to health.[54] The UN General Assembly adopted a resolution on 'the human right to water and sanitation' in 2010, and recognized 'the right to safe and clean drinking water and sanitation as a human right that is essential for the full enjoyment of life and all human rights'.[55]

While the UN Covenant on Economic, Social and Cultural Rights does not explicitly refer to the right to water, in November 2002 the Committee on Economic, Social and Cultural Rights adopted its General Comment No. 15 on the right to water, where it interprets the right to water as a necessary precondition for the realization of the right to an adequate standard of living, the right to the highest attainable standard of health, and the rights to adequate housing and adequate food.[56] The General Comment provides an authoritative, but not a legally binding, interpretation of the right to water under the International Covenant on Economic, Social and Cultural Rights.

In the General Comment, the Committee frames the right to water as an individual right and states that the priority of water uses should go to water for survival and basic needs. It briefly covers water for subsistence farming and agriculture as it is essential for survival. According to the General Comment, water for survival and dignity (water for basic needs) is the primary element of the 'core content' of the right to water. As to the 'scope of the right', it includes all other elements of the right, which are not considered to be core. They are of a lesser priority in terms of the progressive realization of the right than its core elements. The use of water for agriculture (except for the special case of an agrarian society) is an element within the scope of the right to water.[57] The Committee on

2; Water Code 2005 (Mauritania), art. 5; Law on Water Resources 2007 (Paraguay), art. 3; Water Resources Act 2009 (Peru), arts 3, 35.

54 As examples we can cite the Convention on the Elimination of All Forms of Discrimination Against Women, Dec. 18, 1979, 1249 UNTS 13, art. 24(2)(c); Convention on the Rights of the Child, Nov. 20, 1989, 1577 UNTS 3, arts 20, 26, 29, 46. The Geneva Conventions and Additional Protocols I and II outline the fundamental importance of access to safe drinking water and sanitation in armed conflicts.

55 The Human Right to Water and Sanitation, GA Res. 64/292, 108th plen. mtg., UN Doc. A/RES/64/292 (Jul. 28, 2010). Turkey abstained from voting on the Resolution.

56 Article 11 of the Covenant states that everyone has the right to an adequate standard of living, including food, clothing and housing. The open-endedness of this wording – in particular the word 'including' – allowed the Committee the interpretative freedom to recognize comparable basic rights.

57 Drawing such a sharp distinction between the 'water for basic needs' and 'water for agriculture', between the 'water' and the 'food' seems to be problematic. The UN Food and Agriculture Organization argues that 'the role of water for traditional livelihoods and the specific situation of pastoralists and people in societies where livestock is of overarching importance should be considered as a separate issue. In these contexts a

Economic, Social and Cultural Rights refrained from declaring that private sector participation in water provision is contrary to the right to water.[58]

Bakker argues that '"rights talk" offers us an unimaginative language for thinking about new community economies' and explains that, by contrast, the 'commons' is an effective strategy for combating privatization because 'it correctly opposes a collective property right to private property rights'.[59] In this context, I want to investigate the possibility and the actual discussions for the formulation of a right to water that embraces the commons' approach and asserts the ties that water maintains with ecosystems through the hydrological cycle.

Within the existing texts of international human rights law a collective right to water could, in the first place, be formulated in the framework of 'peoples' rights' to the means of subsistence as well as of their 'right to self-determination'. The International Covenant on Civil and Political Rights and the International Covenant on Economic, Social and Cultural Rights provide in their first articles that 'a people cannot be deprived of its own means of subsistence' and that 'all peoples may for their own ends freely dispose of their natural wealth and resources'. Furthermore, ILO Convention no. 169 guarantees indigenous peoples' right to the natural resources pertaining to their lands.[60]

As a collective right, the right to water can also be claimed in conjunction with the emergent concept of 'peasants' rights'. *La Via Campesina*[61] has worked actively over recent years to bring the Declaration of the Rights of Peasants to the UN Human Rights Council.[62] These efforts have recently brought results in the context of the UN human rights system's responses to the 2008 global food crisis. In February 2012, the Human Rights Council Advisory Committee submitted a final study to the Human Rights Council on the advancement of the rights of peasants and other people working in rural areas.[63] The study endorsed fully *La*

sharp differentiation and different prioritization of water for human consumption and of water for food production does not reflect the peculiarities of pastoral systems'. Food and Agriculture Organization, Draft General Comment No. 15, submission to the Day of General Discussion on the General Comment on the Right to Water, UN CESCR 29th sess., Geneva, November 22, 2002.

58 But according to the General Comment, the involvement of the private sector must be consistent with the democratic principles, particularly the right to participation.

59 Bakker, 'The "Commons" versus the "Commodity"', 448–449.

60 Convention Concerning Indigenous and Tribal Peoples in Independent Countries, art. 15, Jun. 27, 1989, ILO C169.

61 *La Via Campesina*, founded in 1993, is the largest movement of peasant organizations, and actually comprises about 150 local and national organizations in 70 countries from Africa, Asia, Europe and the Americas. It allegedly represents more than 200 million peasants.

62 *La Via Campesina* adopted the 'Declaration of Rights of Peasants – Women and Men' in 2008. The Declaration provides in art. VI/4 that 'peasants (women and men) have the right to water for irrigation and agricultural production in sustainable production systems controlled by local communities'.

63 UN Human Rights Council Advisory Committee, *Final Study on the Advancement of the Rights of Peasants and Other People Working in Rural Areas*, HRC 8th sess., February 20–24, 2012, UN Doc. A/HRC/AC/8/6.

Via Campesina's Declaration of the Rights of Peasants – Men and Women, adopted in 2008, and urged the elaboration of a new international human rights instrument. According to the Advisory Committee, the new instrument should recognize the new rights of peasants and other people working in rural areas, such as the rights to land, to seeds and to the means of production.[64] The Committee therefore proposed a draft declaration on the rights of peasants. The draft declaration defines 'peasants' in a way that represents them as an important part of the transnational working class and provides that peasants have the right to safe drinking water and the right to water for farming, fishing and livestock keeping[65] as well as the right, individually or collectively, to the lands and water bodies.[66]

In its work for the adoption of peasants' rights in a UN declaration, *La Via Campesina* takes the existing legal order and its institutions into account for reasons of expediency and adopts tactics to transcend the liberal individual conception of rights. Its strategic aim is to ensure the control of peasants and other people working in the rural areas on the means of agricultural production. *La Via Campesina*'s work for the UN declaration is an important attempt to use existing law and human rights concepts in a form of 'principled opportunism' (following Knox).

The adoption of a human-centered right to water leaves unresolved the inherent conflict between human needs and the requirements of nature. Several commentators argue that this conflict would be reconciled if we look and see the needs of ecosystems as 'common needs'.[67] Every aquatic ecosystem requires a certain amount of water to maintain its ecological integrity. The water requirements for ecosystem functioning also have social and economic content associated

64 In September 2012, the Human Rights Council decided to establish an open-ended intergovernmental working group with the mandate of negotiating, finalizing and submitting a draft UN Declaration on the rights of peasants on the basis of the draft submitted by the Advisory Committee (Human Rights Council, 2012). The first session of the working group took place in July 2013 during which the opposition of the United States and the European states blocked the negotiations of the draft. The second session of the intergovernmental group on the rights of peasants and other people working in rural areas was held in February 2015. A revised draft Declaration was presented. The new draft takes up most of the proposals put forward by *La Via Campesina* and includes the right to land and other natural resources, the right to means of production, the right to seeds and the right to water.

65 The draft declaration defines the term peasant in its first article as 'a man or woman of the land, who has a direct and special relationship with the land and nature through the production of food or other agricultural products'. 'The term peasant can apply to any person engaged in agriculture, cattle-raising, pastoralism, handicrafts related to agriculture or a similar occupation in a rural area. This includes indigenous people working on the land'. According to the draft the term also applies to the landless.

66 Draft UN Declaration on the Rights of Peasants and Other People Working in Rural Areas, art. 24 on 'Rights to water and sanitation' and art. 19 on 'Right to land and other natural resources'.

67 See Dinara Ziganshina, 'Rethinking the Concept of the Human Right to Water', *Santa Clara Journal of International Law* 6, no. 1 (2008): 113–128.

with the food security and livelihood of millions of poor people in developing countries.[68] Thus, the river could be framed as a 'common reserve'.

The General Comment of the UN Committee on Economic, Social and Cultural Rights provides that 'the manner of the realization of the right to water must also be sustainable ensuring that the right can be realized for present and future generations'. As Dinara Ziganshina points out,[69] the environmental oriented approach to the right to water also contributes to the realization of the rights of future generations.

The idea of 'common needs' or 'common reserve' is integrated in the national water policy of some countries as well as in some proposals developed by nongovernmental organizations (NGOs) for an international convention for the recognition of the right to water. The proposal by the Global Framework Convention for the Right to Water, for example, provides that the 'right to water' means the fundamental right of access to 'water for life'. This latter concept includes a 'sufficient water flow needed to maintain the regime and health of rivers, streams and aquatic ecosystems'.[70] The principle also appears in the national water legislation of South Africa and is currently being implemented.[71] The Constitution of Ecuador of 2008 is the first in the world to codify legally enforceable Rights of Nature (*Pacha Mama*). The Constitution recognizes nature as a right-bearing entity, assigns liability for damage to nature and recognizes the authority of people to complain on behalf of the ecosystem.[72] As another example of the recognition of the legal personality of the natural world, we should cite the agreement concluded in 2012 between the Whanganui iwi community and the New Zealand government, which recognized personhood status for the Whanganui River that is the third longest river in New Zealand and is considered as sacred by the Whanganui iwi Community.[73]

68 V.U. Smakhtin, *Environmental Water Needs and Impacts of Irrigated Agriculture in River Basins: A Framework for A New Research Program*, working paper no. 42 (Colombo: International Water Management Institute, 2002), 3.
69 Ziganshina, 'Rethinking the Concept', 127.
70 Green Cross International, *Fundamental Principles for a Framework Convention on the Right to Water*, 2005, http://www.watertreaty.org/convention.php
71 The South African National Water Act contains provisions on the 'reserve', which includes the 'basic human needs reserve' and the 'ecological reserve'. The latter relates to the water required to protect the aquatic ecosytems of the water resource. National Water Act of 1998, pt. 3.
72 Constitution of Ecuador, arts 10, 71–74. The Constitution recognizes also the 'food sovereignty', which entails according to art. 281, the state responsibility for promoting 'redistributive politics to permit access to farmers to soil, water and other productive resources'. (For the text of the Constitution in English, see http://pdba.georgetown.edu/Constitutions/Ecuador/english08.html)
73 Under the agreement the river is given legal status under the name Te Awa Tupua – two guardians, one from the Crown and one from a Whanganui River iwi, will be given the role of protecting the river. See Alison Fairbrother, 'New Zealand's Whanganui River Gains a Legal Voice', *Huffington Post Green*, last updated October 15, 2012, http://www.huffingtonpost.com/2012/09/18/new-zealand-whanganui-river_n_1894893.html

The different comments, texts and drafts relating to the definition of the normative content of the right to water, emanating from diverse organs and commissions, in particular in the UN apparatus, indicates a hegemonic struggle. Within the context of the work of the Economic, Social and Cultural Rights Committee, the right to water is accepted as an individual right essential for the enjoyment of the right to adequate standard of living, the right to the highest attainable standard of health and right to adequate food. However, simultaneously, discussions are taking place and proposals being adopted within the framework of the UN Human Rights Council for the definition of the right to water as a collective right under the peasants' right to the means of production. The normative efforts for overcoming the anthropocentrism of human rights discourse and thereby defining the right to water as an incident of nature seem to be limited to the national legislations of some states. Nevertheless, these examples are important since they demonstrate that the normative models recognizing the natural world as a right-bearing entity are juridically enforceable.

The recognition of the collective character of the peasants' rights could remain an important issue of dispute during the future negotiations of the UN working group on the draft Peasants' Rights Declaration, given the conflict between the UN's conception of individual rights and the emphasis on the collective dimension of peasants' rights prevalent in *La Via Campesina*'s declaration that is endorsed by the working group. Hence, from the beginning, the protection of peasants' rights is presented in the United Nations as an indispensable measure for the protection of a vulnerable group against discrimination in the context of the right to food. Defined in this framework of anti-discrimination, peasants rights are recognized as individual rights that can be exercised collectively,[74] whereas *La Via Campesina* articulates an alternative conception of rights. In particular, through its claim for the 'right of peoples to food sovereignty', it emphasizes this collective dimension in order to provide the tools to fight neoliberalism in agriculture and to put forward the movement's transformative social and political project.

In the next section I will investigate whether these normative actions in the UN apparatus, in particular the struggle leaded by *La Via Campesina* for the legal formulation of peasants' rights to water, have repercussions on the local understandings of the right to water in the local movement against HPPs in Turkey.

Right to water in anti-HPP movement in Turkey

The campaign against the construction of the river type HPPs in Turkey was born in the late 1990s and expanded during the 2000s, in the course of the same period that the abovementioned normative international discussions were taking place in the institutional setting of the United Nations.

74 Christophe Golay, 'Legal Reflections on the Rights of Peasants and Other People Working in Rural Areas' (background paper, First Session of the Working Group on the Rights of Peasants and Other People Working in Rural Areas, July 15–19, 2013).

The concept of the 'right to water' was inserted into the language of the anti-HPP movement almost a decade after the movement had started. To be more precise: it was during the NGOs' preparatory meetings before the Fifth World Water Forum that took place in Turkey in 2009. The concept was used as an argument by some NGOs struggling against the HPPs, but was severely criticized by other associations in the anti-HPP movement.[75] Their criticism focused on the fact that these NGOs had financial links with enterprises involved in water-related activities and that they based their argumentation on the EU directives, whereas the EU is considered by many associations in the movement as an organization centrally involved in regulating the privatization of water. Therefore, most of the actors in the anti-HPP movement reacted negatively to the concept of a right to water or they made use of it only with much caution.

Individual activists and lawyers define the anti-HPP resistance as a struggle of 'survival' for local people. This is not only because the local people need those rivers' waters for personal and domestic use or for subsistence farming, but also because the protection and preservation of these rivers in their natural state constitutes a cultural and, in some regions such as the Munzur Valley, a religious issue.[76]

It seems that many activists in the anti-HPP movement, with the exception of the Farmer Unions' Confederation, do not follow the international discussions going on in intergovernmental or nongovernmental spheres for the formulation of the content of the right to water. Some leading associations in the movement consider the United Nations a pioneering actor for commodification of water, and hence they have no confidence in or expectation of any negotiation under the auspices of this organization.[77] Nevertheless, they remain interested in the

75 For example, TEMA (The Turkish Foundation for Combating Soil Erosion, for Reforestation and the Protection of Natural Habitats) and Doğa Derneği (Nature Association). Doğa Derneği is one of the leading NGOs in the Turkish Water Assembly as well as in the 'Right to Water' Campaign. Activist in No to the Commercialization of Water Platform, Üstün, interview with author; Munzur Şen, interview with author.

76 In the associations opposing Munzur Valley HPPs, the Kurdish-Alevi identity is very important. Dersim in Munzur Valley is a city marked by its long history of violently repressed rebellions and enforced displacements. The population of Dersim is Kurdish and Alevi. Water has sacred importance for the Alevi religion, and several Alevi religious sites are situated along flowing water to honor water as the source of life. More than ten HPPs are under construction or in the planning phase over the Munzur River where the most famous Alevi sacred sites are located, including the *Gola Çetu* (the *Gola Çetu* is a holy water source, a place of pilgrimage situated at the intersection of the Munzur and Pülümür rivers. It has recently been affected by the construction of an HPP).

77 This approach is particularly prevalent in the 'No to Commercialization of Water Platform'. They stress that by qualifying water as an economic good, UN Earth Summit and the Dublin Statement have instigated its privatization and commercialization and the United Nations has also initiated the establishment of the World Water Council. Furthermore, the World Bank encourages the construction of hydropower plants through the privatization of water resources in developing countries. See Gaye Yılmaz, *Suyun Metalaşması: Kıtlığın Nedeni Kıtlığa Çare Olabilir mi?* (Istanbul: Evrensel Basım Yayın, 2013).

domestic initiatives to constitutionalize the right to water in other countries (as discussed above).

Interviews conducted with the actors and lawyers in the movement reveal that the 'right to water' is mainly perceived as a liberal concept that connotes the idea of appropriation. The 'agreements on the right to use water' signed by the General Directorate of State Hydraulic Works with the private companies, for example, are legitimized as a transfer of the right to water. This fact probably reinforces the anti-HPP movement's skeptical approach to the idea of legal formulations of any right over the water.

As explained above, the anti-HPP movement in Turkey does not share a common ideological, social or cultural identity. Swyngedouw indicates that the social struggles around tactics of dispossession, such as the struggle for water, show specific and often highly localized forms of choreography, usually centered on questions of ownership, control, participation and community interests.[78] This can complicate attempts to form trans-local coalitions because both the stakes and the conflicts may be vastly different from place to place. As Claeys argues, rights discourse can facilitate 'the integration of multiple ideologies and help export claims to movements with divergent ideological, political or cultural references and which belong to different geographical contexts'.[79] Hence, as a counter-hegemonic instrument, 'rights talk' could potentially provide the means for expanding the struggle in other localities with divergent political and cultural backgrounds as well as construct its legitimacy in the general public's eye, mobilizing the 'common sense'.

Curtis Kline remarks that the re-conceptualization of what makes a human rights claim is closely linked with identities with a shared experience of suppression and marginalization as well as a claim for their respect, public legitimacy and recognition for their marginalized identities.[80] In many cases the engagement with human rights worked at strengthening the movements in their identities. Since the human rights discourse potentially provides a common language to different groups and communities that are politically, culturally and ideologically diverse, it could facilitate the articulation of diverse social movements.

However, in practice, making use of the 'right to water' has not functioned to strengthen the anti-HPP movement, but on the contrary has marked an ideological fracture line within different groups and activists in the movement. Some associations campaigning against HPPs center their arguments directly on the

78 Swyngedouw, 'Dispossing H_2O', 97–98.

79 Priscilla Claeys, 'From Food Sovereignty to Peasants' Rights: An Overview of La Via Campesina's Rights-Based Claims over the Last 20 Years' (paper presented at the International Conference on Food Sovereignty: A Critical Dialogue, Yale University, September 14–15, 2013), 1–2.

80 Curtis Kline, 'Human Rights and Emerging Actors: Indigenous Peoples and Peasants Redefining the Issues' (paper presented at the Social Practice of Human Rights: Charting the Frontiers of Research and Advocacy conference, University of Dayton, October 3–5, 2013).

right to water.[81] But some other associations in the movement find ideologically problematic the use of the right to water as a central concept for organizing resistance. According to them, because this concept is framed in liberal individualist rights language, it could in many senses impair the anti-capitalist emphasis of the movement. Additionally, the right to water is perceived as an exclusively anthropocentric concept that elevates the human over the ecosystem. According to this point of view, the human rights-based strategy denotes a human-centered, as opposed to nature-centered system of values, and ignores the HPPs' impact on the environment and ecosystem.[82]

Horuş, an activist lawyer in the movement, points out that in the anti-HPP resistance in Turkey local people do not formulate an express claim for the 'use of water', but fight against an assault targeting their 'living space'. They conceive water as the symbol of this living space.[83] He thinks that the citizens' rights do not provide an adequate framework for dealing with ecology-related problems. According to him, the concept of right to water which is currently instrumentalized only for political and practical reasons could not have any concrete impact in the anti-HPP struggle.

The Farmer Unions' Confederation of Turkey (Çiftci-Sen), a member of the 'No to the Commercialization of Water Platform', does not use the concept of 'right to water' but rather the 'right for the use of water'. Aysu, president of the Confederation, reminds us that the ecological cycle of water unites us all and affirms that no one could have a right to water or could dominate water.[84] According to the Confederation's point of view, farmers, like other living creatures in the ecosystem, claim only the 'right for the use of water'.

It appears that different actors in the local anti-HPP movements have different conceptions concerning the 'subject' of the right to water or the 'right for use of water'. Within the Munzur Valley movement, the concept of the right to water is not very central and it is understood as a right belonging to the ecosystem in its entirety, to all living creatures in the concerned river basin. Şen from the Munzur Valley Movement explains that 'they conceive the subject of the right in that way, because they have not lost their water yet. A peasant in a valley in the Black Sea region who cannot irrigate his/her land, because the right for the use of water is sold to a private company could legitimately think that the right to water belongs to him or her'.[85] Kalın, a lawyer active in the Black Sea region anti-HPP movement affirms that in principle. He believes that the subject of this right should be the ecosystem itself. But he states that in this region the right to water is

81 The 'Right to Water' campaign is conducted by Association of Social Change, Hasankeyf Conservation Initiative, The Global Action Group and the Social Democracy Foundation. For detailed information on the campaign, see Su Hakkı, http://www.suhakki.org/en/

82 Üstün.

83 Horuş.

84 A. Aysu, electronic communication with author, May 20, 2013.

85 Şen.

understood and instrumentalized as a right belonging to the local people, to the traditional users of the water.[86]

Arguments framed around the 'right to life' are more easily welcomed in the anti-HPP movement, because it comprises a holistic approach that considers the human being together with all living and non-living elements of nature. The 'right to life' serves as a reference in the courtrooms for claiming the annulment of HPP projects, but it is also instrumentalized in the field for organizing resistance, since the HPPs are regarded as an 'assault on life' and the anti-HPP movement is a struggle for the survival and for the 'defense of life'.

Given the fact that the right to water is not recognized as a self-standing right in Turkey's legislation, claiming its protection under the constitution could be a challenging operation. On the other hand, the recent Latin American examples instanced above demonstrate that constitutional protection *can* be given to the rights of nature.

The Turkish National Assembly was preoccupied with drafting a new Constitution between 2011 and 2013.[87] This drafting process could create an opportunity for the formulation of a constitutional provision for the protection of a collective right to water with reference to the water requirements for the functioning of the ecosystem as 'common needs' or 'common reserve'. The possibilities for a constitutional formulation have been discussed within the 'No to the Commercialization of Water Platform.' However, the Platform did not carry on this work.[88] On the other hand, an Initiative for an Ecological Constitution (IEC), including some leading figures of the anti-HPP movement, started in February 2011 with the objective of intervening into the constitutional debate with ecological demands. By taking Bolivia and Ecuador's models, the IEC submitted drafted articles to the Parliamentary Constitutional Reconciliation Commission in January 2012. The draft recognizes water as an integral part of Nature and provides the right of all living species to clean water.[89] Since the Parliamentary Commission's drafting negotiations were officially deadlocked in November 2013, the fate of the ecological demands for the new constitution is unknown.[90]

86 Kalın.

87 As the ruling party (AK Party) does not hold the required majority for a constitutional amendment, it needs the support of other parties. The Parliamentary Constitutional Reconciliation Commission has been established for the drafting of the new constitution by means of negotiation between the parties represented in the Parliament.

88 Beyza Üstün states they left their work on the constitutional formulations, because they decided not to formulate any proposal within the dominant legal system (Üstün).

89 For the draft, see 'Ekolojik Anayasa için Madde Önerileri', *Ekolojik Anayasa Girişimi*, http://www.stgm.org.tr/tr/icerik/detay/ekolojik-anayasa-icin-madde-oner ileri-2, accessed December 5, 2015.

90 The Parliamentary Reconciliation Commission failed to reach a consensus on the majority of the articles on which it had been working during the writing process of 25 months. In November 2013, the ruling party declared that the Commission had practically come to an end.

Conclusion

Private sector participation in the construction and management of water infrastructure is understood as an important new ground of enclosure of the commons implemented by global and national neoliberal policies. However, the cultural, religious and also symbolic power of water for the survival of all living species in the ecosystem makes it as an ultimate frontier to the commodification of the commons.

Law, legal concepts and in particular human rights language are used to resist water privatization in different contexts including in the anti-HPP movement in Turkey. My contention in this chapter has been that legal concepts in general, and human rights concepts in particular, bear a counter-hegemonic potential. With a Gramscian terminology, the counter-hegemonic struggle can materialize through the deconstruction, retorsion and reconstruction of the concepts that are already being used by the prevailing hegemony. The re-articulation of the right to water could be considered as fertile terrain for the counter-hegemonic use of the human rights language since the right to water is still without a completely fixed legal scope and content.

The universal right to water, which is in *statu nascendi*, could be articulated with elements of neo-liberal discourse for the commodification of water resources. But it also permits different forms of definition and redefinition for better articulating and strengthening the peoples' rights to the means of subsistence and self-determination, indigenous peoples' rights to their lands, and peasants' rights to the means of production or the rights of nature.

The experience of the instrumentalization of legal concepts and of the right to water in the anti-HPP struggle in Turkey reveals the necessity but at the same time the operational difficulties of the implementation of the 'principled opportunism' for political movements. In the case of the anti-HPP movement, the resistance is simultaneously carried on in the courtrooms and in the field where the activists are organizing local people and occasionally confront the police and military forces protecting HPPs' construction sites.

In this context the tactical use of legal concepts and of human rights language first serves the conjunctural aim of having a court ruling in order to suspend the project provisionally and hence to free up time for local organizing. The positive court rulings state the legitimacy of the movements' claims in the eyes of the general public and also encourage local people to resist in the field. Moreover, the movement also tactically deploys human rights discourse outside the courtrooms in the localities affected by the HPPs. But activists diverge on the selection of the concepts that will serve their conjunctural aims of forming trans-local coalitions and exporting claims to individuals with divergent ethnic, political, cultural and religious references and which belong to different geographical contexts. The right to life and the right to environment are the concepts that the movement's leading figures agree on as the tactical tools.

The concepts deployed by or constitutive of the prevailing hegemony bear strong ideological connotations for subordinate classes and communities.

Therefore, the adoption and the acceptance of these concepts by the subalterns in their own vocabulary, for their subsequent political and sociological reconstruction, are achieved with difficulty. The hesitant approach of the Turkey's anti-HPP movement vis-à-vis the right to water concept demonstrates these difficulties.

Another conclusion of my study is that the adoption of legal concepts as tactical tools depends largely on the conviction of the social movements on the possibilities for detaching the ideological ties of the concerned concept with the prevailing hegemonic language and subsequently attaching them in an alternative or opposing discourse. The controversial positions adopted by different actors in the anti-HPP campaign for the instrumentalization of the right to water constitute an example in this respect.

The right to water is a concept used by the proponents of the privatization of water supply and management. The concept is already in the conceptual battlefield and its content is gradually being constructed in the UN system. Different movements and activists struggling against the commodification of water attempt to seize upon the concept and frame its content in national constitutions or else work within UN organs so as to advance a communal approach towards this right.

The prevalent opinion in the anti-HPP movement in Turkey is that the right to water is a concept that cannot be seized upon and tactically used against the national and international water sector. Many leading activists in the movement think that even its use for tactical reasons will undermine the anti-HPP movement's systemic anti-capitalist objectives (and of course, for them, the integration of this concept in the language of the movement is unacceptable in strategic terms). Nevertheless, the movement seems to have a much more positive approach toward adopting rights language through other concepts that, according to them, make a more holistic approach without an exclusive human-centered emphasis. The articulation of right to life in the movement and the formulation of the rights of nature concretized in the proposal for the ecological constitution demonstrate that the tactical use of the right discourse is not rejected when it is believed that the concepts adopted are not problematic in strategic terms.

Index

For Product Safety Concerns and Information please contact our EU representative GPSR@taylorandfrancis.com
Taylor & Francis Verlag GmbH, Kaufingerstraße 24, 80331 München, Germany

www.ingramcontent.com/pod-product-compliance
Ingram Content Group UK Ltd.
Pitfield, Milton Keynes, MK11 3LW, UK
UKHW021303190926
475701UK00009B/620
9780367191825